Urban Environments

Urban Environments

Elisabetta G Mapelli

WILEY-ACADEMY

Acknowledgement

Special thanks are due to Giovanni Narici of Editrice Libreria Dedalo,
Rome, Italy, for the idea that inspired these compilations.

Page 2: Adriaan Geuze, Wastelands, Prix de Rome, Vinkeveen Holland

First published in Great Britain in 2001 by
WILEY-ACADEMY

a division of
JOHN WILEY & SONS LTD
Baffins Lane
Chichester
West Sussex PO19 1UD

ISBN 0-471-49806-8

Other Wiley Editorial Offices
New York • Weinheim • Brisbane • Singapore • Toronto

Cover design: Mario Bettella, Klára Smith

Layout and Prepress: ARTMEDIA PRESS Ltd, London

Printed and bound in Italy

Contents

JUST WHERE DO YOU THINK YOU ARE GOING?

One generation's ground-breaking science-fiction usually becomes the accepted norm of the next. Advances in materials and techniques over the century have eventually caused that which years ago was set firmly in the realms of the imagination to become reality.. . . The present era of futuristic design encompasses a desire to test materials and shapes as well as scientific theories. Frank Gehry's New Guggenheim Museum in Bilbao and the planned Victoria & Albert Museum Extension by Daniel Libeskind begin to give us a sense of future possibilities. . . . As we move towards 2001, the year pinpointed by Stanley Kubrick in his film *2001, a Space Odyssey*, made in 1968, the styles of that space-obsessed era are being re-introduced. In much the same way that 1984 gave us an opportunity to access the state's control over us, and to note that George Orwell's vision was not so far from the truth, the millennium is giving us the impetus to reassess the achievements of the century and look forward optimistically to the design style of the future.

Maggie Toy

URBAN ENVIRONMENTS

Elisabetta G Mapelli

Where Were We . . .   Where Are We . . .   Where Will We Be . . .

Predicting the environment people will be living in during the next millennium is not an easy task, even if at all possible. Film makers continually portray baffling urban decay where chaos takes over amidst convulsive and apparently uncontrollable growth. When this is coupled with a grotesque transformation of human relationships – the consequence of a generalised mistrust in mankind's capacity to cope with the many implications that are the result of radical modifications to interpersonal communication and the introduction of the 'virtual' dimension of 'being' – one can only feel disconcerted.

Why are these scenarios apocalyptic? Why have they superseded the tranquillity of the 1960s' cartoon family's life-in-space? Why do we feel a sense of relief only when we contemplate the burning ashes of our present civilisation?

Could it be because of an excessive acceleration in the way we live, with which we feel unable to cope?

Could it be because this acceleration means we lose control over events and actions in our lives, so that we are incapable of grasping and reuniting the scattered fragments of our existence?

The destruction in the overgrown distorted visions of society portrayed by film makers means that it is necessary to stop, take a deep breath and start again. It is all about regaining control over our actions.

Undoubtedly, since the late 1990s the architectural scene, characterised on a planetary scale by the coexistence of many *isms* and the progressive accumulation of Deconstructivist-derived approaches to design, has become overcrowded. New ideas are fragmented and presented in unusual formats, which makes them difficult to grasp and understand. Changes are so rapid, and novelties so frequent, that their effect tends to be neutralised. The extent and persistence of media coverage is provoking visual saturation.

Because developing theories and forms are experimental there is all too often uncertainty as to whether they are contributing positively to the future of our built environment (and therefore to society as a whole). The result is that many people develop a sceptical attitude towards design.

'Haunting' versus 'exciting' expectations of future urban and non-urban environments therefore dominate the scene and, it could be said, split the world of design into four different categories: traditionalists; perpetrators of the various *isms* from Modernism to Post-Modernism to Deconstructivism; exponents of a new avant-garde that springs from Deconstructivism and projects into the world of non-Euclidean geometry and cyberspace; and, last but absolutely not least, environment-conscious designers preoccupied with the sustainability of future developments.

These four categories actually constitute two bigger clusters. The first two look for order in past tradition, or in the images and theories of the recent past – for example, Mies van der Rohe's 'less is more' – and are now more or less accepted by the general public. The latter two look to the future for a new order: the first by establishing new frontiers in design science that bypass the physical conception of space in a transcultural, multimedia society; the second through a new consciousness of earthly resources, which may provide the basis for gradually transforming crystallised building types, and critically analyses how we live.

In this volume, glimpses of forecasts that have been made over the years, from Hablik and Sant'Elia through Archigram, will be compared with what is currently being produced in the built and non-built architectural design world.

The subject for this overview is the house, taken first as a specific object and then contextualised, thus extending these observations to the city; the instruments are the pages of *Architectural Design*, in a selection of articles from the late 1980s to the year 2000, with excerpts from the imaginative late 1960s.

Why the house?

Because it is a constant throughout the evolution of the built environment.

Because dwellings, old and new, constitute the greater part of the environment we live in.

Because in a culture where work- and travel-related issues are the ones that are most relevant, where work- and travel-related spaces appear to be the new relational references, where mass production for developed global markets can satisfy all voluptuary needs at relatively low costs, there is a major difficulty in providing a shelter that is not just a roof over our heads (and many times not even that!) but is, rather, a defined environment suitable for developing human relationships in all their complexity.

'Only if we are capable of dwelling, only then can we build,' says Heidegger in his formulation of the definition of dwelling, a statement which, as Patrick Keiller recalls,[1] Kenneth Frampton refers to as defining a quality of experience which many believe most modern buildings have lost – a loss which is the reason why people tend to reject modern architecture.

Although we must draw a clear distinction between architect-designed modern homes and a housing market hungry for big earnings through mass production at low costs, it is true that the advances in design that are currently being explored by many architects are having little or no effect on the housing market; and architects are often criticised for designing houses that are impossible to live in.[2] Instead, we witness the proliferation of buildings *in stile* because, mainly, 'they sell better'. The reason why they do is probably because, in the turbulence of modern life, this form of contextualism still accepts the survival of linguistic expressions that are closely related to tradition.

This translates into a constant reference to the vernacular which seems to be legitimised by theory on the one hand, thanks to the fragmentation of the once-unified spirit of the Modern Movement; and by 'popular' thought on the other, because of the necessity to envision architecture as an all-inclusive discipline that is able to accept and accommodate the spontaneous, the repetitive and the contradictions of everyday life. 'Any discipline which denies the everyday will be denied everyday.'[3]

The average man or woman is unaware that through contextualism they are operating a deep critical revision of the modern and of the utopian visions of its prophets who are thought to be responsible, in their rejection of historic forms, for loss of memory and identity. Contextualism substitutes the strong model of the architect-creator for another that is softer, more gentle: the architect as a kind of doctor who, having abandoned aspirations towards protagonism, tries to understand, cure and improve what already exists. This is confirmed by the success of the classicists' interpretation of urban form through the design of buildings that appear traditional and yet are suitable for a modern way of life: an image-of-the-past shell with a highly technological interior? In the words of Adorno:

> Tradition derives from *tradere*, to convey. What is intended are the links between different generations, heritage flowing from one member to the other . . . tradition contrasts with the rational, though the latter is formed within the former. The means for this is not conscience, but the binding character given, unplanned, by precise social configurations. The presence of the past is a character which transfers immediately to the spiritual.[4]

Past and future should therefore coexist in the mind as a continuum:

> Architects today are pathologically devoted to change, considering it something either to hinder or to pursue . . . this occurs because they tend to separate the past from the future, with the result that the present becomes emotionally inaccessible, without a temporal dimension.[5]

Psychologically, for the generations who experience the ever-changing multiplicity of images, opinions, trends and information that mould our built environment, what 'was' remains the only certainty. There is a growing gap between what we acquire through experience and what we define as tradition. Recovering tradition by reproducing its image and all the 'cute'-nesses that follow leads to the creation of a false tradition[6] that has no authority because it lacks a convincing form. Our relations with nature and with the 'physical' world as we have known it until now have lost their original ties and become informal and abstract; they are therefore no longer the consequence of direct experience.

Surely this means that we must search for our true environment not in theme parks representing the past, but within the emerging values of modern society. Through the action of design architects must enhance both aesthetic and ethical inquiry, in the face of the need of the client and society to recognise and comprehend, in a creatively dynamic process of give and take aimed at discovering, understanding and accepting the inevitably new conditions of contemporaneity.

For example, Deconstructivism, expresses this new perspective well by abandoning preconceived fixed schemes and admitting not only multiplicity but also difference. Progress today coincides with discovering and affirming the possible positive coming together of diverse and complex ideas. As Mies wrote:

> What renders buildings of the past so significant to us is not the architectural form in itself, but the fact that the ancient temples, the Roman basilicas and the cathedrals of the Middle Ages alike, are not the work of one man, but the creation of an entire era. Who, in front of these buildings, asks the name of their constructor? What extra meaning could a single identity add? These constructions are, for their nature, absolutely impersonal. They are pure expressions of the spirit of the time . . .

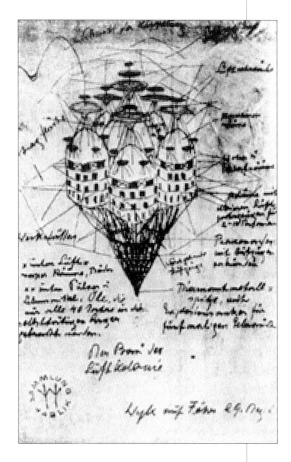

The Building of the Air Colony by Wenzel Hablik

Architecture is the will of an age translated into space, nothing more. Until this simple truth is generally accepted, it will be impossible to firmly set the foundations of a new architecture; up to then, we will be caught in a chaos of disorganised forces . . .
Every architecture is tied to its time and can only emerge in vital tasks by using the instruments available within it.[7]

It should be clear that if there is a future in architecture, it will not have its genesis in a new method of designing the house, be in a new way of conceiving in the sense of 'thinking': an alternative cultural tendency, one that includes the different, the private, the error the sustainable and, especially, one that is capable of self-criticism. These are our conceptual instruments, undoubtedly marking an important break with the past; what means do we have to translate them into our built environment?

New developments have changed the boundaries of design and are coming to our aid: information technology on the one hand and globalisation on the other. If the latter, which essentially concerns people, includes and expands our conceptual instruments and therefore constitutes the new cultural background to how we conceive our designs, then the former provides the practical instruments we use to develop architectural form.

The expressive potential of this technological revolution, as it passes from its quantitative phase (as an instrumental aid to drafting, computing and new techniques of representation) to a qualitative phase of design science, is now starting to become apparent. The growing interest in, and research into, complex mathematics through the study of generative or multidimensional spaces, non-Euclidean geometry, topology, the theory of fractals, Mandelbrot sets, quantum physics, transfers from biological research (and more doubtful references to theories of chaos and turbulence) is pointing the way to new methods of design: scaling, folding, morphing and others.[8]

The other significant element in this revolution – one that is a true discovery – is the introduction of 'virtual reality'. This will have inevitable and important repercussions (which are anyway developing spontaneously) on the order of things: on the one hand the virtualisation of architectural space for communication and working will cause a profound revision of what constitutes present-day physical space; on the other, designing the tectonics of virtual environments will become a new discipline in the third millennium.

It must be understood that all that is new is not necessarily 'good'; nor is all that is old 'bad'. But it is necessary to explore what is brought about by the expanding possibilities of modern-age technology in order to try to *evolve*, and not *involve* for fear of facing the unknown future. 'The future will not be good or bad, but both.'[9] After all, electricity, automobiles, aeroplanes and telephones (to mention just a few modern inventions) evolved from being elements of wonder and disturbance in the architectural context of their introduction to become necessities that are naturally part of an integrated vision of our urban environment. New frontiers in communication can only open up new horizons which give new meaning physically and virtually, to architectural space and social relations within it.

Edwin A Abbott's exhortation in 1882, in the final pages of *Flatlandia – A Romance of Many Dimensions*, couldn't have made more sense then than it does at present. It is expressed through the words of the Square, its protagonist who is jailed for having spoken about the existence of a third dimension (inconceivable for the two-dimensional kingdom of Flatland) which he discovered by simply observing the motion of a sphere in his two-dimensional world (a plane) through its progressively increasing and decreasing section (from point to circle to point). The Square recommends future generations not to fear what is discovered, for it has always existed; it is just that no one had the knowledge to perceive it, let alone understand it.[10]

'Advance into the future must be striven for before it can be achieved.'[11]

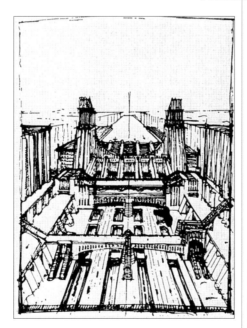

Sant' Elia's visions of an urban metropolis

Rethinking the house: The physical and the virtual

To eradicate generalised suspicion about design research, especially when it is applied to the home, it is necessary to create new and convincing role models, thus overturning attitudes that cling to past images in order to find a comfortable identity.[12]

The consequences of new forms, and new ways of thinking, are yet to be revealed.

It is probable that our way of thinking and our language are more out of date than the object of which we speak. It would therefore perhaps be best not to try and force the new into past schemes, but instead try progressively to adapt past schemes towards a gradual understanding of the new.[13]

One aspect of readdressing acquired concepts and definitions in a domestic context may be found, for example, in the work of the Kolatan/Macdonald Studio. In the Ost/Kuttner Apartments in Vienna the identity of the objects found in a home are read topographically and cross-referenced electronically to constitute a kind of 'domestic scape'.

> [This] domestic scape, unlike the domestic space (the room) or the domestic object (the furniture), cannot be identified through categorical classification. Rather, like a particular landscape, its identification is contingent on the presence of idiosyncratic features. In the case of the bed this would mean that a plateau of a certain measurement can be identified as, but would not be limited to, a potential sleeping area. This is very different from the concept of a 'bed' or 'bedroom' which are both categorical designations of identity and therefore fixed in their programmatic associations.[14]

What underlies this project is that 'domestic scapes are always situated across the boundaries of domestic spaces'.[15]

The similarities, both conceptual and aesthetic, between the integrated design of the domestic space of Archigram's 'Living, 1990' exhibition project in the late 1960s and the Ost/Kuttner project of the late 1990s give new meaning to E Duffy's prophecy that 'architecture lies well outside the orbit of technological forecasting – the ability to look forward further ahead than you can see – but inevitably and eventually it will be pressurised into a more receptive position.'[16] Thirty years of sedimentation separate what was once thought of as 'far out' and what is now perhaps adventurous, but possible. Is this a consequence of pressure or of experimental evolution?

In another Kolatan/Macdonald project, the Raybould House addition, the shape of the house is determined by singling out and cross-referencing elements of interest in its surroundings: the existing house, the landscape and the car. There seems to be an intention to cancel the boundaries between nature and artificiality by electronically crossing the natural with the artificial.

But if this game of denaturalisation affects the physical world, and its continuation towards total abstraction is therefore limited by the limits of materials and the necessity to divide what is 'in' and what is 'out', what happens when we relate to, or even step into, the world of virtuality? Relating to the virtual world by remaining in the real one causes a drastic shift in the configuration of physical environmental boundaries. Inside these boundaries, the virtual becomes the psychological; it is where all actions take place, it is the 'active' part of life. Outside them is the physical; it unites landscape and house and is indifferent to the significance of their boundaries and form in the real world.

'Cyberspace exploration contacts the imageless body.'[17] The reconsideration of the dwelling for the next millennium must therefore not be separated from reflections on the pervasive use of technology in the home.

Informational geometry is forcing a new meaning on the relationship between space and time[18] and so simultaneously causing the dismantling of Euclidean settings for human space. It is a matter of redefining the visual relationship with the object, and this greatly affects the sphere of perception. Subject and object belong to different environments, and the particular qualities of the virtual environment of the object provide new levels of significance that go beyond what we are capable of representing in our physical environment.

In the Möbius House study by Perrella and Carpenter the transversal membrane that defines the design is an interwrapping median which follows binary laws and defines no interior space or exterior form. That is, it tends to characterise the complex ways new interfaces will occur and reconfigure us; it is a hypersurface.[19] But this study, along with others – for example, of the generation of form through the 'collaborative evolution of a virtual environment by global participation on the internet',[20] has to do with pure research, looking for the 'primary generator' in the conception of a design.[21]

Möbius House is an abstraction that identifies a clear attitude towards the concept of future dwellings but tends to 'virtualise the domestic'. Would it not be destabilising to think human life could be floating into something without boundaries? The house, in the physical world, defines a space which gives importance and shelter to *me* as opposed to *the rest*. Whether it is a cardboard box or a mansion, it is a question of creating individual reference points.

Foreign Office Architects and Decoi Architects don't lose touch with our three-dimensional set of references and bring back the question of, shall we say, 'domesticating the virtual'.[22] In the projects featured in *Architectural Design* their researches are concerned with numerically generated designs and the manipulation of matter. Both apparently believe in the potential of virtuality to unfold or inherit a series of lineages[23] and, while searching for a recognisable form, they play with domestic spatial phenomenology. But while FOA's virtual house, in its redefinition of opposites – inside/outside, front/back, up/down – is destined, at least for the time being, to represent a manipulation of reality in the virtual realm, Decoi Architects' numerical manipulating of geometry and materials translates into a global process that is not suspended in the generative phase, but reaches a final form. Research, in this case, is not all-inclusive but concentrates on the definition of the shell, exposing outwardly an otherwise non-innovative inside.

The problem is: will the virtual always be dissociated from the physical? Is there a way of physically experiencing virtuality? Maybe Arakawa and Madeline Gins try to suggest a partial answer through the Critical Resemblance House and the Elliptic Field game: detachment from the sure references of the three-dimensional world by introducing disarray at a psychological level.

The truth is that giving real form and assigning true materials to virtuality crystallises a generative form and reduces it to the mere representation of its physical and quantifiable components. It is stripped from its original environment and set into a space which hosts it without being able to reproduce the effects that time has on the perception of naturally evolving virtual space.

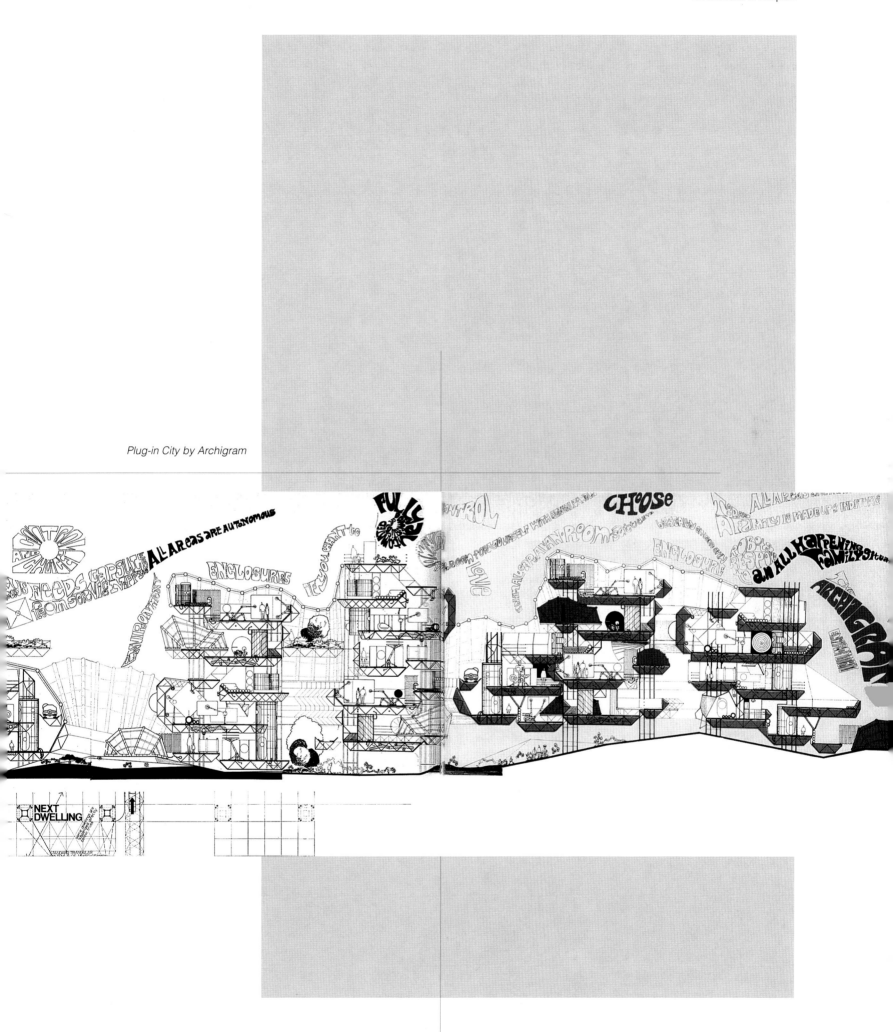

Plug-in City by Archigram

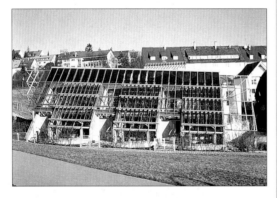

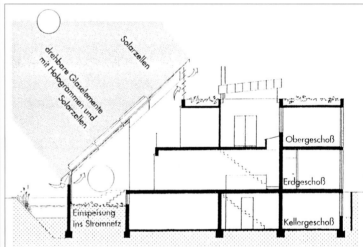

HHS Planners – Hausgruppe 5 – IGA Stuttgart '93
To think of natural energy as a building component is
to think of the elements that could bring about a new
way of defining the elements of design. Solar cells as
chromatic variables in new facade decoration

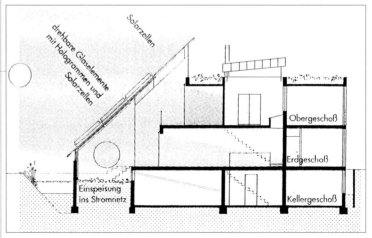

Rethinking the house: Ubi natura, ibi geometrie[24]

Different approaches to a respectful interaction with the environment can range from simple visual object integration to sustainable buildings that are often complex operating organisms.

The definition of 'sustainability' in the Bruntland Report (World Commission 1987) is that it is a process of change in which exploitation of natural resources through investments and technological development coexist in harmony, and may therefore enhance the present and future capacity to satisfy all human needs and aspirations. But the coming into being of a sustainable environment does not rely only on political institutions and big investors. The evolution of technology permits concepts and instruments of sustainability to enter our everyday lives and our homes. We must therefore rethink our relationship with nature as well as our interactions with the city, in the context of plain quotidian actions that respond to the environment. This, obviously, means doing more than keeping front lawns and flower gardens neat, however visually acceptable this may be.

Sustainability is more complex. It deals mainly with energy consumption versus energy production and the consequences on the local and global environment (pollution, global warming, reduction of the ozone layer, etc); but also with the extensive occupation of land, which has often compromised and destroyed vital ecosystems, and with the question of waste. There is a strong necessity to develop comprehensive frameworks for understanding the interrelations between built systems and ecosystems, thus allowing people in various fields to act in concert[25] on the one hand and, on the other, to bring about a diffused eco-responsive way of thinking in the average man and woman.

Since the object of our discussion is rethinking the house, let us investigate the possible consequences of an environment-responsive reformulation of living. Solar panels for heating, wind towers for refreshing, earth inertia, shading, transpirant and natural materials are just small pieces in a bigger, complex mosaic which needs a coordinating design if it is to be effectively complete. It is a matter of efficiency, obtained by the correct interrelation between technology and materials.

The result of this would be the progressive typological modification of current house schemes: the dislocation of day/night grouping of spaces according to orientation, and the consequent opportunity to use glass panelling; the increased use of strategically located lightwells which may also function as hot-air chimneys in summer; or the introduction of winter gardens with a (hopefully) selected arrangement of greenery for microclimate control. Ultimately, this means adapting to a new interpretation of the spatial qualities of the houses we live in, and therefore to the development of a new repertory of images with which we define 'home'.

Many architects are gaining knowledge of a new eco-philosophy of design, from Thomas Herzog, a veteran at first hand in developing and experimenting with new materials and technologies, to younger practitioners like Log ID and Mario Cucinella Architects who are increasingly experienced in this type of design. However, there are margins of uncertainty as to whether architects in general have the instruments and preparation to pursue good results in this expanding field and actively advance research through design.

Gunnarshaung – Hausgruppe 3 – IGA Stuttgart '93

East-west orientation and varying light games throughout the usually 'dark areas' of row houses through south oriented glass-panelled roof slope. Northern roofing covered with earth and greenery for insulation

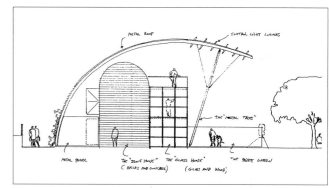

Jourda et Perraudin – Hausgruppe 6 – IGA Stuttgart '93
The Winter Brick vs. Summer Glass House: a seasonal nomadic
shift in living spaces within the home

The Internationale Gartenbau Austellung in Stuttgart in 1993 was significant in its reflection of the more general state of the art at the beginning of the 1990s. A selected group of architects from across Europe was invited to participate in proposing prototype eco-responsive housing in either row-house or block configuration. Among them were Jourda et Perraudin, Karla Sytzkovitz-Kovalsky, HHS and Mecanoo, all of whom developed interesting designs on environment-conscious themes, enhancing one or more aspects of sustainability. Overall, though, architects have tended to demonstrate a pro-environment design intention without completely mastering the complex mechanisms of sustainability in the house.

Another subject of enquiry in environment-responsive architecture is the relationship between a new construction and the intrinsic qualities of its immediate surroundings – the impact it may have on the local ecosystem. The *genius loci*. In a rural context, for example, a house hidden under a tree has a modest visual impact, its imprint on the ground and the delimitation of its garden may develop into a major disturbance to the equilibrium of existing fauna and flora. Obviously not a question of hiding a construction, but is one of integrating it.

Sytzkovitz Kovalsky – Hausgruppe 4 – IGA Stuttgart '93
The necessity to keep the cold out and let heat and light in without splitting the
house into separate blocks breaks the standard plan in moving through north
small and cosy winter spaces to the three level winter-garden on the south in
an attempt to reconquer expressiveness

We could say we are in a research-through-design phase of experimentation in sustainability which is starting to lead us towards a new reality in architectural conception.

The Living Pod by David Green: model showing folding viewing seals; plan of the upper level

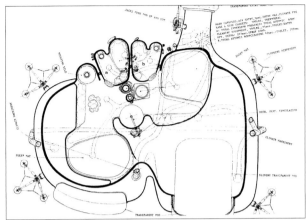

Rethinking the house: Forget it! Let's get out of here.

While most of the world's population strives for a house that will give them roots, self-identity and recognition in a defined social enclave, there are plenty of people who prefer to live on the outskirts of civilisation, as nomads. Whether they do so permanently, for long periods or for a quick break, the gene that underlies the philosophy of living on the road defines a different way of conceiving of the house: one that allows them the possibility to pack it instantly, change their scenario and leave no trace.

From tents to caravans, different levels of ephemerality and movability have different meanings in dwelling and community living which inspire either general enthusiasm or negative prejudice among city dwellers. At one extreme, the tent, the portable, the ephemeral; something that can be easily folded and taken away, an object linked to the idea of freedom and poetic integration with the wilderness. The personal, individual self, packed into a rucksack and taken wherever. At the other extreme is the caravan. Very American in its idealised reproduction of the standardised interiors of the 'static' dream home, its exterior does almost nothing to mask the instability of being on wheels.

Could 'living on the outside' be read as a refusal to be part of, or a challenge to, the Western social structure? Is living in a mobile home a choice for freedom or a consequence of necessity? Since most of the people who live in caravans are low-income workers who tend not to use their homes for travelling although they could do so, it is probably a merging of the two. For those who might otherwise be living as forgotten numbers in some bleak city expansion, the re-creation of a parallel, human-size community where the property-linked social hierarchy no longer exists provides a second chance in gaining social identity. This applies particularly to the United States. In Europe it is difficult to find similar social configurations, and those that there are differ in size to those in the US. Gypsy communities and camper-tourism are by no means comparable as they have different cultural premises and therefore belong to totally different spheres of reality.

Between the two extremes, *Architectural Design* featured the developing scheme of a drive-in house in the late 1960s. The concept was very simple: provide the fixed furnishings of the house, drive the rest around and make pit stops only when necessary. After observing the computer models of its 1990s reinterpretation, and after viewing Luc Besson's *The Fifth Element*, it is difficult not to conclude that the real drive-in house is still to come. Only when we are able to hover in our little shuttle homes and fly directly into our all-equipped personal shell homes, thus abolishing the cranes which limit our freedom of movement – only then will the drive-in house come into its own.

GRP Igloo by Cohos, De Lesalle and Evamy of Calgary, Alberta

Rethinking the house: What city?

'It was heartbreaking, if not obscene . . . to have to imagine here, a city.'[26] So wrote Koolhaas over a peaceful two-page panoramic view of an ordered piece of French countryside in *S,M,L,XL*.

But what city? Through the pages of *Architectural Design* we are given a clear perception of the ever-more complex issues we must consider when we examine our urban environment. Dispersed, intelligent, soft, reversible, dynamic, sustainable, fractal, stretched and so on. All adjectives that are applicable to any 'cityscape', defining multiplicity and complexity. What then will our future cities resemble?

How to deal positively with the restless phenomenon of inurbation has been an important aspect of planning since the reconstruction after the Second World War. But at present, along with reflections on where and how to choose and plan sites for new towns or peripheral expansion, there are three new major components to consider.

The first is the question of sustainability that arises from excessive energy consumption, waste production, pollution and other negative aspects of modern living. The second is the necessity to rehabilitate large urban voids that have been left open and abandoned mainly because of industrial decentralisation (but also as a result of war or political unrest). The Moll de la Fusta seafront in Barcelona, London's docklands, Bercy and Rive Gauche in Paris, Euralille station in Lille, the historic Fiat automobile factory in Turin and the Bicocca-Falck-Breda areas in Milan are just a few of the urban areas that were once beyond the outskirts but which have, with urban sprawl, been included in the consolidated built area. All these redevelopment schemes include housing programmes but, intelligently enough, housing is not all they consist of. Planners and designers have made a special effort to understand the nature of the interaction between microeconomies at a neighbourhood level and the possibility of juxtaposing organisms that work at a regional, national or international level on dense local relational patterns.

The third component is as important as these first two, and is the redefinition of the relational habits that have been enhanced by the new forms of communication and travel that are available to us. Time and distance assume a totally new meaning in a globalised, informational society. On the one hand, as a result of the significantly diminishing transfer times involved in physical forms of transport, much of the population is constantly on the move; on the other, informational technology allows us to travel the world while physically sitting behind a home-computer. This is introducing a significant shift in our values when we consider the spatial qualities of the built environment and, especially, it is changing our local references within cities. New places for interaction are therefore developing, both in expanding physical space and virtual space, and will be among the key considerations in planning for the communication age.

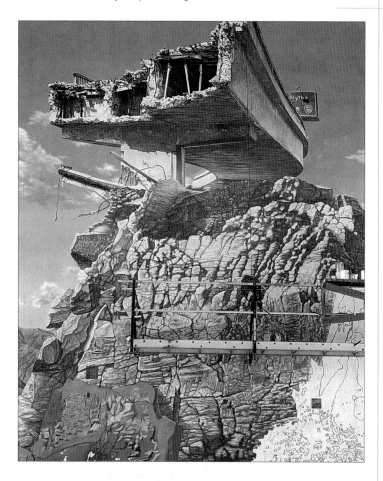

Tomorrow's Yesterday: City of Armageddon

Yesterday's Tomorrow: Argosy by Robert McCall

Rethinking the house: What about them?

As cities sprawl and the rich get richer, while we reflect on non-Euclidean space and sustainability, while we envision space colonies and shuttle houses, while we take time to experiment with evolving new ways of interpreting domestic and urban environments, who, in the present, stops to think about those who, from choice or necessity – but ever more for the latter reason – cannot afford to buy a house and are not eligible to obtain a dwelling in a social housing scheme?

Architecture participates heavily in the moulding of society. It is the theatre of life's actions. It therefore has an enormous responsibility towards every segment in the social scale, including the homeless, and every aspect of everyday life.

You, who explore the surroundings and see the signs, you should tell me toward which of these futures the favours of the winds are directing us.

Through these ports I would not know how to trace the course on the map, nor fix the date of the landing. It seems to me, at times, that a glimpse of the middle of an incongruous landscape, the surfacing of lights in the fog, the dialogue between passers-by who meet in the bustle, would be enough to begin to assemble the perfect city, piece by piece, made of fragments composed with the rest, of instants divided by intervals, of signals sent by those who do not know the receiver. If I tell you that the city I seek through my voyage is discontinuous in space and time, sometimes more rarefied other times more dense, you must not think it possible to stop searching.[27]

During the winter of 1940/41

Notes

1 P Keiller, 'The Dilapidated Dwelling', p 20.

2 M Toy, Editorial, *AD* profile 137: *Des-Res Architecture*, pp 7–9.

3 S Wigglesworth, J Till, 'The Everyday and Architecture', *AD* profile 134: *The Everyday and Architecture*, p 7.

4 TW Adorno, *Parva Aesthetica* (Milan), 1979, p 27. Translated from the German: *Ohne Leitbild* (Frankfurt am Main), 1967.

5 A van Eyck, in Forum (1967); cited in K Frampton, *Modern Architecture: A Critical History*, Thames and Hudson (London), 1985.

6 TW Adorno, *Dialettica Negativa* (Turin), 1980, p 48. Translated from the German: *Negative Dialektik* (Frankfurt am Main), 1966.

7 Mies van der Rohe, 'Baukunst und Zeitville', *Der Querschnitt*, 4 (1924), pp 31–2.

8 Cf L Sacchi, 'Tre tendenze e due ipotesi sull'architettura di oggi', *Op.cit.*, 103 (September 1998), pp 11–12.

9 N Negroponte, *Being Digital*, Hodder and Stoughton (London), 1995, p.20.

10 EA Abbott, *Flatlandia – A Romance of Many Dimensions*, first edition, 1882.

11 Toy, op cit, p 9.

12 Ibid., pp 7–9.

13 L Benevolo, *Storia dell'Architettura Moderna*, Laterza (Bari), 1960, p 11.

14 Kolatan/Macdonald Studio, 'Ost/Kuttner Apartments', p 68.

15 Ibid.

16 E Duffy, 'Looking Back Looking Forward', *AD* profile 137: *Des-Res Architecture*, p ii.

17 N Land, 'Cyberspace Anarchitecture as Jungle-War', *AD* profile 118: *Architects in Cyberspace*, p 58.

18 M Toy, op cit, pp 7–9.

19 S Perrella with Dennis Pang, 'The Haptic Horizon', *AD* profile 133: *Hypersurface Architecture.*

20 J Frazer, M Rastogi and P Graham, 'The Interactivator', p 78.

21 This reference is to the evolution of design science and specifically to Jane Darke's theory of the 'primary generator'.

22 Because of the way time's technological impact on domesticity has evolved, we have voluntarily substituted 'virtual' for 'industrial' in freely taking from the essay by E Duffy, op cit, which explained technological understanding of the house by the Eames Partnership, who wanted, and obtained, a 'domestication of the industrial' as opposed to the 'industrialisation of the domestic'.

23 Foreign Office Architects, 'Virtual House: Potential Beyond the Future', p 80.

24 Thomas Herzog's reply to those who feel that his architectural approach to the question of sustainability leads towards a dissolution of the boundaries between nature and artifice. In A Battisti and F Tucci, *Ambiente e Cultura dell'Abitare*, Editrice Librerie Dedalo (Rome), 2000.

25 K Yeang, *The Green Skyscraper*, Prestel (Munich), 1999.

26 R Koolhaas and B Mau, *S,M,L,XL*, The Monacelli Press (New York), 1995, pp 972–3.

27 I Calvino, *Le Città Invisibili*, Mondadori (Milan), 1993, p 163.

JANET CARSTEN AND STEPHEN HUGH-JONES
ABOUT THE HOUSE, LÉVI-STRAUSS AND BEYOND

This extract is taken from the Introduction to About the House,[1] *which examines ideas about the house as a specific form of social organisation discussed by Claude Lévi-Strauss in* Anthropology and Myth[2] *and* The Way of the Masks.[3]

The real value of Lévi-Strauss' idea of the house as a specific form of social organisation lies in providing a jumping-off point allowing a move towards a more holistic anthropology of architecture which might take its theoretical place alongside the anthropology of the body.

The house and the body are intimately linked. The house is an extension of the person; like an extra skin, carapace or second layer of clothes, it serves as much to reveal and display as it does to hide and protect. House, body and mind are in continuous interaction, the physical structure, furnishing, social conventions and mental images of the house at once enabling, moulding, informing and constraining the activities and ideas which unfold within its bounds. A ready-made environment fashioned by a previous generation and lived in long before it becomes an object of thought, the house is a prime agent of socialisation. Moving in ordered space, the body 'reads' the house which serves as a mnemonic for the embodied person. Through habit and inhabiting, each person builds up a practical mastery of the fundamental schemes of their culture.

Houses are frequently thought of as bodies, sharing with them a common anatomy and common life history. If people construct houses and make them in their own image, so also do they use these houses and house-images to construct themselves as individuals and as groups. At some level or other, the notion that houses are people is one of the universals of architecture. If the house is an extension of the person, it is also an extension of the self. As Bachelard reminds us, the space of the house is inhabited not just in daily life, but also in the imagination. It is a 'topography of our intimate being', a 'felicitous space' with protective and comforting association, a rich and varied poetic image which 'emerges into the consciousness as a direct product of the heart, soul and being of man, apprehended in his actuality'.[4] Western children's drawings of houses with two windows and a door – two eyes and a mouth – underline this projection of the self in the house, but there are surprisingly few anthropological explorations of this identity between house and self in non-Western societies.

Intimately linked both physically and conceptually, the body and the house are the loci for dense webs of signification and affect and serve as basic cognitive models used to structure, think and experience the world. Yet if the body has long been a focus of anthropological research which has revitalised the study of kinship and has had a major impact on other disciplines, the same cannot be said for the house. As Caroline Humphrey observes, 'architecture has been curiously neglected by academic anthropology'.[5] Indeed, much of the more comparative and theoretical work on the anthropology of architecture has been done not by anthropologists but by architects and art historians.

One reason for this neglect is that houses get taken for granted. Like our bodies, the houses in which we live are so commonplace, so familiar, so much a part of the way things are, that we often hardly seem to notice them. It is only under exceptional circumstances – house-moving, wars, fires, family rows, lost jobs or no money – that we are forcibly reminded of the house's central role and fundamental significance. Anthropological field research is another such exceptional circumstance. To enter another culture is to stand nervously in front of an alien house and to enter a world of unfamiliar objects and strange people, a maze of spatial conventions whose invisible lines get easily scuffed and trampled by ignorant foreign feet. But these first, revealing, architectural impressions, reinforced by the painful process of learning who is who, who and what lives where, and what to do where and when, soon fade into the background to become merely the context and environment for the increasingly abstract and wordy conversation of ethnographic research.

Institutional divisions and specialisations also underlie anthropology's neglect of architecture – what might have been a more holistic anthropology of the house has been fragmented between various sub-disciplines and theoretical traditions. Family and household are basic units of analysis in studies of demography and kinship; economic anthropology deals with the physical and mental activities implied by the notion of 'housekeeping', treating the household as a basic unit of production and consumption; cultural ecologists deal with subsistence as an adaptation to an environment whose architecture, the result of human activities and perceptions, is often masked by the term 'natural'. We have not considered here the relationship between the house and the landscape in which it is situated. Ingold suggests a homology between the relations body: house: landscape, and organism: dwelling: environment. The former set emphasises form, the latter function. This provokes the further question of where each entity in the sets begins and ends.

Architectural works focused on the more material aspects of dwellings typically say much about environmental conditions, resources, technology, techniques of construction and types of building, and about the spatial organisation, symbolism and aesthetic values of buildings, but they often say relatively little about the social organisation of the people who live inside.

It was Lévi-Strauss who first drew attention to the potential theoretical significance of the house, who saw in house societies a specific and widespread social type, and who emphasised the significance of the indigenous category of house in the study of systems of social organisation which appeared to make no sense when seen in terms of the categories of conventional kinship analysis. His writings on the house were inspired by the noble houses of medieval Europe. He argues that the Yurok house was a central feature of their social organisation, perpetual establishments whose names, taken from their location, decorations or ceremonial function, were used in turn by the house owners.

Noting the similarity between these institutions and European noble house, Lévi-Strauss points out that 'in order to recognise the house, it would have been necessary for ethnologists to look towards history'.[6] He stresses that the house as a grouping endures through time, continuity being assured not simply through succession and replacement of its human resources but also through holding on to fixed or movable property and through the transmission of the names, titles and prerogatives which are integral to its existence and identity. He moves away from a theory in which genealogy is primary, to one where it is displaced by other symbols and to a consideration of systems in which the criteria of wealth, power and status, normally associated with literate and class-based societies, begin to play an increasingly important role in the constitution of social groupings.

Lévi-Strauss talks of the 'borrowing' and 'subversion' of the language of kinship in the pursuance of political and economic interests, but nowhere discusses how the naturalisation of status differences is achieved. In fact, a striking omission from his writing is any detailed attention to the most obvious feature of houses: their physical characteristics. The architectural features of houses are usually ignored and no consideration is given to the association of rank with architecture. This point is graphically illustrated in *The Way of the Masks* which contains Lévi-Strauss' original discussion of 'house societies'. The photographs of painted house fronts and elaborately carved house posts might suggest that, for Northwest Coast Indians, the sociological significance of the house is reflected in the care and attention lavished on buildings. Yet in his discussion of the Kwakiutl *numayma* or 'house', Lévi-Strauss makes no mention of their architecture.

Internal features of the house such as the division of space often serve as vehicles for the symbolic elaboration of systems of hierarchy which may mirror or transform those represented by the house as a whole. At the same time, decorative elaboration of the house's external facade, sometimes taken to extreme proportions, may serve as a sign for the inhabitants' identity, wealth and powers and as a vehicle for the conspicuous display of mythologically sanctioned powers and prerogatives reminiscent of the heraldic devices of medieval houses. Referring briefly to the elaborate houses of the Atoni and Batak, Lévi-Strauss does invoke the fetishistic quality of buildings as illusory objectifications of unstable alliance. The usage is suggestive but comes nowhere near to doing justice to the complexity of the issues involved. The house is a representation not just of unity but also of various kinds of hierarchy and division.

The significance of a focus on the house is that it brings together aspects of social life which have previously been ignored or treated separately. Crucially, we would consider architectural features of houses as an aspect of their importance as social units in both life and thought. Rather than seeing in the house the birth of a new analytic type, the anthropological child of alliance and descent, it is this holistic potential of viewing houses 'in the round' which we would emphasise. The relation between building and group is multifaceted and contextually determined, the house's role as a complex idiom for social groupings, as a vehicle to naturalise rank, and as a source of symbolic power being inseparable from the building itself.

Despite the historical element in Lévi-Strauss' analysis of house societies, his notion of the house often appears paradoxically static. The very language used to describe the house, how it 'solidifies' an unstable relation of alliance, or 'transfixes' irreconcilable oppositions, reveals a tendency, shared by others, to see the house in static terms. Houses are dynamic entities. Their vitality comes from a number of sources – most obviously from the people who live in them, but also from the materials used in building, from life-giving rituals, or from the movement of the heavenly bodies which often determine their orientation. But it is often expressed in much stronger terms. In certain cultures, houses are far from being merely static material structures. They have animate qualities; they are endowed with spirits or souls, and are imagined in terms of the human body. In going beyond Lévi-Strauss' formulations, we would place these qualities at the centre of an anthropology of the house which considers houses and their inhabitants as part of one process of living.

There is a tendency in anthropology, not limited to Lévi-Strauss, to focus on the ritual aspects of social life. But the house has another side. It is an ordinary group of people concerned with their day-to-day affairs, sharing consumption and living in the shared space of a domestic dwelling. It is out of these everyday activities, carried on without ritual, reflection or fuss and, significantly, often by women, that the house is built. This house, all too easily taken for granted, is one that anthropologists have tended to ignore. One conclusion we would emphasise is the need for further research on an anthropology of everyday life which might both balance, and eventually be incorporated into, studies of ritual and ideology.

Notes

Janet Carsten is a Lecturer in Social Anthropology at the University of Edinburgh and the author of articles on Malaysia. Stephen Hugh-Jones is a Lecturer in Social Anthropology at the University of Cambridge who is currently researching the architecture of North-west Amazonia.

1 Janet Carsten and Stephen Hugh-Jones, *About the House*, Cambridge University Press (Cambridge), 1995.

2 Claude Lévi-Strauss, *Anthropology and Myth: Lectures 1951-82*, Blackwell (Oxford), 1987.

3 Claude Lévi-Strauss, *The Way of the Masks*, S Modelski (trans), Jonathan Cape (London), 1983.

4 Gaston Bachelard, *The Poetics of Space*, Orion Press (New York), 1964, xxxiii.

5 Caroline Humphrey, 'No Place Like Home in Anthropology: the Neglect of Architecture', *Anthropology Today*, vol 4, no 1, 1988, pp16-18.

6 Op cit, Claude Lévi-Strauss, *The Way of the Masks*.

PATRICK KEILLER
THE DILAPIDATED DWELLING

Where I live, there seem to be two kinds of space. There is *new space*, in which none of the buildings are more than about ten years old, and there is *old space*, in which most of the buildings are at least 20 years old, a lot of them over 90 years old, and all are more-or-less dilapidated. Most of the *old space* is residential, but there are also small shops, banks, cafés, public houses, a health centre, a library, a social security office, schools and so on. Most of the *new space* is occupied by large corporations of one sort or another, a few of them international in scope, and it is not urban in the conventional sense. It includes retail sheds, supermarkets, fast food restaurants, a *Travel Inn*, a business park, distribution warehouses, tyre, exhaust and windscreen service centres. Most of these places have large car parks and security cameras. There is a lot of new space under construction, it goes up fast, and more is proposed. Buildings in *new space* do not have to last very long. In some of the older *new space* the original buildings have already been replaced by new ones.

The *old space* looks poor, even when it isn't. Much of it is poor, but when it isn't, the dilapidation is still striking. *Old space* appears to be difficult to maintain. A lot of the shops don't look as if they're doing very well. The cybercafé didn't last very long. The public institutions, if they are lucky, manage to maintain their buildings. The public lavatories are in a terrible state, though they are very photogenic. In the street, there is a fair amount of outdoor drinking, and according to the police who attend burglaries, there is a lot of heroin about. Many houses have burglar alarms. Some have cable television or Internet access.

At the moment, the residential property market is busy. There are always a lot of builders working, but they don't have the skills, the materials or the time to be particularly conscientious about anything beyond short-term performance. The conservationist is, as always, frustrated, and if anyone is responsible for the surfaces of *old space*, it is these builders and their clients.

In *old space*, apart from the smaller branches of banks and supermarket chains, the activities of large corporations are not very visible. A local estate agent, for example, is likely to be a major bank, building society or insurance company in disguise. Dilapidated houses are bought with mortgages from building societies, banks and other large corporations. A lot of small shops are franchises. The utility companies' installations are mostly underground, or in anonymous boxes which one tends not to notice. TV aerials and satellite dishes quickly blend with the domestic scene.

The dilapidation of *old space* seems to have increased, in an Orwellian way, with the centralisation of media and political power – by the disempowerment of local government, for instance. At the same time, experience of dilapidation is tempered by the promise of immediate virtual or imminent actual presence elsewhere, through telematics and cheap travel. As I stand at the bus stop with my carrier bags in the rain, I can window-shop cheap tickets to Bali, or contemplate Hong Kong, Antarctica or Santa Cruz as webcam images on my Nokia; or I could if I had one – the virtual elsewhere seems, if anything, most effective as mere possibility, as a *frisson*.

New space is mostly work space. An increasing proportion of 'economically active' people work in *new space*. Most of those who are not 'economically active' visit it fairly frequently, at least for the weekly shop, but they do not spend much time there. A very large number of people are not 'economically active' – they are physically or mentally ill, children, non-working parents, 'voluntary' carers, the unemployed, pop stars in waiting, unpublished novelists, the early or otherwise retired and other non-employed people. For these people, everyday surroundings are *old space*, and *old space* is mostly residential space – houses and flats. Residential space has a visiting workforce: the window cleaner, the decorator, the meter reader, the washing-machine engineer, the plumber, the small builder; as well as on-site earners slaving away at Christmas crackers, clothes, poetry or television research. Despite the talk about corporate homeworking and the long expected 'death of the office' most of the above are likely to be self-employed, and very few of them at all well paid. The real economic activity of residential space – housework, most of it involved with child-rearing – is not paid at all. It was recently estimated that the real value of housework in the UK is £739 billion, 22 per cent more than the current value of the country's GDP.[1] On average, people in the UK only spend 12 per cent of their total time in paid work.[2] Although unpaid, child-rearing is presumably the most significant of all economic activities in that it shapes – though not always directly – the values and attitudes of the next generation of wealth creators. *New space*, on the other hand, is mostly corporate, company-car territory. There are plenty of women working in *new space*, often in senior roles, but the structures and work patterns in these places do not easily accommodate active parenthood. Most flexible part-time work suited to the child-rearer pays under four pounds an hour.

In the UK, housing takes up around 70 per cent of urban land.[3] Its housing stock is the oldest in Europe with an average age estimated at about 60 years. A quarter of the stock was built before the end of the First World War.[4] There are about 24 million dwellings in all,[5] but in the last 20 years the rate of new house building has fallen to only 150,000 per year, largely because of the elimination of public-sector house building.[6] Most new housing is built by developers for sale on completion, and is widely criticised as unsophisticated and over-priced.[7] In other developed economies, house production occurs in different ways, but if the UK is taken as the extreme example of a *laissez-faire* system operating in a built-up landscape with a restricted land supply, one can perhaps discern a general tendency in that under advanced capitalism it is increasingly difficult to produce and maintain *the dwelling*. This is especially odd given that dwellings constitute the greater part of the built environment, that they are the spaces where most people spend most of their time, and where what is arguably the real 'work' of society is done. Modernity, it seems, is exemplified not so much by the business park or the airport, but by the dilapidated dwelling.

During the last 20 years or so domestic life has been transformed in many more-or-less electronic ways: supermarket distribution, increased unemployment and early retirement, programmable gas heating, computerised banking, new TV, video, audio, telecommunications, the personal computer and the Internet. Most of these things make it easier to stay at home, and many of them make it more difficult to go out, but the house itself has changed very little. The supermarkets, with computerised distribution and warehousing, and big trucks on modern roads, have transformed the UK's food market and shopping habits, for example creating a mass market in cosmopolitan food and drink that was previously only available in a few parts of London. In the same period, house production has merely declined, though, supermarkets now offer mortgages. For the corporate economy, the house seems to exist only as a given, a destination for sales of consumable materials and services.

There are many reasons why this might be the case. Firstly, houses last a long time. House building is also by its nature a very local undertaking, even for the largest producers. Wimpey, who claim to be the largest house builders in the world, only seem to advertise their developments locally. The tendencies in production that have brought Ford to the Mondeo – the world car – have never been widely applied to house production. Despite the best efforts of several generations of architects, houses are still not manufactured off site and are not generally susceptible to *distribution*. When they are available in this way, the purchaser is faced with the problem of finding a site on which to erect a single house, which in the UK is very difficult. IKEA have started to produce prefabricated dwellings, but so far they have erected the product themselves on their own development sites. There have been many impressive examples of factory-produced houses since the 18th century, but never in very large numbers.

In the middle of the 19th century, less than one per cent of the UK's national income was spent on house building.[8] Since before the time of Engels, industrial capitalism has been more usually accompanied by the production of large but insufficient numbers of poor-quality houses, palatial workplaces, and a small number of millionaires' mansions: the Rothschilds' houses of Mentmore and Waddesdon, for example, or Bill Gates' $50 million house on the shore of Lake Washington, near Seattle. It seems that, for capitalism, houses are a means of centralising wealth, rather than products to be distributed. In the last 100 years, relative to earnings, food and most manufactured goods have become much cheaper, but houses have become more expensive both to build and to buy. Industrial production has not been very successful at producing houses for the people who are otherwise

its consumers: most of the best housing developments of the last century or so seem to have been undertaken outside the market, by philanthropic employers, civic bodies or committed individuals and groups.

Since the late 1970s, 'housing' has been an unfashionable subject for architects and theorists. With a few notable exceptions – the architecture of Walter Segal, for instance – there has been very little house building of any architectural interest in the UK beyond a few one-off houses, these often for architects themselves. Among theorists and other writers, the very idea of *dwelling* has been recognised as problematic, for example:

Architects have long been attacking the idea that architecture should be essentially stable, material and anchored to a particular location in space. One of the main targets for those who would make architecture more dynamic is of course that bulwark of inertia and confinement, the outer casing of our dwelling place that we call a house. Which explains why, as early as 1914, the Futurists put their main emphasis – at least in theory – on the complex places of transit.

'We are . . . [the men] of big hotels, railway stations, immense roads, colossal ports, covered markets, brilliantly lit galleries . . .'

We are dissatisfied because we are no longer able to come up with a truly promising form of architecture in which we would like to live. We have become nomads, restlessly wandering about, even if we are sedentary and our wanderings consist of flipping through the television channels . . .'[9]

On the other hand:

Bridges and hangars, stadiums and power stations are buildings but not dwellings; railway stations and highways, dams and market halls are built, but they are not dwelling places. Even so, these buildings are in the domain of our dwelling. That domain extends over these buildings and yet is not limited to the dwelling place.[10]

In a culture in which so much of the space of work and transit is new, modern and professionally produced, but so much home space is old, amateurish and artlessly hand-made, one tends to forget that, like the industrial landscapes that inspired the modernist avant-garde, the corporate economy only exists because it has been able to develop global markets in the necessities and longings of domestic life. The dominant narratives of modernity – mobility and instant communication – appear to be about *work* and *travel*, not *home*. They are constructions of a work-oriented academic élite about a work-oriented business élite. However, as Saskia Sassen points out:

A large share of the jobs involved in finance are lowly paid clerical and manual jobs, many held by women and immigrants' . . . the city concentrates diversity. Its spaces are inscribed with the dominant corporate culture but also with a multiplicity of other cultures and identities. The dominant

Victoria Street, Reading, 'Reading in England was a sleepy biscuit- and beer-making town until it was invaded by decentralised offices from London and high-technology factories from California.'[18]

L to R: Rear of signs: 'COMING SOON ON THIS SITE, A WARNER BROTHERS 9-SCREEN MULTIPLEX CINEMA, OPENING EASTER 1996'

Bus shelter, Great Bridge Street, West Bromwich, 'For amid the Ridley Scott images of world cities, the writing about skyscraper fortresses, the Baudrillard visions of hyper-space . . . most people actually live in places like Harlesden or West Brom. Much of life for many people, even in the heart of the first world, still consists of waiting in a bus shelter with your shopping for a bus that never comes.'[19]

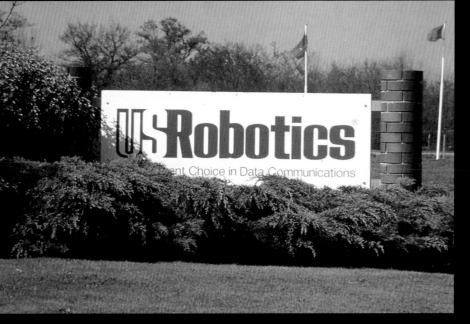

US Robotics, Winnersh Triangle business and distribution park, between Reading and Wokingham. Microsoft and Digital also have sites at Winnersh and Microsoft are building a large new site nearby at Thames Valley Park, Reading

and '40TH AND TESS PASSED IT. WELL DONE', opposite houses in Ripple Road, Dagenham – the A13 to Tilbury and the Dartford Tunnel

Sign to Midpoint distribution park, near Junction 18 of the M6 at Middlewich, Cheshire. Tesco has a 37,500-square-metre distribution centre at Midpoint, built in 1993; it has 33,000 pallet positions and a holding capacity of 43 million cases, or nine days' stock for 120 stores in an area which extends as far as Gateshead; each store receives between one and four deliveries per day

Images are frame enlargements from Robinson in Space (Patrick Keiller, 1997, 83 min), a BBC film distributed by the British Film Institute and available as a Connoiseur/Academy Video

culture can encompass only part of the city. And while corporate power inscribes non-corporate cultures and identities with 'otherness', thereby devaluing them, they are present everywhere. This presence is especially strong in our major cities which also have the largest concentrations of corporate power. We see here an interesting correspondence between great concentrations of corporate power and large concentrations of 'others'. It invites us to see that globalisation is not only constituted in terms of capital and the new international corporate culture (international finance, telecommunications, information flows) but also in terms of people and non-corporate cultures. There is a whole infrastructure of low-wage, non-professional jobs and activities that constitute a crucial part of the so-called corporate economy.[11]

Dwellings are rarely corporate space (see Billy Wilder's *The Apartment*). Are dwellings 'other'? The 'other' space in the city centres, where corporate power is concentrated, is usually the dwelling space of 'other' cultures and identities. The dwellings of corporate insiders are usually located at a distance, but even they live in homes that represent a level of investment per square metre that is only a fraction of that made in their workplaces. At the same time, domesticity is characterised by intimacy, the 'nearness' that Kenneth Frampton noted as increasingly absent from architecture,[12] presumably most of all from corporate architecture. Perhaps these qualities of domesticity are 'other' to the corporate economy, even in the homes of corporate insiders? Perhaps we are all *others* when we are at home?

> Marginality is today no longer limited to minority groups, but is rather massive and pervasive; this cultural activity of the non-producers of culture, an activity that is unsigned, unreadable and unsymbolised, remains the only one possible for all those who nevertheless buy and pay for the showy products through which a productivist economy articulates itself. Marginality is becoming universal. A marginal group has now become a silent majority.[13]

Heidegger's formulation of *dwelling* certainly sounds unfashionable in the late 20th century:

> *Only if we are capable of dwelling, only then can we build.* Let us think for a while of a farmhouse in the Black Forest, which was built some 200 years ago by the dwelling of peasants. Here the self-sufficiency of the power to let earth and heaven, divinities and mortals enter *in simple oneness* into things, ordered the house. It placed the farm on the wind-sheltered mountain slope looking south, among the meadows close to the spring. It gave it the wide overhanging shingle roof whose proper slope bears up under the burden of snow, and which, reaching deep down, shields the chambers against the storms of the long winter nights. It did not forget the altar corner behind the community table; it made room in its chamber for the hallowed places of childbed and the 'tree of the dead' – for that is what they call a coffin there: the *Totenbaum* – and in this way it designed for the different generations under one roof the character of their journey through time. A craft which, itself sprung from dwelling, still uses its tools and frames as things, built the farmhouse.[14]

This essay was invoked by Frampton towards the end of his *Modern Architecture – A Critical History* as a recognition of a quality of experience that many believed most modern building had lost. This loss being, they said, why many people had

rejected modern architecture, and why, perhaps, we have speculative house builders who build houses for sale that are supposed to resemble the tied cottages of Victorian farm workers.

Richard Sennett, in a lecture in 1992, pointed out that Heidegger neglected the *stupefying* nature of *dwelling*, and that in fact *dwelling* and *thinking* are antithetical. The creativity of cities, said Sennett, arises from their being sites of unresolved conflict between *thinking* and *dwelling*.

It is easy to poke fun at Heidegger's notion of dwelling – so nostalgic, so conservative, so *agricultural* – so at odds with a quasi-nomadic hunter-gatherer present as to be unhelpful, if not actually undesirable, especially in the context of his involvement with Nazism in the 1930s. Although the house he evokes is exemplary as a work of *architecture* (and has the required longevity), the social fabric – the *dwelling* – that produced it is almost unattainable, unsupportable, though perhaps not quite. In a letter responding to some of these questions, a friend wrote:

> Recently we visited together with students of architecture the small village Halen in Switzerland, designed by Atelier 5, still located in an unspoiled forest. The extremely narrow terraced houses with small private courtyards and a central public place, built more than 30 years ago, were in a perfect state, well kept, partly modernised (insulation of the external walls). The common installations like the shop in the piazza, the petrol station, the swimming pool and the tennis lawn were still working and in good condition. The community, now living in the houses, were to a high percentage the children and grandchildren of the initial owners. They have returned after they first had left the houses of their parents.

Frampton has described Halen as, 'one of the most seminal pieces of land settlement built in Europe since the Second World War . . . a model for reconciling development with place-creation and the maintenance of ecological balance'.[15] If Halen represents something approaching the modern attainment of Heidegger's *dwelling*, as Frampton seems to suggest by his subsequent reference to Heidegger, it is intriguing to learn that many of those who live there occupy the houses of their parents.

We are more familiar with this kind of *dwelling* in the context of its loss. In a World Service radio interview, a Bosnian refugee in Mostar longs to return to his house in Stolac, 50 kilometres away, from which he was evicted by his Croat neighbours, even though the town is still under Croat control: 'My family has lived in Stolac for centuries . . . I love the smell of the river . . .' For most of us, there is another kind of *dwelling*:

> The purpose of this work is to . . . bring to light the models of action characteristic of users whose status as the dominated element in society (a status that does not mean that they are either passive or docile) is concealed by the euphemistic term 'consumers'.

> In our societies, as local stabilities break down, it is as if, no longer fixed by a circumscribed community, tactics wander out of orbit, making consumers into immigrants in a system too vast to be their own, too tightly woven for them to escape from it.

> Increasingly constrained, yet less and less concerned with these vast frameworks, the individual detaches himself from them without being able to escape them and can henceforth only try to outwit them, to pull tricks on them, to rediscover, within an electronicised and computerised megalopolis, the 'art' of the hunters and rural folk of earlier days.[16]

If we think of ourselves as *consumers* in this way, perhaps our difficulties with housing are easier to understand. How is housing *consumed*?

In the context of the urban home in the UK, De Certeau's notion of 'tactics' as a response to the predicament of being a consumer evokes not so much do-it-yourself – currently a bigger market in the UK than new house building – but the way that the character of the public-sector housing 'estate' is changing 'as local stabilities break down'. In Inner London and elsewhere, the system of allocating public-sector housing on a basis which reflected its philanthropic origins in the 19th century has been fractured since the 1970s by ideas like the 'hard-to-let' flat, by the 'right to buy' and by an increase in social mobility generally. Public-sector housing was financed by 60-year loans, and was often designed by critically respected architects. It aimed to be of far better quality than that produced by the private sector. Often the more architecturally ambitious developments (including some influenced by the model of Halen) were difficult to build and were regarded as problematic early in their history, but some of them have aged well and have gradually accumulated populations who find them attractive as places to live.

Whatever the wider implications, perhaps architects can take some comfort from this. The notion of 'the everyday' in architecture offers a welcome relief from conventional interpretations of architectural value, especially in a culture where most 'everyday' building is not produced with much architectural intention, but it seems to affirm the spatial quality and detail of architects' architecture where it exists. Similarly, the subjective transformations of spatial experience characteristic of both the Surrealists and the Situationists might seem to promise a way of transcending assumptions of spatial poverty, of transforming 'even the most colourless localities', as Breton said of Aragon's 'spellbinding romantic inventiveness',[17] but in practice both groups were quite selective about the sites they favoured. In the long run, spatial and other architectural qualities seem to survive, though often not in the way that was expected.

The UK's new Labour government seems to be prepared to leave house building to the private sector, even for the showcase 'Millennium Village' development next to the dome at Greenwich. The long-term success of the Lansbury estate in Poplar, which was built as the housing showcase for the 1951 Festival of Britain, has not prompted Labour to recall that its commitment to public-sector housing produced so many internationally acclaimed housing developments between 1945 and the early

1970s. Not long before the 1997 election, Richard, Lord Rogers, newly ennobled in preparation for a Labour victory, presented an edition of the BBC's *Building Sites* – in which celebrities present favourite buildings – for which he selected the former London County Council's Alton Estate at Roehampton in southwest London – the Modern Movement landmark of 1952-59. This timely endorsement of the heroic period of public-sector housing seems not to have awakened any enthusiasm among members of the new government.

So far (at the time of writing), Labour has said little about housing, but appears to be giving tacit support to various private-sector proposals for 'super-villages': 5,200 new houses near Peterborough; 3,000 at Micheldever in Hampshire; between 5,000 and 10,000 houses west of Stevenage; 3,300 houses in three new villages near Cambridge. The latter have been 'masterplanned' by the architect Terry Farrell for a consortium of Alfred McAlpine, Bryant and Bovis in 'Cambridgeshire vernacular', an attempt to create 'a traditional village, with village greens with cricket pavilions, local shops and pubs' and a 69,677 square metre business park. With or without cricket pavilions, none of these developments sound as if they will have much chance of either 'reconciling development with place-creation and the maintenance of ecological balance' or attempting to reconfigure the house as something approaching a successful industrial product.

Labour's belief in finding an accommodation with the market seems to preclude a revival of public-sector house building on anything like its former scale, but the history of house building suggests that the market will never be able to modernise *dwelling* on its own, and Labour is committed to modernisation. If there is to be any possibility for a more promising approach to *dwelling*, it is very unlikely to come from the conventional house-building industry. Some of the most successful house-building projects in the UK during the last two decades have been non-commercial initiatives which included houses for sale. In the Netherlands, the government's VINEX policy aims to build 800,000 dwellings by the year 2,000 in a planned programme with commitments to credible architectural design and environmental and transport policies. This approach produces domestic architecture for sale of a quality that house buyers in the UK can only dream about. If house production in the UK is to undergo any kind of consumer-led reform, it looks as if this can only happen in the context of similar collectivist initiatives.

Notes

1 Announcement by the Office for National Statistics, reported in *The Guardian*, October 7 1997. The figure is for unpaid work valued at the same average rate as paid employment.

2 Ibid.

3 Michael Ball, *Housing and Construction: A Troubled Relationship*, Policy Press (Bristol), 1996, p1.

4 Philip Leather and Tanya Morrison, *The State of UK Housing*, Policy Press (Bristol), 1997, p21.

5 Central Statistical Office, *Regional Trends*, 1995 edition, HMSO (London), p94.

6 Ball, op cit, p7.

7 Ibid, p47.

8 Ibid, p8.

9 Florian Rötzer, 'Space and Virtuality: Some Observations on Architecture', in *The Future of Space*, Bernd Meurer (ed), Campus Verlag (Frankfurt/New York), 1994, pp205-206, 217.

10 Martin Heidegger, 'Building Dwelling Thinking', in *Poetry, Language, Thought*, Albert Hofstadter (trans), Harper and Row (New York), 1975, p145.

11 Saskia Sassen, 'Economy and Culture in the Global City', in *The Future of Space*, Campus Verlag (Frankfurt and New York), 1994, p74.

12 Kenneth Frampton, *Modern Architecture – A Critical History*, Thames and Hudson (London), 1980, p312.

13 Michel de Certeau, *The Practice of Everyday Life*, Steven Randall (trans), University of California Press (Berkeley), 1984, p.xvii. *L'Invention du quotidien, 2. Habiter, cuisiner*, by Luce Giard and Pierre Mayol, was published in French in 1980, and deals, writes Steven Randall, with 'a "fine art of dwelling", in which places are organised in a network of history and relationships, and a "fine art of cooking", in which everyday skill turns nourishment into a language of the body and the body's memories.'

14 Heidegger, op cit, p160.

15 Frampton, op cit, p311.

16 De Certeau, op cit, ppxi-xii, xx, xxiv.

17 André Breton, quoted from a radio interview in Simon Watson Taylor's introduction to his translation of Louis Aragon, *Paris Peasant*, Picador (London), 1980, p10.

18 Peter Hall, 'The Geography of the Fifth Kondratieff', in *Uneven Re-development*, Doreen Massey and John Allen (eds), Hodder & Stoughton (London), 1988, p52.

19 Doreen Massey, 'A Place Called Home?', in *Space, Place and Gender*, Polity Press (Cambridge), 1994, p163.

URBAN SENSE

Half a century of planning activity has transformed the built environment, but has failed to capture the public's sympathies. The disillusionment with modernist town proposals has been particularly evident in the last two decades. Projects once hailed as manifestations of a brave new global vision have shown themselves to be inadequate as long-term settlements. Most conspicuous in post-war developments has been the absence of a sense of place. By zoning towns into distinct and unrelated sectors, modernist planning divided and polarised community life.

The growing public disaffection has helped to bring about alternative views in the architectural and planning professions, views which embrace traditional towns as models for new developments. These older models have been carefully studied by a new generation of professionals who introduce into urban design the idea of neighbourhoods with a diversity of communal, commercial and residential functions. The use of traditional urban models has resuscitated age-old questions about continuity and change in the relationship between architecture and the city, the setting of new towns and villages in the natural landscape, and the dialogue between built form and communal open spaces.

Despite the growing public support that new traditional towns have enjoyed, some critics have claimed that these models cannot work today, as they fail to address contemporary social and technological issues. What critics have failed to appreciate, however, is that the most viable contemporary urban centres are in fact historical enclaves that evolved not out of *tabula-rasa* attitudes like those expounded by the Modern Movement, but a wholesome investment in the notion of a 'res publica', or public realm. The question of technology is not posed by the new traditionalists in awe of science, but in practical terms: how it can be harnessed to a common-sensical urbanism, rather than the other way around. Science, then, needs to be used correctly – to warm our houses, aid us in our daily endeavours, expedite our business, if this remains within the bounds of a healthy urban life.

The new attitudes regarding technology are perhaps most evident in the way the problem of the car is being handled. The new traditionalists seek to limit its use to peripheral areas, creating pedestrian neighbourhoods and quarters that will ultimately reduce the reliance on automobiles. More central to the argument, though, is the appreciation of communal or public space as a generator of civic environments. At Belvedere Village in Ascot, Demetri Porphyrios sets up what he call a 'nucleus of a settlement': a pattern of buildings and spaces intended not merely for long-term use but for gradual transformation and adaptation into a larger regional urban centre. At Windsor in Florida, Andres Duany and

Elizabeth Plater-Zyberk have codified the elements of urban growth, setting up a building programme that limits idiosyncrasy in favour of an appreciable pattern of streets, squares, greens and street elevations.

The same attitudes are in evidence in the better-known masterplan for Poundbury by Leon Krier, which displays the entire range of civic amenities necessary for a balanced urban environment. The public spaces are bounded by communal buildings, residential blocks look onto central greens, commercial districts are located always at walking distance within the neighbourhoods.

Not least of the new practices in urban design is the respectful provision of a 'hard edge' along the boundaries of new towns, one which no longer seeks to expand haphazardly into the natural landscape but to treat it as a separate, sovereign entity. For the new traditionalists, *delineation* is paramount; whether one delineates the edges of a square, a green, a park, or the urban periphery, the act derives from the same appreciation of the integrity of every element that constitutes our environment. The Modern Movement purposefully blurred the differences in the city. Potsdamer Platz in Berlin is a point in case, the area having since the war been diluted with the most diverse, eccentric structures – buildings clamouring for attention in a desolate, unaccommodating area that has been reduced to a loosely-knit, confused cluster of interstitial spaces. In their masterplan for the region, Hilmer and Sattler have ventured to reaffirm the historic pattern of streets and squares, setting up the right mix of uses and a system of public spaces that they deem indispensable in any urban proposal.

This issue pulls together the proceeds of the Symposium that was held at the Prince of Wales's Institute of Architecture and the International Forum hosted by the Academy Group and the Royal Academy of Arts on 1st December, 1992. Four presentations – the new town of Windsor at Vero Beach, Florida, by Andres Duany and Elizabeth Plater-Zyberk; the masterplan for Potsdamer and Leipziger Platz in Berlin by Christoph Sattler of Hilmer and Sattler; the Belvedere Village in Ascot by Demetri Porphyrios; and the new town of Poundbury in Dorchester by Leon Krier and the Duchy of Cornwall – were used as a springboard for discussion.

Absent from this group of professionals is the view of the architect as procurer of high-tech panaceas – the new traditionalists choose the more realistic path of collective experience and common sense, refusing to be seduced by industrial iconography or be lured into the guilt-ridden culture of anti-traditional rhetoric. They argue that if there is to be a brighter vision for the city, humanity must learn to make use of the good that is engrained in traditional urban models.   *Richard Economakis*

OPPOSITE: ANDRES DUANY AND ELIZABETH PLATER-ZYBERK, VIEW OF THE NEW TOWN OF WINDSOR, FLORIDA

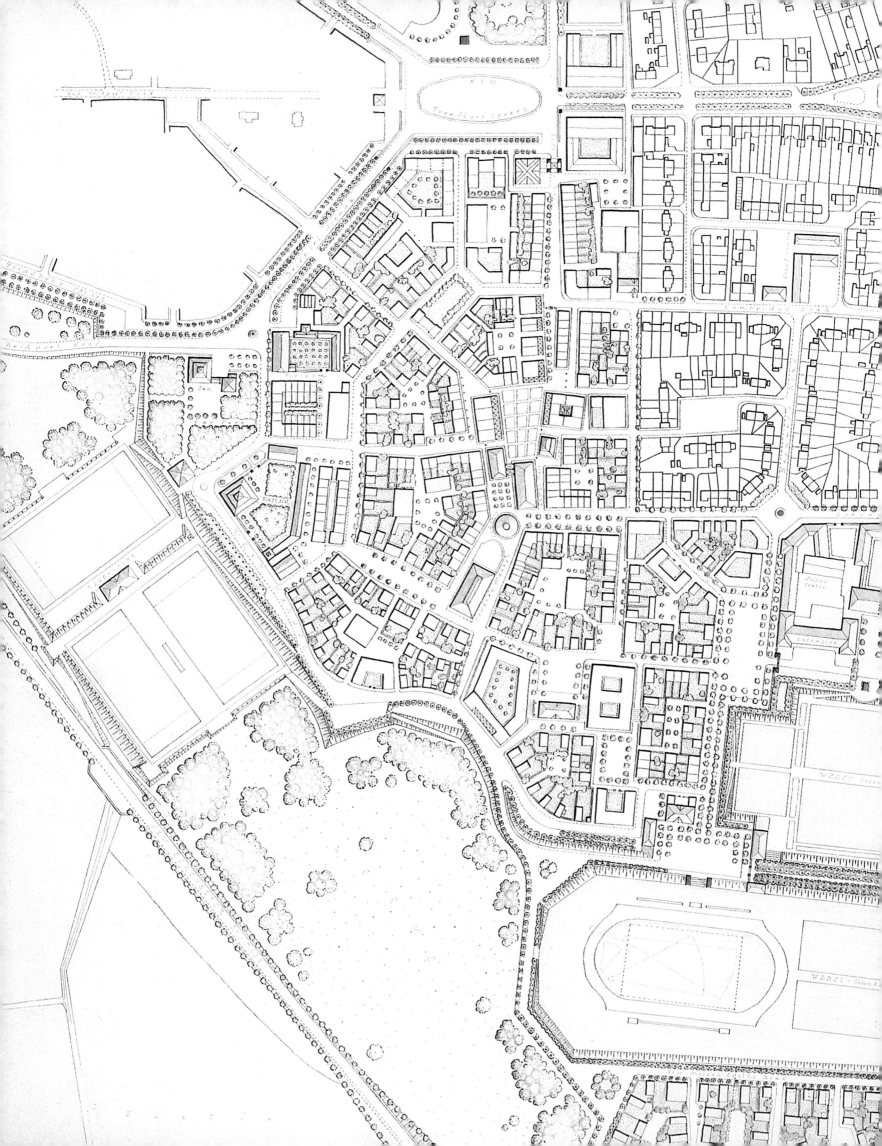

HRH THE PRINCE OF WALES

I have learnt over the years that one can do a certain amount through words. In architecture, however, the power of words alone is limited. This is why I believe that one of the most important tasks for my Institute is to apply theory to the creation of practical examples which can be seen to work. For it is not until you try to turn a theory – a way of looking at the world – into real buildings that the difficulties facing you become fully apparent. And those difficulties – vested interests, established practices, ways of thinking which discourage humility, appropriateness and human scale – can be immense.

Only the architect, engineer or builder who is willing to commit himself actively to a different approach can begin to understand how to turn these forces to positive rather than negative account. The resistance encountered at the outset is remarkable, but by patient and determined action it can be overcome.

I recognise that it is a long-term process. Indeed, when I announced my intention at the Villa Lante in Italy last year to set up an Institute, I said rather rashly that I was quite prepared for the fact that it might take another 50 years to overcome the mistakes made by architects and planners during the last 50. I still am.

All the best architecture has helped humanity better to understand itself and its place in the universe. Part of the reason for the decline and fragmentation of building over recent decades has been the modish disregard amongst many of the profession for the harmony and proportion inherent in the Universe. I feel that this is a particular tragedy, partly because in reality many people have tended to retain a firm belief that a profound Order does exist in the world.

The problem is to find a language which expresses this Order through building. There is no shortage of tools to enable us to begin this task of reinvesting architecture with human significance – not just at the level of how it looks but also at the level of how it is made.

Excerpt from an address given by HRH The Prince of Wales on the occasion of the formal opening of The Prince of Wales's Institute of Architecture, 28 October 1992.

OPPOSITE: LEON KRIER, POUNDBURY, DORCHESTER, PLAN OF MIDDLE FARM QUARTER

ABOVE: AERIAL VIEW OF THE SITE; *BELOW*: PERSPECTIVE VIEW OF THE NEW TOWN; *OPPOSITE*: VIEW OF THE DEVELOPMENT MODEL

ANDRES DUANY AND ELIZABETH PLATER-ZYBERK
THE NEW TOWN OF WINDSOR, FLORIDA
1989

The United States has been largely the creation of developers. Virtually from the beginning the first people who came over were in the business of getting people to settle and in some way acquire land and make money off the acquisition and distribution of land. The reason that this is not perfectly obvious is that some of these developers, in fact virtually all of them, did such a good job that they could barely be noticed. Many of the places which we love, which are equal to the best in the world – places like Washington DC, Annapolis, Maryland, San Francisco and New Orleans – are the result of developers' work. Unfortunately in the last 40 years, by having changed the model they have actually disgraced themselves, and developers in general are no longer welcome. One of the remarkable achievements of the last few decades is that in a country as forward-looking as the United States, virtually everywhere growth is unwelcome; when the developer turns up and says 'here I am' to build this shopping centre or office park or housing-cluster, the population comes out and says 'thank you very much but do it elsewhere'. Clearly we must busy ourselves with changing the model.

Our attempt in projects such as Windsor is to take those elements which are necessary for human life and activity – the places of living, the places of working and the places of shopping which developers have so competently provided for so long – and restore them to the earlier model of villages, towns and neighbourhoods. Windsor happens to be in Florida, and it also happens to be in an extraordinarily beautiful place between the Atlantic Ocean and the Indian River that is unusual but not actually all that special in Florida, which has a seacoast of this quality from top to bottom. What is unusual is the attitude towards what is traded, what in the United States is called the amenity. Windsor is all about the belief that it is not mere quantity that one ought to buy, that it is not just the largest lot with the best view and the most bathrooms and the most square feet and the most shag carpets, but in fact the idea of community, and in order to achieve community, which I think is a highly desirable attribute of Windsor, one intrinsically has to give up the quantities. One does not have the largest lots, one does not have the largest houses, and yet, and this is paradoxical, one is here afforded privacy as well as community.

The site was a dying grapefruit grove; the freezes had been coming down further south every year but there were certain given, pre-existing conditions of landscape which were taken up by the plan. Actually there is so very little in Florida in terms of topography, that everything is precious and one must really try to pick even the small features up. Although the site plan is essentially a grid (and a grid in the raw American condition can be very unsophisticated), it also has a strong capability of variety and picturesqueness. The large streets mostly terminate in vistas of pavilions, civic buildings or special ends of buildings, with streets being deflected by small

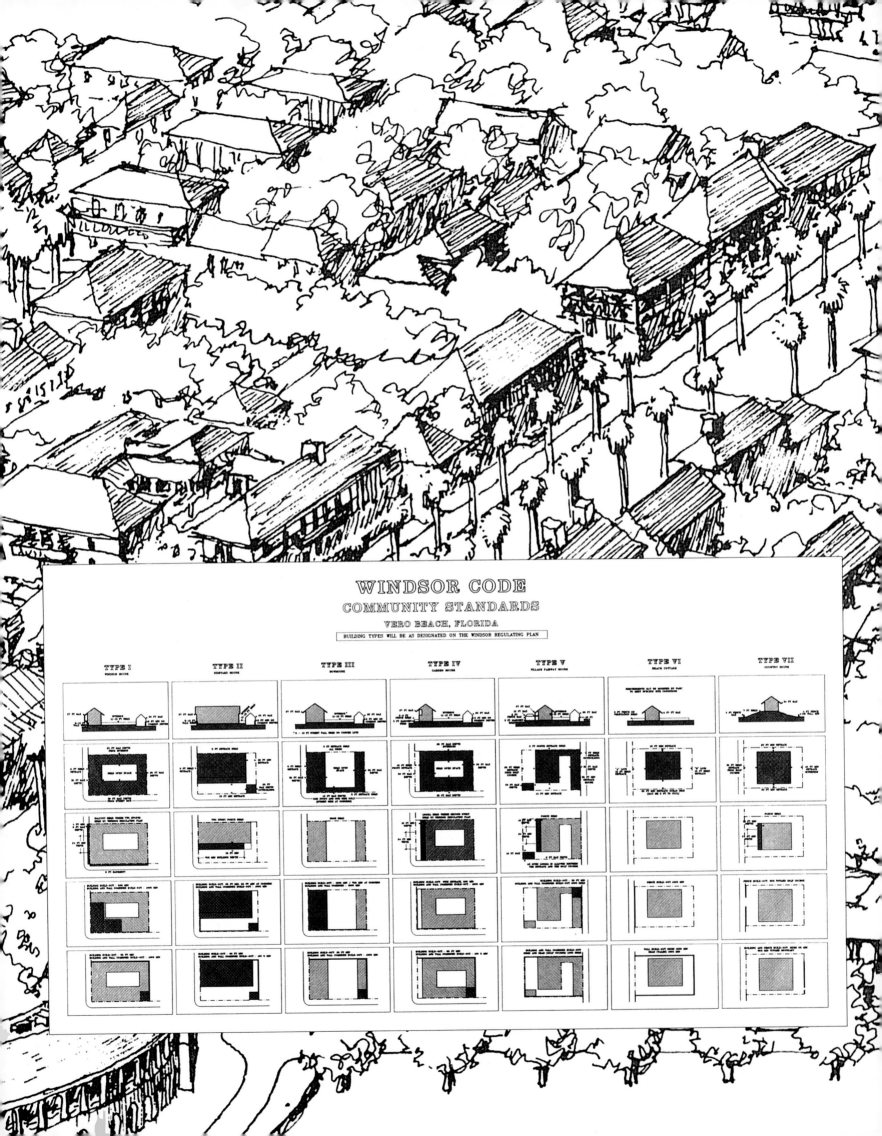

turbulent clauses which are interspersed throughout.

Something which is important yet absent from conventional development, is a variety of street types. In the United States the street is the public space, rather than the square, so there is an unusually large variety of street types; at Windsor all of these are designed, not for the automobile, but for the pedestrian. They are the places of community, which is what one exchanges for quantity. The plan requires discipline of the buildings, which must always come up to certain lines. Particular elements are permitted to encroach on these lines, balconies and so forth, but essentially there is a strong sense of order along the street. Our scheme is all about making space, and by space I mean place. A sense of place requires, we think, a high degree of discipline in the bounding wall – a certain neutrality in the architecture and a high degree of order in the building elevation. The civic buildings are often smaller than the residences, but by being permitted to be developed in a classical manner they establish their hierarchy over the private buildings. Studies were made on how the different building types might be assembled on a block system. What we discovered from this is that one can build right on to the property line, liberating so much of the lot which is normally wasted by front lawns typical of the United States. By doing so, one can achieve a very large perceptual exterior piece and still have relatively small lots. By virtue of the walls, which we coded to be of a certain minimum height, and a certain care in the designation of the way in which the buildings open onto the street, we could achieve a great deal of privacy – which is very difficult to provide when a building stands free in the middle of its lot.

The Windsor plan is entered via the town square; the great green is arranged along a grid which is slanted because of a pre-existing grid of trees. There is a system, albeit subtle, regarding the location of the civic buildings, how one enters these, where these are placed relative to each other, and how they relate to the squares. One of the things about this plan which makes it superior to Seaside is that it operates at the perceptual level; it seems like a much duller plan than Seaside, which is a very hyperactive, explicit kind of place, but Windsor is full of subtleties that can be appreciated by the pedestrian. From the beginning, Windsor was designed perceptually.

As planners we design a masterplan, pull back, write a code, and then invite architects in quantity, perhaps hundreds of architects in an instance like this, to actually design the buildings. We found, much to our consternation, that after the completion of our first project – which was called Charleston Place, a scheme which did in fact achieve streets and squares – we had designed virtually all the buildings. Although we had attempted variety, one could always tell that the buildings were by the same hand. There is no way to falsify that a scheme is by the same hand; it's actually much better to confront this and do the Georgian job of actually having all the buildings look alike. There's nothing, I think, less satisfying than false variety. But we learned that, and now we code our town projects and invite architects to come in.

At Windsor the building fronts are hermetic, designed in consideration of the passer-by who normally cannot tolerate gangs of garage doors. These are located at the back of each block, with guest houses, outbuildings and so forth. Traditional towns are extremely resilient and able to sustain modern life. Don't let any planners tell you that they do not work. In fact, what does not work are the modern suburbs which are congested. We now have become a society that is accustomed to step out of our front door and past the garbage dumpster. We need the traditional street as a public space where both cars and people are comfortable. It is a balanced equation.

The code is a complex instrument consisting of three pieces: urban regulations, the regulating plan, and architectural regulations. The urban regulations identify seven different building types, from courtyard buildings to free-standing villas surrounded by porches. Regulations tell you very simply where to place the building, what you can articulate it with (balconies and so forth), how you must build it, how high you must go, and how to model the interior. The regulating plan shows on every lot exactly where the building must be loaded to; there's a kind of genetic information that goes into something like this – in fact the closest analogy of what a good code does is perhaps the DNA molecule; genetic information that makes the design which one has conceived emerge over time and quite independently of the designer. So long as it is administered properly it will emerge, whatever the quality of the architecture, whether exceptional or absolutely mediocre. We always test the codes with first- and second-year students who have a surplus of enthusiasm and an absolute ignorance of such matters. They tend to try the code more than anyone else. The more controversial parts of the code are the architectural regulations that chart what materials, what configurations and what techniques can be applied to building walls, garden-walls, balconies, porches, roofs, gutters etc.

A code like Windsor has much to do with the region's vernacular architecture. In this case it was the Anglo-Caribbean vernacular, the way the British built when they hit the tropics. This kind of construction makes an enormous amount of sense, being a combination of the heavy masonry base and wood superstructure which tends to be light, full of porches and lodges. In our study sketches we considered the way columns might be used, whether classical elements were to be permitted in the vernacular and so forth, whether the roofs were to be notched, whether the rafters were to show. What we personally prefer is an archetypal vernacular based on the expression of construction. We think that that's what is timeless about architecture: the bringing-down of a building's weight, expressing the small elements which support weight (rafters, brackets and so forth), all of which are highly prized by the code.

At Windsor, the tendency is towards sobriety, to limit expression so that buildings can be harmonious. The buildings are about load-bearing construction, rafters and columns and the simplicity which is derived from these.

No town planner would have the time to lavish care on every building. One of the things that coding and distributing the work does is that it divides the care among people who have the time to apply it.

From the presentation given by Andres Duany at the Royal Academy of Arts, London, 1st December 1992.

OPPOSITE: The Windsor code, sketch perspective of Windsor; OVERLEAF: View of Windsor

ABOVE: ANDRES DUANY AND ELIZABETH PLATER-ZYBERK, DEVELOPMENT SKETCHES AND ELEVATION FOR WINDSOR; *OPPOSITE*: WINDSOR STREET CORNER

SARAH CHAPLIN

AUTHENTICITY AND OTHERNESS

The New Japanese Theme Park

Nobody in Japan, it seems, is afraid to grapple with the issue which is so problematic architecturally in Europe: that of authenticity, especially when it comes to designing a new cultural theme park. If a developer thinks that the Japanese public desires to consume replicas of Shakespearean England or a Turkish Bazaar, then it is simply a matter of hiring the right people, constructing with the right materials, using the proper techniques, and stocking the appropriate imported merchandise in the gift shop. It is about creating a place without caricature but with plenty of attentiveness to detail, in order to suggest a specific cultural resonance, and to make the experience sufficiently exotic or 'other', to generate and satisfy an active curiosity. Ultimately it satisfies Japanese visitors' desire to see something of the world without the necessity to visit say, Stratford-upon-Avon or Topkapi Palace, Istanbul.

For the European visitor it is often difficult to take developments of this type seriously, and indeed they are often seen to represent a curious quirk of the Japanese penchant for consuming generally. However, considered in a more traditional Japanese way of thinking, the approach to building these theme parks is in many respects akin to the way in which Shinto shrines are rebuilt every 20 years or so, and visited regularly throughout the calendar, a thoroughly authentic practice which has existed for hundreds of years. What is celebrated is not the actual antiquity of the structures themselves, but the importance of the site on which they are built and the faithfulness and skill of their ritualised reconstruction.

Since the remarkable Huis den Bosch was built on the southernmost island of Kyushu, the idea of building whole pieces of elsewhere in Japan has spawned a form of virtual tourism: consuming foreign architecture on home territory. Huis den Bosch is not just a reconstructed bit of a Dutch city but a complete resort, popular with Japanese honeymooners, which now boasts 58 restaurants, 14 museums and 67 shops, presents nightly laser shows and firework displays, and features the Hotel Europe, modelled on Amsterdam's Hotel de L'Europe but built on a grander scale, with interiors by a Dutch designer. This is consuming architecture on an ambitious level, and ironically, it has been said that because of Huis den Bosch, a proper record of traditional Dutch architecture now exists which will remain untouched by the ravages of history. By comparison, the actual architectural examples in Holland on which Huis den Bosch is based, are likely to be altered by continual use as the Dutch adapt their built fabric to suit the needs of the next century.

There are many other examples of the Japanese actively consuming foreign architecture which date significantly from the mid-1980s: Philippe Starck's Asahi Beer Hall in Asakusa, or Nigel Coates' Wall project in Roppongi both parade their signature designs using imported skills and ideas, and stand out in the street as 'other'. This is similar to the way in which many English or French words have been incorporated into everyday speech,

but are written in a different script, *katakana*, compared to indigenous vocabulary, making them immediately visible in a page of text. Even the concept of the theme park has been rendered in *katakana* as Japanese English: pronounced *taimu parku*, it is marked out linguistically as a Western notion, which began with the invention of Disneyland.

During the economic bubble of the 1980s there was a tendency in Japan to consume all things imported: beers, cars, novelists, trends. Such items were part of the conspicuous display of wealth by corporations and individuals alike, where architecture was just one element of a whole shopping basket of appropriation. At the time, such acts of consumption brought added kudos: everyone knew import taxes were high. There is also a certain eroticism for the Japanese concerning European architecture: it is often the turreted palaces and castles such as Neuschwannstein that are evoked in the designs for Love Hotels, and this romantic connotation is deliberately employed to enhance the desirability of these establishments in the eyes of the younger generation who frequent them: they offer the prospect of real sex in the context of virtual tourism.

Nowadays, consuming foreign architecture in the form of theme parks has a stronger educational emphasis in Japan, and demonstrates a different kind of commitment to developing Japan's cosmopolitan outlook as a nation. Rather than using architectural otherness to aggrandise the identity of a few entrepreneurs and their respective punters, the Japanese in the 1990s now seem more curious to learn and teach about other cultures through hosting or staging them, where before they sought foreignness for its own sake. With Japanese theme park developers now engaging with the process of cultural representation more actively, some interesting zones of cultural reinterpretation are opening up.

Ultimately, what is desired in Japan in terms of an array of pre-prepared, almost pre-digested architectures to consume, is an experience of intensification: mediated images of other parts of the world dominate the popular imagination, and demand that leisure space be colonised by bits of Merrie Englande, remnants of the Ottoman empire, or an assortment of carnivalesque.

Mary Yoko Brannen, in an article about Tokyo Disneyland,[1] argues that while its Japanese owners, the Oriental Land Company, requested an exact replica of the original Disneyland, subtle alterations occurred in the process of importing the model for their theme park, to do with the specifics of the way Japanese behave in public; for example, not eating while walking along accounts for fewer fast food outlets around the park. She argues that the theme park aesthetic in Japan coincides with the current consumer trend of *yuttari*, meaning easy, comfortable, calm. The commodified cultural artefacts are recontextualised in Japanese terms at Tokyo Disneyland, consisting of two forms of cultural consumption: 'making the exotic familiar and keeping the exotic exotic.'[2] Brannen considers that this entails both American

Kashiwazaki Turkish Culture Village, roofscape

Suleymaniye Mosque, Istanbul, roofscape

Kashiwazaki Turkish Culture Village, art gallery

Topkapi Palace, Istanbul, inner courtyard

Kashiwazaki Turkish Culture Village, traditional Turkish dancing

Kashiwazaki Turkish Culture Village, Turkish bazaar

and Japanese forms of cultural imperialism working together, and not necessarily at odds with each other.

Similarly, with the two projects reviewed here, there is a level of hybridised cultural imperialism in evidence, producing a complex situation for the consumer, who is simultaneously consuming two types of environment: one explicit, the representational architecture, and the other implicit, to do with the consumers' expected code of behaviour.

Shakespeare Country Park, Maruyama, Chiba Prefecture

Ove Arup and Partners' commission to work with architects Julian Bicknell and Associates, Fujiwara Sekkei (co-architects) and John Romayne (exhibition installation designer) to design a Shakespeare Country Park, was completed in March 1997, and had 10,000 visitors in the first two weeks after its opening day on 23 April (Shakespeare's birthday). The client, Maruyama City, wanted to present a kind of abstraction of Elizabethan culture, which was achieved by distilling the project down to the building types of the period: farm, townhouse, inn, theatre, village green, physic garden, and by demonstrating their connections to or effects on literature, theatre, and the visual arts through exhibits and shows. The overall intention was to create a place of recreation that provided a clear educational context through which to understand the meaning of Shakespeare's work.

Searching for an authentic link to Shakespeare, Maruyama town's press release refers to their symbol, Rosemary, a plant 'much loved and referred to by Shakespeare'. This herb therefore features prominently in the landscaping of the Park. Authenticity was also assured by the use of traditional timber building techniques, and the construction company, Border Oak, took great care to adapt Elizabethan detailing to suit local conditions which are invariably more humid than in England, and where typhoons often occur.

Julian Bicknell writes about the project:

In Europe we might expect a Shakespearean theme park to be an exercise in cynical opportunism and commercial exploitation – a romanticised and watered-down version of Stratford-upon-Avon . . . or worse still a cartoon caricature in the Disney manner. In Japan both the expectation and the finished product are quite different. The Shakespeare Country Park fits neatly into the Japanese tradition of recreational pilgrimage. Shakespeare's name is, amazingly, known to most Japanese school children (who in Europe has heard of Chikamatsu, or any other famous Japanese poet or playwright?). Tourists from Japan visit the Shakespearean properties in Stratford-upon-Avon in greater numbers than from any other country. They have brought the same diligence and curiosity to the new Shakespearean village at Maruyama. They are not discouraged by not seeing the original – after all many of the famous shrines of Japan have been rebuilt, moved, and reproduced, without any loss in their spiritual power.

Kashiwazaki Turkish Culture Village, Niigata Prefecture

Turkish Airlines has sponsored the creation of a sampler of Turkish culture on the west coast of Japan, comprising a bazaar full of produce straight from Istanbul, a restaurant serving Turkish cuisine, an art gallery of contemporary Turkish artworks, a plaza in which Turkish dancing is performed at intervals, landscaped gardens containing a Turkish breed of dog tied up by its kennel, and a minaret, from which announcements are made over the PA system as to when the next dance show will be performed. This 'culture village' adds up to more than a collection of spaces and artefacts: the whole experience has been designed and carefully orchestrated, right down to the Turkish-speaking attendants in traditional costume who greet the visitor and offer cologne with typical Turkish hospitality.

Here the exotic is made familiar through a certain Japanisation in the design of signage at the entrance, the escalator up the steep hill, even the 'bento-isation' of Turkish dishes in the restaurant to resemble the layout of a traditional Japanese meal. The exotic is kept exotic by excluding any Japanese-made merchandise, hoards of carpets, Turkish delight, rosaries, decorated plates, tea sets and jewellery, all piled high in a dark, vaulted interior, and the elaborate detailing and materials used in the architecture. There are no rides or guided tours, and Japanese visitors wander through the spaces in the same way they would leisurely encounter a foreign city. In comparing images of Kashiwazaki with views of Istanbul and Topkapi Palace in particular, it is also apparent that the overall setting with glimpses of water in the distance over domed rooftops, and the tiled colonnades reproduce some of the urban conditions found in old Constantinople, albeit operating at a subliminal level.

Whether Turkish Airlines intends this cultural sampling to act as an inducement to a visit to the real Turkey, or whether it is an acknowledgement of the fact that what is now wanted by tourists is a planned series of edited highlights as a preferred substitute for the so-called 'real thing' is unclear, but the effect is to provide, by means of a cultural outpost, a form of cultural representation far more effective than the closed world of an embassy, and more available to the public as an active consumer experience.

Notes

1 Mary Yoko Brannen, 'Bwana Mickey: Constructing Cultural Consumption at Tokyo Disneyland', in *Remade in Japan*, Joseph Tobin (ed), Yale University (New Haven and London), 1992.
2 Ibid, p219.

FORUM

THE MYTH OF HIGH TECH

Royal Academy of Arts, London, June 1998

Paul Finch: The title of this afternoon's discussion: 'The Myth of High Tech', came out of a conversation between a small group of people who plan these events. Charles Jencks argued strongly that it should not be merely 'The Myth of High Tech', but 'The Myth and Beauty of High Tech', and I dare say the question of high tech as relating – how can I say this without the risk of getting eggs thrown at me immediately – in some senses to the Baroque, being about beautiful decoration independent of whatever else it may be, will arise during the course of the afternoon.

Robert Maxwell: Whether high tech is a style or not seems to depend on whether we view it from the inside or the outside. The insider sees it as a technique that responds directly to the needs of the client and puts no obstacle to their realisation. The outsider sees a series of obsessive artefacts that, in the words of the poet Robert Herrick, 'are too precise in every part'. Whatever else they do, they present the image of the machine, and that is to eliminate everything human except the immediate purpose. There are certain practical aspects of high-tech building that militate against this clarity. In the Pompidou Centre, for instance, the need to spray on fire protection results in a coarse structure. In order to restore the technical precision, it has to be further encased in aluminium or stainless steel tubing. This is neither cheap nor aesthetically consistent with the idea of exposing an underlying reality.

Paul Finch: Would anybody like to raise any point immediately following that, or pursue any issue with Bob before we move on?

Ian Ritchie: Just to add to that I think Bob's comments are appropriate to the Beaubourg, in the sense that the dream of this kind of future flexibility came face to face with the fire officer and that world of reality and actual public safety that the architect was supposedly serving.

Dalibor Vesely: May I make one little comment about flexibility? That dream was definitely cultivated to a certain point, but suddenly it was dropped. And yet the building as it stands at the moment is expected to be what I would call flexible. Now, we can push that aside, but I would ask, how flexible do we need it to be? If you go there, you see practically all the possible requirements in play. You see exhibitions coming and going. There's a floor with an information centre and a library. Nothing's changed there. They are quite content with the original layout. Some years ago one of our students undertook some research, and part of the research was the very question of exhibiting. The most flexible piece of the building, I have no doubt, is the temporary exhibition centre.

Robert Maxwell: The flexible 'shed' space, such as we see in the Sainsbury Centre at UEA and in an elongated vertical form at the Hong Kong and Shanghai Bank, is a form that is close to the

classical. I've compared the design of the Sainsbury Centre at UEA with the Palazzo dei Congressi in a suburb of Rome to show that there are big similarities. I've always claimed that the shed leads back through history to… well, King's College Chapel is a shed, isn't it?

Peter Blundell Jones: But Foster is rather careless about the number of bays – that always seems to me to be the case. Stansted is presented as though it's an accident that it's square, that there are 11 bays each way, because it's supposed to be extendable. You're supposed to have as many bays as you like. No classical architect, least of all Mies, would be indifferent to that. Even his housing blocks look like prototypes – a kind of serial repetitive device that you could then run off the production line. That's the paradox with Mies. The ideology of flexibility and repetition was taken up by all his followers and was the great ideology of the 50s and 60s, and behind it is this monumentalist ideology stating that the buildings have to be finite, classical, and so transcendent they can't have anything to do with their function. They have to be completely clean.

Robert Maxwell: Well, the chapel at King's College is a sort of clean machine in that sense – pretty well empty.

Paul Finch: There's just one other point that I'd like raise before asking Colin Davies to speak, which is the extent to which the sort of buildings you spoke about are pushing technology, or are trying to do things with technology for which it's not quite ready. The first people to pursue these sorts of things always run up against certain practical difficulties. But by the time they're capable of being resolved, of course, you wouldn't be designing the same building in the same way anyway because things have moved on. Although it's a myth that you can't do it, actually it's not a myth in the sense that you *can* do it. You could do precisely those things that were being laid claim to.

Robert Maxwell: There was over-excitement about flexibility. It was exaggerated as an idea. It seemed as if architects could really treat their buildings as something that need not be an obstacle; then they would open up to all kinds of human futures. It was another 10 or 15 years before a survey of working spaces in London revealed that 99 per cent of all needs could be satisfied by a space 10 foot by 8 foot by 20 foot and that human bodies in fact always do exactly the same thing, such as stand up and sit down. And the flexibility that we thought was around the corner in 1972 didn't in fact arrive.

Paul Finch: I'm going to bring Colin in now.

Colin Davies: In my introduction to my book on high-tech architecture, I tried to point out its main characteristics: that its typical materials were metal and glass, that it adhered to a strict code of honesty in expression, that it usually embodied ideas about industrial production, that it used industries other than the building industry as sources both of technology and of imagery, and that it put a high priority on flexibility of use – what we've just been talking about. As far as I could see, high tech, as practised predominantly by UK architects Foster, Rogers and Grimshaw, lasted between 1967 and 1987; then it was all over – or, at least, it seemed like an exciting idea in 1988 that high tech might have come to and end and was possibly about to be superseded by something else. So I thought I'd write it as history.

Paul Finch: Actually, *Time* magazine has already listed the architects who made a difference. Norman Foster was the only British architect included, and, indeed, it was for the Hong Kong and Shanghai Bank.

It's quite interesting that Grimshaw's Eden project is both a hymn to nature and probably one of the most successful Lottery schemes, because it's doing something absolutely new, as opposed to accretial modernism which 'does up' the British Museum or 'does up' a power station. The question I wanted to ask you is whether you think that the high-tech architects have now used nature explicitly as a way, not simply of thinking about the design – taking biological models and so on and so forth – but of validating and justifying what they're doing?

Norman Foster says that his Reichstag project will be powered by a little power station that will take care of the local district. What is the fuel for this? Vegetable oil, which will be cropped in the fields nearby. So all of a sudden this project isn't simply about the restoration of one of the great symbolic buildings of the 20th century; it's all about rapeseed oil and sinking tubes 70 metres into the ground to cool them down. The main thing about this is that energy-wise it's just about as good as you can get.

Ian Ritchie: I'd just like to add something to that, having been at press conferences in Europe with the directors of Foster's where they put forward the case for the high-performance ecological skin to the building. It starts with the preconception: I like glass. How do I make it work? How do I make this entire building work? And it has been proven, not just at Commerz Bank but at other buildings, that having three or four levels of glass is absolute nonsense in terms of the cost in relation to the life of the building. There is again this desire for an image of a building. With certain architects that starts with glass in its totality: how can I make this thing work? What stories can I build into it that can, if you like, continue the myth?

Robert Maxwell: This myth of the image is demonstrated by the Sydney Opera House, which cost so much they had to invent the idea of a lottery in order to pay for it. When it was discovered that the structure couldn't stand up, an engineer had to find a way of resolving this, and when it was found that it didn't have the desired acoustic properties, a second building had to be built inside it. But that building generated enormous interest; its image made the architect famous and has become a source of new architecture. This demonstrates the power of image.

Architecture is becoming increasingly dumbed down – looking at it from the professional functionalist point of view – because now what catches is what goes. Any image that attracts the public generates entrance money. That's where the purely commercial values of global capitalism give you a situation that intellectuals mistake for, and call, 'the post-modern condition', where nothing is true except what sells.

Colin Davies: I believe that high tech went through the three usual phases: early phase, high phase and mannerist phase. It did become incredibly mannered, but something fundamental survived and was reapplied. It found a new job saving energy – just as illusory as the job it had dragging the building industry into the 20th century. It had to have a job to do. It always does. The discovery of green issues by Foster, Rogers and Grimshaw may be laughable, but certainly the market's right.

Dalibor Vesely: As an outsider, I find it interesting that the English are high-tech – very, very amusing indeed. When you come to this country the last thing you see is high-tech architecture being the dominating phenomenon in the UK. It is quite interesting to remember that when you read Prince Albert's speeches about the Great Exhibition, he says something like, 'the science and the knowledge can come from Germany, the art can come from France, and we're going to make and put it together'. So that's British high tech: the process.

David Turnbull: The questions of ecology and building performance become rather pathetic when they're considered solely in relation to the building rather than in relation to the larger territories or regions or organisations within the city. I've just been in Cairo, where the population is growing by one million people per year. The conditions of density in the city are quite extraordinary – sometimes 1,000 people per hectare – with very few high-rise buildings. These are incredible issues that really demand some kind of reflection on the condition of the city and on the status of technology in relation to that city.

Robert Maxwell: When we saw Colin Davies' slide of Lethaby's Brockhampton church, I had a strange feeling in my stomach. It's a beautiful church. If Lethaby was able to talk about construction and myth, which he did, it was because he was a very religious man. Arts and Crafts was essentially a religious movement, referring back to the wholeness of life under belief. If you think of the Pre-Raphaelites in England and the Nazarenes earlier on in Germany, those people really thought that there was a need to

regenerate society; that a Christian story, a Christian myth, would somehow remake society. That the high-tech people can use the idea of the Arts and Crafts Movement as a justification for their obsessive military machines offends me, frankly. It's an undue expenditure of money in a world where we have to think about the untold millions. I think that bringing up the city is another way of bringing up the relationship between architecture and culture. The high tech, as an expensive style, is good for a certain kind of images and therefore sales. That's all it's good for. It's not really architecture.

Paul Finch: I'm going to ask Andy Bow to say a few words as the apostolic representative of Sir Norman this afternoon.

Andy Bow: Rather than talking about the myth of the high tech, I'd like to offer some of my thoughts on the way technology is used within our office now, by referring to three different projects that I'm working on. Firstly, in terms of space – to use Nick Grimshaw's analogy of space, skin and structure – with world squares, the analysis of Trafalgar Square and Parliament Square, the very first thing we did was go to Bill Hillier's Unit at the Bartlet School of Architecture to understand the way in which people moved around all of these spaces that we've all come to know and love. Without this analysis it would have been impossible for us to even begin to contemplate how to deal with a master plan for that area. So straight away very advanced computer technologies for understanding the ways in which people moved through the city helped us in that process.

Secondly, the skin: at Albion Wharf, next to our office, there is a rising crescent. It's a mixed-use development. We have a facade that faces north, south, east and west, where we're trying to create glass balustrades that are 7 metres wide, and we have open-bowl glass that, with the flick of a switch, moves away.

And finally, in terms of structure, on the millennium footbridge, wind is an issue. There were many suggestions that we might begin to make glass balustrades, but they would be difficult to maintain and the structure would become three or four times as big. The solution that we've come up with is technology transfer – it's from motor racing: the air foil sections at the back of cars. So the balustrades are emerging as an air foil in section. Now, for me it's quite natural to learn from technology transfer. I have daily conversations with Norman Foster, and our conversations are about philosophy, humanity, scale, rhythm, colour, texture. The conversations every day of the week are not about nuts and bolts like facades, and I think that it's very important to say that. Technology in our office is the servant of the concept. You're only as good as the last idea that you drew; the pencil is everything, and it's as basic as that. I feel uncomfortable with accusations of being liars. Problems evolve, and we try to find the right solutions, and ultimately we're in search of the most beautiful solution. That's really the stage that we're at now.

Paul Finch: And now we're going to hear from Ram Ahronov, who worked for six years as a project architect at Richard Rogers' and then was an associate at Foster and Partners.

Ram Ahronov: I thought I'd pick up on the role of visual art, which, I think, is a very important aspect of the aesthetics and meaning of what we call 'high tech'. Take Stansted Airport, whose roof is almost the area of two football pitches. One of the big problems was what to do with the rainwater. Either you

channel it through the diagonal or through the gutter. Now, neither of these fairly conventional solutions was suitable for this particular case. The solution that we were able to find after about three years' research was from Finland. There, they've developed a UV system that allows you to take the rainwater pipe horizontally by using a siphon system. You see a kind of flexible covered pipe and inside the building a panel system that covers the whole ceiling of the terminal. This gave us two elements: on the one hand we could take all the water horizontally – you see nothing at all on the building – on the other, the pipe can be exposed once you take off the panel, so for maintenance and repair it's always open. We brought those ideas together, but the major concept was the aesthetic aspect.

Paul Finch: I think we'll move straight on to Chris McCarthy, who is an engineer, formerly with Ove Arup and now with the thriving and ever-expanding practice of Battle McCarthy. They're best known for their advanced work on extreme energy-saving systems and the use of nature as part of building structures and services.

Chris McCarthy: I was taken to Mippin at the beginning of the year – that's where you end up with 10,000 planners and surveyors – and they were all debating the 'big deal'. It suddenly occurred to me that it was all about looking at cities as 'the deal', and the way that transactions relating to our urban environment, and all our architectural decisions now are taken very quickly. One of the developers came over to me. I was talking about the work I've done, and he said, 'Oh, yes, that was great stuff, but that was just about space and throwing the services and structure outside the building to get maximum space'. It was depressing that here were the people making 90 per cent of the decisions about the future of architecture, and structure, quality of space and energy weren't on the agenda.

Shortly afterwards, I went to a conference on land-fill sites, which I thought was quite similar. They were talking about waste management of the material, something called 'site fabrication'. These are the real issues, and these are the people who are going to make the decisions about the future of technology, not architects. They went on to say that the *biggest* issue affecting land-fill sites, building construction and reduction of waste is adaptability; not flexibility but adaptability. Why are you building car parks that you can't adapt in the future into homes?

What I'm going to be talking about is the engineer as a kind of high priest of technology. What is the role of the engineer? You could say that architects are about applied art and we're about applied science. As applied scientists, our agenda, our brief, is to maximise use of materials, energy and skills to the benefit of mankind. The other issue that we're faced with as structural engineers is the role of myth; we were trying to do things that were unnaturally real. At the same time we were becoming aware that the structures we were creating were bigger than they needed to be, and there was more energy associated with those.

Taking a step back, if there is a need to close one door in architecture, you can open another, ie close the door of the 'high tech' and open the door of the 'new tech'. It's really going to be 'energy tech'. From working with architects on different projects, I've discovered that you are great space planners. As a structural engineer I've been rediscovering the atom. Moving into the area of nano-technology and separating atoms is also all about space. You can't cram them in. You've got to come up with three-dimensional space relations between atoms.

Bernard Tschumi Architects, Performance Hall and Exhibition Centre, Rouen, France

45

The actual technology is so much simpler to understand than a building, ie understanding how these different molecules compare. This is the sort of thing architecture should be moving into: starting to think about the relationship between molecules, and expanding that out to a cornice. Or, conversely, you can say, 'This is a performance delight. I want this to do this; I want that to do that', which is then involving industry in the conversation. If you go to ICI, where they've been doing all this work, they call it architecture, but they've never had an architect visit them.

I think the role of the architect and of the engineer in the field of nano-technology, atomic technology or genetic engineering is going to become part of our field. It does exist. We've been involved in designing composite footbridges and plastic footbridges for Lisbon. We understand that there is a need. There is a value in this technology transfer from a conventional steel bridge to the new technology. The bit that isn't so clear is the area where, for example, we did the review for Greenpeace on the Dome. Should it be PTFE or should it be PVC? It's a very unnerving and risky subject. Where is the architect? We're now saying these new materials are going to be created; we must debate them openly with people like Greenpeace. We must look at these materials and see if there is a future for them. If in the future we need to close the door so that high tech can go forward, I think the appeal of genetic engineering should open the debate. This is something that should be discussed openly amongst architects, because it will lead you into the issue of the plastic pipe that Ram specified earlier.

Paul Finch: The idea that the architect should know about molecules just when the schools of architecture thought they could knock a year off the course is going to mean that they'll have to put two or three on!

Ian Ritchie: Picking up on Chris' point about molecules, I think what's interesting for an architect interested in duct industry and the nano aspects of it, is that it requires finance from industry. Industry won't finance it because it has its own little secret research programmes. An architect is a very humble little being, and the market-place for building materials, as seen by the big industrialists, is actually fairly insignificant. Therefore, the ability of architects to have a signficant influence raises fundamental questions about one's ability to actually do something about it.

Chris McCarthy: I feel that the architect's conversation is very much about the final product. There is a question, a moral issue, that concerns the Dome. If you use, say, a PVC-membrane roof, you're upsetting the Green Party, and if you investigate the basis of their argument, it's not founded. The greatest thing the high-tech engineers can do for architects – and I've always done this – is to give them a vision of the future. I think you're in the business of looking at what you've done and what you're going to do and how that will affect the future. The scientists that I work with don't see beyond their lab. They work in a test-tube. Certain people just can't see tomorrow. I think the great success of high tech was in communicating technology to the public.

Robert Maxwell: But I think you're far too optimistic to think that architects are anywhere near taking on what you've defined.

Paul Finch: It's a bit like the battle over whether steel or concrete can produce the most economical or strongest bridge.

Alan Jones: I don't think it's necessarily true that high tech means new materials. Many of the examples we saw earlier actually used old materials in new ways, and that, in some ways, can be seen as high tech as well. The way that it becomes high tech, if that's the right expression, is through the integration of thought that we're talking about now. By bringing those thought processes together and by the transfer of technology you produce something that is new, that is different, that has a style of its own. I'm not sure whether the Dome is actually high tech. It uses materials that are established; it doesn't use them in a particularly different way. Other examples take materials and use them in different ways. The Eden project was not built because it was looking for somewhere to go: it's in the right place at the right time. It's in Cornwall; it's in a quarry because that provides the right sort of climate to do what they want to do within that building; it's in a very sheltered location.

Paul Finch: Iann Barron has an extraordinary CV, which I commend to you all if you haven't already read it. He designed his first computer when he was still at Cambridge and was running the first mini-computer company in the UK in the mid-60s. I suppose we shouldn't be too surprised that at the moment he's involved with a virtual reality company called the Vision Group, which, as I understand it, supplies programmes or software – 'kit', to use the loosest term. The company is also involved in what might loosely be called the design of that kit.

Iann Barron: I must say that I speak to you with more than my normal diffidence. I too, am an architect, but I'm a computer architect. I don't think that I work in a different way from any other architect: I have a problem; I have a lot of issues, and I synthesise them. Actually – and this is the point that I want to make – I think that good scientists, good technologists, use exactly the same processes as architects. We choose beautiful solutions. It may not be obvious to anybody outside. Sometimes beauty is in the eye of the architect anyway. I don't think there is that gulf between one profession and another. We're really trying to do the same sort of thing; it's just that our problem area concerns different materials. I sympathise with all of you. I have a hell of a lot of problems designing things.

Dalibor Vesely: What's also interesting is that science, if you follow its development in the last few decades, goes from physics to something like polymers, for instance. Nowadays it's almost impossible to say whether you're in physics or biology. Some decades ago, it was clear-cut. What I'm really saying is that science itself moves from, say, physics – from physical structures – to biological structures and eventually, probably, to certain kinds of human structures. You are, in one sense, almost moving into psychiatry. About seven years before he died, Louis Kahn received a letter from NASA asking him to come down to Houston. He replied saying, 'I'm sorry, you've probably got the wrong person; it's not me'. They said, 'No, we know exactly who we want; we want you'. They wanted him to work with the people designing the interior of the capsule. They especially wanted him because, they said, 'We've been working on it for a number of years and we're now convinced that we're not getting anywhere, and you may be able to help', which he did. I remember when I finished engineering my teachers said, 'When you go up the stairs to architecture, don't forget. The architect will be moving towards engineering', and we didn't believe them.

Andy Bow: Ten years ago I hadn't designed a building with inflatable structures; I have now. I worked on a 200-metre-long wind canopy in Plymouth with Peter Rice. I hadn't worked on membrane structures before. I'm quite convinced that those of us who are spared the next ten years and who assemble in this room in a decade's time will see that the whole thing has moved on again. I'm absolutely convinced of that fact. I think it's enormously exciting. The gap between architecture and engineering is minuscule. We're very lucky in London, because the best engineers in the world are here.

Ian Ritchie: I was interested in Iann Barron's reference to the real world of building as being somewhat bespoke, as against the Ford analogy. I remember Geoffrey Broadbent saying that the nearest thing an architect could deal with in terms of, let's say, computer architecture is to print a silicon chip on a bigger scale on a bit of glass from which to make a balustrade. There's a relationship between that flow of information and a couple of things that come together, which are the virtual world and the real world. More and more, as architects work all day in front of screens, there's a desensitising of the humanity. I know that from experience, having worked on 3-D computers for the last 15 years (and not Apple Macs) and having extreme difficulty training people on them, getting information distributed and knowing where the difficulties are – it's a virtual world. It's tasteless, untouchable, non-smelly. It's a very strong illusion. It's also an extremely strong architecture that is real. It exists in the minds of all these people who invent it. One can take the analogy that I think Martin Pawley once made: 'He said, "You're going to live in a virtual world", and I asked him, "And where am I going to piss?"' But 50 per cent, certainly, of my life is in this virtual world. A translation of that into the real one, which I think Chris was moving into, is that there is through that technology a fluid and natural, rather than a mechanical Victorian, idea, which one sees in high tech, that will emerge in future architecture. That, I feel, is certain.

Robert Maxwell: I do agree with that, and I would just like to say that I hope the fact that I proposed the demise of the high tech doesn't lead you to think that I'm against progress. Of course, we can't avoid progress; it's inevitable. People will always look for quicker, neater, cheaper and more effective ways of doing things, so I don't want to stop science. In attacking the high tech I was not attacking the march of science, but I do see, at the same time, that as science uncovers for us a more and more complex universe – nature – the question of what kind of human structure we can fit to that, which will hold social coherence, becomes more and more crucial. In classical architecture, for instance, decoration was derived from a metaphor for structure, and all the parts of that decoration fitted together in an ordered hierarchy. Nature has become so complex for us, and we're so aware of this, that we no longer have an image of the whole. So, my interest in the high tech has been increased here because I see it as a rather naïve, a rather rough-and-ready, a rather Victorian way of trying to come to terms with the future. In terms of the perspective that you've raised here, it actually becomes fetchingly whimsical and human because it's concerned with the problems of every day. I really was touched by Ram's account of the rainwater pipe, which is a superb piece of design in itself. There is a very, very long distance from understanding the complexity of nature and decoding it, and being able to create on our side a complexity that is deeply human.

Paul Finch: It's an impossible afternoon to sum up, not least because there's a whole series of other things that we might have talked about with more time. If Charles Jencks had been here he would have had plenty to say about decoration and his view that, say in the work of Eva Jiricna or some aspects of Richard Rogers', this is our equivalent of the Baroque at its highest. We didn't talk much about the divorce between high-tech architecture and the idea of technology and replication or repeatability, except for the point about buildings being bespoke. There's a notion that high-tech buildings cannot deliver their promise of cheapness and affordability because they never replicate. That's why they're such expensive prototypes in the first place.

I'd like to end with – I think we touched on it very briefly – what for me is a very interesting building that relates to a whole series of the arguments and conversations this afternoon: Frank Gehry's new Guggenheim Museum in Bilbao. As regards the relationship between high tech and the Arts and Crafts, here is a building in which every single titanium panel has come out of a standardised process and yet each one is different; each is pre-formed to go onto a specific point on the structure. As a result of the miracle of computer technology, the design information can go down wires, the jigs can be set without human intervention, and what you get are things that in other industries are becoming bespoke and standard at the same time, such as the Nike trainer where your foot has been digitalised and your trainer is just slightly different from the next one coming off the line; and it doesn't really cost you that much more, if any more at all. The relationship between the standardised and the customised starts to vanish, and at this point the idea of the hand-crafted and the machine-crafted start to converge. Arts and Crafts meets the vision of technology, prefabrication and standardisation in a new way.

The outcome, as it happens, goes right back to Iann's earlier point. Here is the building that has become *the* architectural image of this year and possibly this decade. Why so? It's partly to do with the fact that it looks so different. It has shades of Sydney Opera House, but this is Sydney Opera House with a bit of chaos thrown into the structure and, of course, with the most expensive metal (until palladium recently overtook it), titanium, used to an extravagant extent – millimetres thick on the outside. It has been photographed; it has become advertising architecture. Now, how does the client respond to that? In an interesting way. The museum has registered the architecture and, as a consequence, the artefact – not what's inside, but the building itself – as an artwork. It now has copyright. If you want to go and take a photograph of that building, which you then sell for profit, you'll be breaking copyright law, and they can sue you.

This is a coming together of Arts and Crafts, high tech and standardisation. Yet going back to what it is that we've created, we've created an artistic image which is, I think, a metaphor for what we've been discussing.

ALBERTO CAMPO BAEZA

MORE WITH LESS
Essentiality

I propose an ESSENTIAL Architecture of IDEA, LIGHT and SPACE

IDEA

An Architecture that is born of an IDEA

Without an IDEA, Architecture would be pointless, only empty form

An IDEA which is capable of: serving (function), responding to a place (context), resolving itself geometrically (composition), materialising itself physically (construction)

Architecture is always a built IDEA. The History of Architecture is the History of built IDEAS. Forms change, they crumble, but the IDEAS remain, they are eternal

LIGHT

An Architecture is brought into existence by LIGHT

Without LIGHT Architecture is nothing

LIGHT is an essential material in the construction of Architecture

LIGHT is that which creates a relation, a tension between man and Architectural space

SPACE

An Architecture is translated into an ESSENTIAL SPACE

SPACE is shaped by FORM through the minimal, indispensable number of elements capable of translating the IDEA with precision

A SPACE is capable of touching people

More with Less

This Architecture, born of an IDEA, shaped by ESSENTIAL spaces and tensed by LIGHT, allows people to find in it the BEAUTY that only Architecture is capable of offering them. That BEAUTY which is always the final stop on this long journey towards Liberty, which is CREATION

With these notes on IDEA, LIGHT and ESSENTIALITY, I offer here some of my work in which I have attempted to translate this simple principle of 'MORE WITH LESS'

PRECISIONS I

About ESSENTIALITY

ESSENTIAL Architecture (Not Essentialist) is NOT MINIMALISM

ESSENTIALITY
is NOT	EssentialISM
is NOT an	ISM
is NOT a	MinimalISM
is	ESSENTIALITY
is	Precision
is something more than only a	
question of Form	
is a	BUILT IDEA
is	POETIC
is	MORE WITH LESS

ESSENTIAL ARCHITECTURE is NOT cold and cruel
is NOT perfectionist and untouchable
is NOT imposing and overwhelming
is NOT only to be photographed

is	CLEAN and SIMPLE
is	NATURAL and OPEN
is	FREE and LIBERATING
is	FOR LIVING

I would like my ARCHITECTURE to be:
as PRECISE as Bernini's, as luminous
as NATURAL as Barragan's, architecture for the man
as DESHABILLÉ as Le Corbusier's, as strong and powerful

not for the purpose of becoming famous
but making man happy

not only for this time
but forever

not to be photographed
but to be lived

PRECISIONS II

About the perfect perfectionist work

(Praise of IMPERFECTION)

I think, like Heidegger, that architectural spaces tensed up by the LIGHT are to be inhabited by the man

I think, like Barragan, that creation is of cleaner and more free spaces, it s not the creation of hard, cold and untouchable ones. Architectural spaces are to be inhabited (they are not freezers)

I think, like Le Corbusier, that the creation of spaces for man calls for a level of imperfection (deshabillé) which underlines the power of architecture

Architectural spaces should house man not expel him. In this way the Parthenon, the Hagia Sofia or the Pantheon have all housed man in History (they are admirably corroded)

And even more than perfect and unpolluted houses, I prefer:

The imperfect Villa Savoie by Le Corbusier
The decorticated houses by Barragan
The huddled Villa Malaparte by Libera
and
Melnikov's own defective house in Moscow
Utzon's own corroded house in Palma

And I discover in them that the History of Architecture is the History of IDEAS, of BUILT IDEAS, of magnificent imperfect works with magnificent LIGHT which provokes a magnificent life, Emotion in man and intelligent Beauty!

ALBERTO CAMPO BAEZA

GARCIA MARCOS HOUSE
Valdemoro, Madrid

This single-family house in a conventional suburb on the outskirts of Valdemoro, Madrid, is sited on a 15 x 21 metre corner plot with two street facades.

The site is enclosed by ceramic brick walls, like a box open to the sky. In the centre, complying with set-back requirements, is a white prism with a rectangular base of 8 x 14 metres, divided transversally into three parts. The ceiling of the central, double-height sitting room is perforated by a long, horizontal skylight near the interior wall, through which light is admitted vertically. A large window, piercing the exterior wall at its lowest part, extends from side to side, echoing the horizontal plane. The resulting diagonal light creates a tension within the space.

Two other rooms are articulated around the central area. The stairs, kitchen and bathrooms are also situated on both sides of the main axis. The floors are of under-heated limestone and the flat roof incorporates a washing area, drying place and solarium. A garage is situated in the basement.

Through careful exploitation of light and proportion, a small, closed house is converted into a grand, open living space where anything is possible: a miracle box.

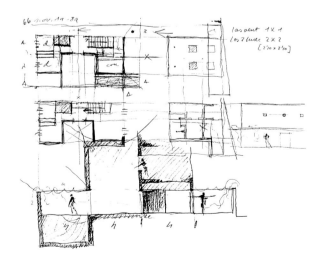

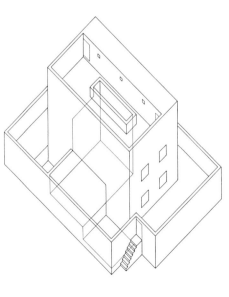

LEFT AND RIGHT: Sketch; axonometric

CLAUDIO SILVESTRIN
RIVERSIDE ONE APARTMENT
London

Claudio Silvestrin and Adam and Carolyn Barker-Mill first met on the south bank of the river Arno in Florence at the opening of the Victoria Miro gallery, designed by Silvestrin for contemporary art amidst the Renaissance splendour of the city.

In the summer of 1991, the Barker-Mills acquired a 232-metre-square apartment in Battersea, also overlooking a river, this time in London on the south bank of the Thames, between Albert and Battersea bridges. Set within the glass-block building constructed by Sir Norman Foster in the late 1980s, it offered panoramic views of the city, but very little else. In November, they wrote Silvestrin a note:

> We have been discussing the idea of redesigning the interior of our flat at Riverside One and we were wondering if you would like to create a Silvestrin masterpiece.

So Silvestrin set about his task, creating, in 1993, a peaceful space despite the frustration of being unable to intervene in the existing structure, with its low ceilings and perimeter windows. His first step was to open up the north-south axis (flanked on one side by a long stretch of floating, solid-white wall), through which the cityscape projects uninterrupted from one end of the apartment to the other. Flowing across the entire space, large slabs of Tuscan *pietra serena* stone echo the calm grey ribbon of the Thames.

A floor-to-ceiling, curved, satin-glass screen separates the doorless kitchen and bedroom areas from the more public spaces of the living room and study, yet also reveals and unites the elements on either side through their shadows and silhouettes, cast against its surface. To the west, floor-to-ceiling, satin-glass screens act both as barrier to, and enhancer of, the outside light. Solid and stretched interior wall expanses incorporate Adam Barker-Mill's light sculptures.

The geometric pieces of furniture are one-off designs by Silvestrin, as are the fixtures and fittings, from the flush lighting discs and elegant wooden tap fittings to the stone kitchen island, bathroom basins and pear-wood tables and benches.

Countless sophisticated details veil the technology, all the functions being concealed behind fully stretched glass screens, floor-to-ceiling cupboard doors and walls. This creates an air of silence and abstraction. The choice of natural materials is rigorous, their qualities coming alive to the senses due to the monolithic, pure forms through which they are presented.

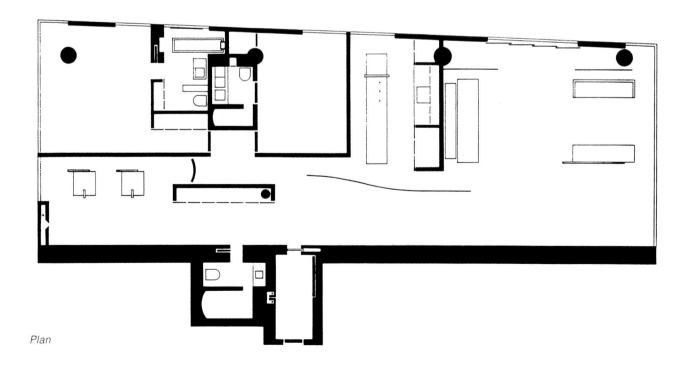

Plan

CLARE MELHUISH
ON MINIMALISM IN ARCHITECTURE

If someone bothered to feed the facts into a computer – and maybe someone has – it would probably be possible to predict in exactly which of the years ahead skirts would be long, mid length or short, trousers narrow or flared, colours pastel or vivid, and cuts sharp or relaxed, allowing clothes to be put away in the wardrobe with a ticket indicating when they would next be in vogue. Such is the mechanism of fashion: an even turning of the wheel from one polarity to the other in rhythmic accordance with the time it takes for humans to tire of one thing and crave its opposite.

Fashion holds sway in architecture and design as well, although because each part of the cycle takes longer to come to maturity, the wheel turns more slowly, and its movement not perceived so clearly. So when, amidst a plethora of glossy magazine articles on the same subject, the 'minimal' approach was hailed as 'the style of the nineties' in Jonathan Glancey and Richard Bryant's book *The New Moderns*, it was not entirely surprising, after a decade of excess and conspicuous material consumption by the richer elements of society. As Glancey so aptly put it: 'some wealthy people are tiring of the visual clutter and sheer bulk of too many worldly possessions and discarding these in favour of more austere homes.' The magazines stopped showing the wild and wacky homes of rich eccentrics and fell over themselves to picture cool rectilinear interiors constructed out of natural materials, painted white, or at least in neutral hues, stripped of conventional detailing, bathed in natural light, and cleared of all superfluous furnishing to make way for a single Modern classic, or, alternatively, some piece of ethnic booty from, say, Tahiti, to emphasise the flight of the sophisticated from the consumerism of the developed world. Suddenly it was all very chic: recession chic.

Once society has tired of the austere look, as it moves out of recession in the inevitable economic cycle of boom and slump, it will no doubt revert back to some form of the voluptuous and over-blown. Yet underneath the fashionable froth, beyond the reach of the glossy magazines, there is the steady undertow of a serious international architectural tradition of illustrious descent which has been flowing with renewed strength since well before the beginning of the 1990s – at least ten years before. The term 'minimalism' had had some currency in architectural debate for some

time prior to 1990, in connection with the work of a number of architects emerging around the end of the 1970s, who had espoused a lean, pared-down approach to design. In December 1988 a special issue, entitled 'Minimal', of the Italian architectural magazine *Rassegna* was devoted to an analysis of the phenomenon; it only needed Charles Jencks to launch it officially in popular architectural culture as a distinct new movement in late-20th century architecture.

When Jencks published his book *The New Moderns* [1] almost simultaneously with Glancey and Bryant's volume of the same name, it seemed the moment might have come: a proof that something must be going on beyond what merely 'some wealthy people' were doing, which would be of significance to Jencks' exclusively architectural readership seeking an insight less into lifestyles than into new developments in the architectural debate.

Jencks had previously made use of the term minimalism in his book *Current Architecture*, in 1982, but only in a fairly casual, adjectival, rather than generic sense, with reference to the work of Koolhaas, Hejduk, Eisenman, Campi and Pessina.[2] Confusingly, he uses a capital 'M' on each occasion, but never actually defines what it means – Koolhaas is influenced by the Minimalism of Mies van der Rohe, Hejduk by the 'Minimalist image', and Eisenman by the Minimalism of Donald Judd while Campi and Pessina make use of a 'Minimalist' pediment. In fact it is the simpler, more linear work discussed in the chapter on 'Twenties Revivalism' which seems most closely related to the minimal 'new modernism' outlined by Glancey and Bryant. Surprisingly, this work is hardly mentioned in Jencks' own *New Moderns,* which is more concerned with a fragmented type of architecture – 'Neo Modernism'. Minimalism itself is only briefly defined, as an essentially bourgeois, Late-Modern movement. This definition was repeated a year later, in the new additions to the sixth edition of *The Language of Post-Modern Architecture* (1991). Minimalism was linked to Deconstruction, Avant-Gardism, and silence used to describe the work of architects Antoine Predock and Luis Barragan, but again left largely unexplained.

OPPOSITE: Alberto Campo Baeza, Public School, Cadiz; ABOVE AND BELOW: Donald Judd, The Chinati Foundation, Marfa, Texas

The architects who appear in the Twenties Revival category (which he traces back to the mid-1960s) of Jencks' flow diagram of architectural trends, as published in *New Moderns*, include Tadao Ando, Benson and Forsyth, Tod Williams, Kurokawa, Meier, Holl, Gwathmey Siegel, George Ranalli in the 1980s, and Colquhoun and Miller, Neave Brown, Botta, Lasdun, Hejduk, Aymonino and others in the 1970s bracket. This is a fairly broad range, both stylistically and chronologically, but there are overlaps with the contents of the Glancey/Bryant book, in which Holl, Gwathmey Siegel, Meier and Ando also appear. Jencks however does not include any British architects of the 1980s, while Glancey and Bryant are mainly concerned with precisely that generation of British architecture: Mather, Chipperfield, d'Avoine, Wild, Chassay, Munkenbeck and Marshall and Pawson and Silvestrin – who came to notice in the 1980s.

However, there remains a considerable degree of consensus between Glancey and Bryant's minimal 'new moderns', and Jencks' 'Twenties Revival' architects – although more limited correlation with his sketchy references to minimalism itself (Barragan is probably the only one of Jencks' minimalists who would fit into the Glancey/Bryant new-modern stable, except that his work uses bright colours). Furthermore, Glancey and Bryant specifically refer to Le Corbusier, Neutra, Frank Lloyd Wright and Chareau as influences on the new modern architects they discuss; while Jencks describes Mies van der Rohe himself as a progenitor of Minimalism. The connection with the architecture of the early Modern Movement is thus implicit in the current usage of the term 'minimalism', widely understood as being in some sense a revival of early Modernist aims and forms.

There is a certain amount of truth in this. The interest in openness and continuity of space, generating an essentially horizontal architecture, the reduction of detailing to the minimum, along with the rejection of traditional architectural forms and conventions, and the play of natural light on mainly white surfaces, are common to both generations of architecture, and give the work a certain similarity of appearance. But the key difference is in the concept of the 'minimal' itself.

Although not a term given any currency in connection with the Modern Movement at the time, it has since been used by Alan Colquhoun to describe its failings: 'one of the strongest criticisms of modernism was directed against the architectural version of minimalism, closely tied to the doctrine of functionalism.'[3] In Colquhoun's mind, the concepts of functionalism and minimalism are 'bound together'. But there is a world of difference between the early Modern pursuit of a mechanistic and industrial reinvention of architecture ('the house a machine for living in')

– the functionalism, as an end in itself, which eventually generated such a backlash – and the interest of current, so-called 'minimalist' architects in fulfilment of the functional programme simply as a means to an end, being the corporeal, sensual experience of uncluttered space.

Hence the connection between current architectural 'minimalism' and the ideology of the Modern Movement has to be handled cautiously. The implications of the term as used in the architecture debate, which the Jencks and Glancey/Bryant books extended to a wider, more general audience, have also to be understood in relation to the art movement of the same name, represented by the work of artists such as Donald Judd.

It is notable that in all the serious magazine coverage of the architectural debate on 'minimalism' – *Rassegna*, December 1988, *Lotus* 73, 1992 and *El Croquis* 62-63, 1993 the architectural content is paralleled by substantial discussion of so-called Minimal art, acknowledging and highlighting the strong links between the two disciplines. Minimalism emerged in America in the 1960s, as a new movement which spread into painting from sculpture, led by figures such as Dan Flavin, Carl Andre, Robert Morris, Robert Smithson and Richard Serra as well as Donald Judd. It had been prefigured by the work of Ad Reinhardt, Barnett Newman and David Smith, developing as a new impetus to constructivism, and also called primary structure, or ABC art – in which there are strong overtones of the Bauhaus.

The minimalist sculptors and painters 'aspired to muteness and can be regarded as a further reductionist development in abstract art', according to Frances Spalding, although they never welcomed the name the critics gave them, with its negative overtones, just as most architects now will only reluctantly acknowledge it.[4] Their work paralleled that of the Pop Artists, in that it rejected the ideal of the work of art as either a vehicle for personal expression, or for any other sort of intellectual or metaphysical meaning over and above the 'meaning latent in different materials and in the processes of making' (Michael Craig-Martin, *The Art of Context*).[5] Their strategy, however, was the reverse of the Pop artists': whereas they sought to evade the process of 'interpretation' by choosing a content so obvious and banal that it became meaningless, the minimalists pursued the same aim by reducing all content as far as they could to nothing.

Hence the abstract materiality of the art became paramount – 'the simple, irreducible, irrefutable object', as EC Goosen put it, in an essay for the catalogue to the 1968 exhibition at the Tate, London, aptly entitled *Art of the Real*. The intention was to displace intellectual,

Pierre d'Avoine Architects, White House, London

cerebral perception and understanding of the work in favour of pure physical, corporeal and sensory experience, on the grounds that: 'Words restrict experiences and ideas as well as develop and organise them. We become slaves to the limitations imposed on us by our use of language, at the same time that we organise ourselves in essential ways because of it' (Allen Leepa, in *Experience: The Spectator*).[6]

The phenomenological nature, architectonic purity and relationship to site of the work of the minimalist artists has undoubtedly been extremely influential on the younger generation of contemporary architects throughout the Americas and Europe as they reassess architectural values in the aftermath of Venturi and Post-Modernism. In 1966, two years before the Tate's *Art of the Real* exhibition of American minimalist art, Venturi had published *Complexity and Contradiction in Architecture*, in which he condemned orthodox Modernism, as inculcated by Gropius, Mies van der Rohe and other representatives of the Bauhaus in America after 1937, for idealising 'the primitive and elementary at the expense of the diverse and the sophisticated', and 'puritanically advocat(ing) the separation and exclusion of elements, rather than the inclusion of various requirements and their juxtapositions.' Venturi called for a fresh understanding of architecture as a vehicle of communication, or a 'language', rich in the meaning and signification inherent in cultural and social history: precisely the opposite of what the Minimalist art movement stood for, at precisely the same moment.

In 1972 Venturi published *Learning from Las Vegas*, containing his theory of the 'decorated hut'. Although the reaction against his ideas had already set in, with the emergence in the same year of the New York Five (Eisenman, Graves, Hejduk, Meier and Gwathmey), calling for a return to the first principles of Modernism, the impact of *Las Vegas* was to be felt in architecture across the world for at least the next 10-15 years, achieving, perhaps, its most potent symbolic expression in the architecture of Disneyland, in Florida. The New York Five can arguably be seen as predecessors of contemporary Western 'minimalism', in their early reaction against the post-modernist manifesto for an architectural language based on historical precedent, and their pursuit of a rather self-conscious abstraction in which the austerity associated with the early Modern Movement was tempered by lyricism and a certain fulsome, almost figurative quality. Twenty years on, Richard Meier and Charles Gwathmey are still working in very much the same idiom on a large scale; while Graves has absconded to the camp of Post-Modernism itself, Hejduk has embraced a certain intellectual esotericism apart from building, and Eisenman has diverged away into Deconstructivism.

It is in the substitution of austere functionalism by what can be an almost too consciously composed, too perfectly crafted, poetry of materials in light and forms in space that the significant difference between early Modernism and the new architectural minimalism lies; and, likewise, the firm common ground between architectural minimalism and the minimalist art movement, reinforced by the flight of many architects from the dry, formal intellectualism of Deconstruction – from the need for 'interpretation' – which has succeeded the decorative excesses of Post-Modernism. Hence, although there is still a strong sense of the continuing, mythical 'unfinished project' of Modernism, and although the influence of Le Corbusier and Mies van der Rohe, especially, is still a powerful inspiration, although perhaps now equalled by that of Lloyd Wright and Kahn, and the later work of Corb, there is also a strong awareness of difference and new direction among the contemporary generation.

The minimalist idiom is not then simply a revival of early Modern ideals; and there is a further area of significant difference between the two, beyond, but interconnected with, the rejection of functionalism for materiality and sensual pleasure, which is the powerful influence exerted on the new generation of work by the awareness of different regional architectural traditions, in contradistinction to the universalism espoused by the Modern Movement. Of all of these it is probably the traditional architecture of Japan, and its modern-day interpretation by contemporary Japanese architects such as Tadao Ando, which has been the most profound inspiration to many architects in Europe and America. The effect of the simplicity, lightness and pure planar linearity of this architecture is summed up by Jun'ichiro Tanizaki in his influential essay on aesthetics: 'the beauty of a Japanese room depends on a variation of shadows, heavy shadows against light shadows - it has nothing else': a paradigm for a minimal architecture.[7]

The Japanese tradition seems to have been particularly influential on the work of British-based architects working in the minimalist idiom – perhaps because, geographically, the two countries share the constraints of limited space, and the condition of being surrounded by water, and, temperamentally, both races tend to reserve and, traditionally, an almost formal standard of courtesy. Of these architects, John Pawson, who believes the first use of the term 'minimalist' to describe a certain type of British architecture, was by an American critic in 1983 of the flat he had designed for himself, spent four years in Japan, where he had intended to enter a monastery, before beginning his architectural training at the AA. Here he met Tadao Ando, still at the

Richard Meier & Partners, Canal + Headquarters, Paris

beginning of his career, and forged a close friendship with the architect Shiro Kuramata, who was a strong influence.

Pawson's work during the 1980s consisted mainly of flats and houses in London for rich clients, many of whom were associated with the commercial art world. The work is almost obsessively concerned with the play of unadorned planes and volumes in light, the textures of materials, and the revealing of empty space. Between 1987 and 1989 he worked in partnership with fellow minimalist Claudio Silvestrin, who had established a reputation as a designer of commercial art galleries during a period when most gallerists were moving towards the ideal of the neutral space as the most appropriate setting for art. There is clearly an overlap between the two fields of work, in that many gallerists saw their homes as places for the display of art almost to the same degree as the gallery; but there was also an extension of the ideal beyond the work of art to the person. The human body, too, became an object in space, the architecture its setting. At one level, this represents a positive rediscovery of the body as the subject of architecture: a resurrection of architecture's human purpose after the tyranny of functionalism. But at another, Pawson and Silvestrin's work is of the sort that can seem almost too perfectly composed, too perfectly crafted, and thereby to negate the very physicality and earthiness of the human body. Both architects are aware of this problem. Pawson says, 'the danger is that the work becomes an artwork; then you lose the restraint.' It is the restraint which he regards as essential in creating 'calm spaces, a seamless effect', rather than falling into the trap of 'doing something clever' which he believes is a problem for so many architects – and even for the 'minimalist'.

Despite his experience in Japan, Pawson argues that there are other factors at play, coming from within the European tradition: the notion of casting away material positions for a life of contemplation is common to monastic traditions the world over, and nowhere, perhaps, more inspiringly expressed than in the architecture of the Cistercian monasteries, which he counts, along with the honest, industrial architecture of Halifax, the town of his birth, and the work of Mies van der Rohe, as possibly a greater influence than his experience in Japan.

Pawson and Silvestrin's work is perhaps the most extreme form of what is known as 'minimal' architecture in this country, but since the early 1980s there has been a considerable range of work perceived as belonging, broadly, in this area, largely to distinguish it, for the purposes of the critics, from either the architecture of structural and technological ingenuity and innovation represented by, say, Foster or Rogers, or the architecture of figuration represented in different forms by Farrell or the later work of Stirling.

According to Tony Fretton, the common quality of the so-called 'minimal' work is 'a reductivist quality . . . which is good', but he stresses that beyond the stylistic similarity is a whole range of very diverse ideas, and, unlike John Pawson, finds the term 'minimalism' 'not very useful.' Pierre d'Avoine also reiterates the essential quality of 'paring down' and 'reduction' in the work, but rejects the concept of minimalism as a style or an aesthetic. Both architects agree there is a common vocabulary of detailing across the whole range of the work, which Fretton describes as a rejection of traditional architectural vocabularies, and d'Avoine as 'a sort of mannerism, or inversion' and a reaction to the chunky, DIY-aesthetic detailing of the 1960s and 1970s.

Fretton's best-known work is the Lisson Gallery, designed for very much the same world as Silvestrin's galleries, but quite different in spirit, if not at a cursory viewing. Fretton's architecture is informed by a lively political agenda, and an awareness of its role in the world beyond its walls. The Lisson Gallery incorporates the rough edges of the real world, both within itself, and through the connections forged between the building and its immediate context: a scruffy street market in a still predominantly working-class area of the capital. Fretton is thus forcing the world of refinement and sophisticated taste into some form of engagement with the rough everyday life of the less privileged, and vice versa. This potential for conflict filters through the architecture itself, in total contrast to the calm perfection of Pawson or Silvestrin's work.

Fretton acknowledges the influence on his work of a type of neo-modernism based on the early Modern Movement, along with Louis Kahn's re-working of Modernism through the Japanese tradition. By contrast, d'Avoine, despite considerable experience of working in Japan, believes his work to be explicitly English in its genealogy, in the sense that it is part of a long tradition of leanness and linearity in English art and architecture. Nikolaus Pevsner, in his discussion of this subject, refers to 'the anti-corporeal flatness noticed throughout English architecture and the anti-corporeal intricacies of line noticed in some English architecture and in much later illumination', from Perpendicular architecture and psalter illustration, to Adam, Blake and Soane. He describes the linearity of English art – 'thin, wiry, sinewy . . . flaming or flowing' – as a 'negation of the swelling rotundity of the body' in favour of disembodiment. He also refers to 'a nausea of perfection' which led to the abandonment of the Early English for the Decorated style of architecture.[8]

Like Fretton, d'Avoine abjures the 'perfection' of Pawson or Silvestrin's approach, which he

John Pawson, RK RK shop, London

believes 'subjugates the user', but his work lacks the austerity and rough edges of Fretton's, expressing a potential for transformation rather than tension. Although he shares the predilection for a planar architecture of walls and uncluttered spaces, rather than structure, there is always a sense of latent movement and of the surprising in his work, and also a deep concern for the relationship of the architecture with its physical site. In the case of the White House, in London, an introverted suburban house is opened up in such a way as to transform not only its internal spaces, but also the street on which it is situated.

In view of the quantity of work produced in this country in the minimalist vein, it seems surprising that the British contribution has been almost completely overlooked in serious European coverage of the subject, overshadowed by the very strong Spanish, Italian, and, to a lesser extent, central European movements in this direction. Part of the reason may be that so much of the British work is still internal, while the opportunities to build in the round have been much greater abroad during this period. Part may be that the minimalist approach seems so alien to the Arts and Crafts movement with which Britain is so strongly associated abroad – although in fact the concern with materiality and craftsmanship is an area of common ground between the two – or the structural engineering tradition which is so admired, that the idea is too difficult to entertain.

On the other hand, the British have been deeply inspired by the work of Portuguese and Spanish 'minimalist' architects such as Edouardo Souto de Moura and Alvaro Siza of the Porto school, or Herzog and de Meuron and Diener and Diener of Switzerland – though less so by, say, the Italians Gino Valle or Francesco Venezia – all producing very different buildings, but, again, with the emphasis on 'the suppression of redundancy in artistic practice', as Vittorio Gregotti has put it.[9] The work is clearly related to that of the early Modern Movement, but the significant difference is always in the connection between the building and its site – whether urban or rural – and the craftsmanly, as opposed to industrial, quality of the construction. The mediterranean region has its own indigenous tradition of a simple geometric, strictly rational, whitewashed architecture integrated with the landscape, which José Luis Sert discussed in the 1930s as a basis for a humane contemporary architecture, and the spirit of this tradition seem to permeate the work of these latter-day mediterranean modernists.[10]

Beyond Europe, the most substantial amount of new architecture in the minimal vein is found in Japan, but the work produced by architects such as Ando, Shinohara, Maki or Isozaki is arguably a different thing from western 'minimalism', being so much a part of a centuries'-old indigenous architectural tradition rather than a specifically new development. In America, there seems to be surprisingly little current minimal work by the younger generation, though George Ranalli's interiors, and some of Steven Holl's, constructed out of simple geometric, white-painted volumes inserted into existing spaces could be included in the survey. It seems possible that the reason for this may be the fact that the origins of the Modern Movement in America were always imported, and that since then a reaction in favour of rediscovering a truly American, non-European architectural idiom has taken place, in which the more dynamic, expressive work of architects such as Frank Gehry has attracted most attention.

Ultimately the question with current minimalism is how long it will sustain its current appeal for younger architects. Undoubtedly its flowering has been closely associated with the escalation of world-wide economic recession and the steady growth of awareness of the need to conserve the world's resources if ecological collapse is to be avoided. In this context, minimalism, as an architecture of restraint and limited means, against over abundance and squander, has exercised a deep appeal. But as the cycle turns it seems not unlikely that reaction will set in, and the urge to make more dynamic, more exciting, more actively communicative architecture will return again. On the other hand, the qualities and ideals of minimal architecture may prove to be enduring; for as life itself becomes increasingly fragmented, intangible and uncertain, the innate human desire for the calm space, the comfort of solid materials and the contemplation of slow-moving nature, may become ever more powerful.

Notes

1 Charles Jencks, *The New Moderns*, Academy Editions, London, 1990.
2 Reprinted and expanded as *Architecture Today*, Academy Editions, London, 1988 and 1993.
3 Alan Colquhoun, *Modernity and the Classical Tradition*, MIT Press, Cambridge, Mass, USA, 1989.
4 Frances Spalding, *British Art Since 1900*, Thames & Hudson, London, 1986.
5 *Minimalism: Collection Display*, Tate Gallery, Liverpool catalogue, March 1989-Feb 1990.
6 *Ibid*.
7 Jun'Ichiro Tanizaki, *In Praise of Shadows*, Leete's Island Books, 1977.
8 Nikolaus Pevsner, *The Englishness of English Art*, Penguin, London, 1956.
9 Vittorio Gregotti, 'Minimal', *Rassegna*, Dec 1988.
10 José Luis Sert, *Mediterranean Architecture*, Poligrafa, 1974.

Claudio Silvestrin, Johan Menswear shop, Graz, Austria

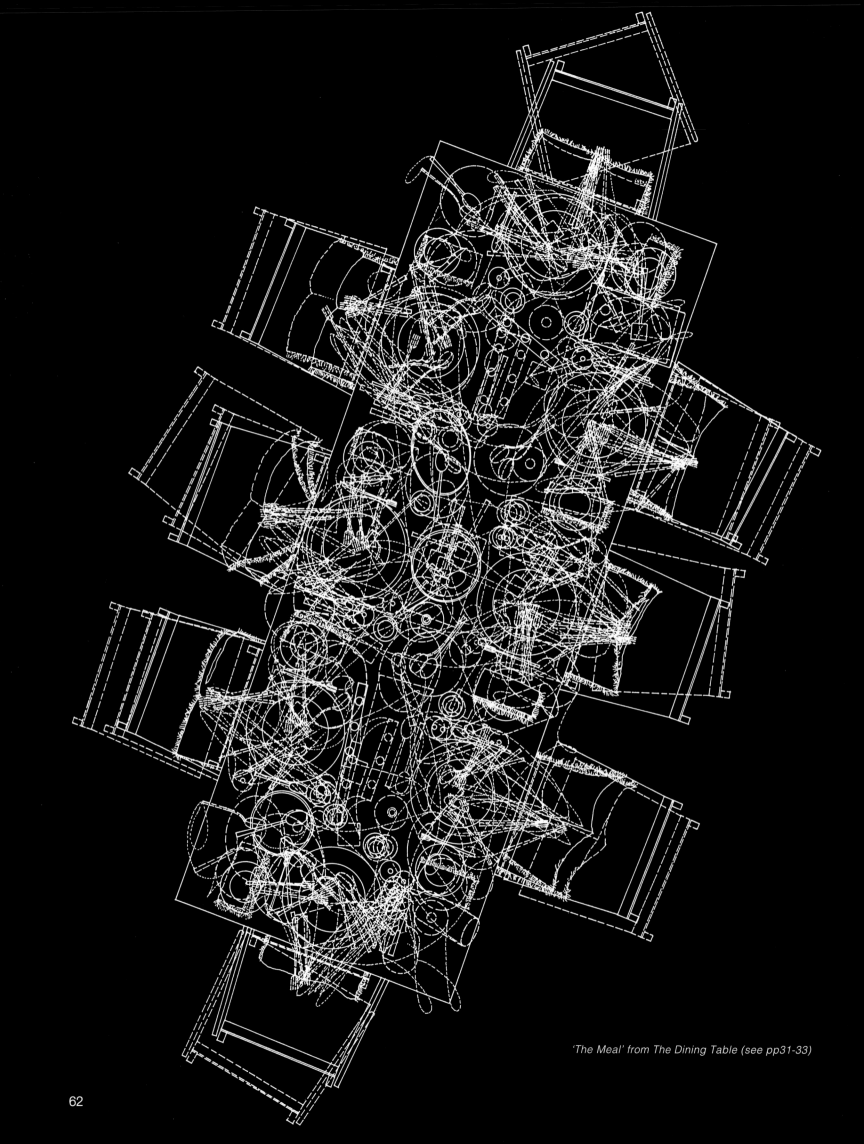

'The Meal' from The Dining Table (see pp31-33)

SARAH WIGGLESWORTH AND JEREMY TILL
TABLE MANNERS

Four stories; four different narratives about a project whose subject is the relationship between work and home.

Story 1. The Dining Table

Faced with a blank sheet of paper and a couple of buildings to design, where do you start? Any novelist will tell you: write about what you know. What we know is that living and working from the same building means our two lives (work and home) are never easily distinguished, but rather are irrevocably intertwined. An architect's response to this might be: separate the two physically; clarify zones; keep activities distinct; apply order. The person who lives and works there knows this is impossible. The Dining Table shows why.

The Dining Table sits in the centre of our 'parlour', the front room of our terraced house. On it stand items of everyday domestic use such as salt cellar and pepper mill, vases of flowers, fruit bowl and candlesticks. On an average day it collects the detritus of domestic life: letters and mailshots, magazines, keys, bike lights and small change. At regular intervals it becomes the site for meals, gathering over time the marks of the food and drink spilled on its surface. At other times it is the venue for office meetings, because our office is not large enough to accommodate more than four

people. At such times it is to be found scattered with pieces of paper, models, drawings, pens and other evidence of office life. The surface retains the patina of time, the traces of past events indelibly etched into the surface. At no time can the Dining Table be said exclusively to represent one side of life more than another. This ambiguity is an essential motif in the reinvention of the new house and office. In this process, the Dining Table itself is the starting point for the project, acting as a trope for the design of spaces which inscribe home and work simultaneously.

The Dining Room in the new scheme occupies a space which positions the table ambiguously between the house and the office, recognising the claims of both to the use of its surface. At times the space is used as a conference room for the office, the place of official business. At other times it can be united with the house and plays the role of the formal dining room.

Above the table hangs a chandelier of broken milk bottles: discarded domestic artefacts fashioned into a status symbol. The chandelier signifies the formal nature of this space; yet as a mediating world it symbolises the conditions of real life, reminding us in the gentlest way that we have several identities, often co-existent.

Our Dining Table

The Lay of the Table

An architectural ordering of place, status and function
A frozen moment of perfection.

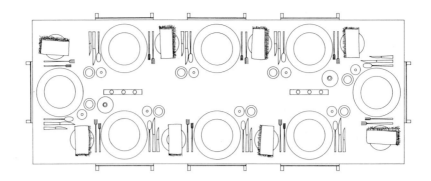

The Meal

Use begins to undermine the apparent stability of the (architectural) order
Traces of occupation in time
The recognition of life's disorder.

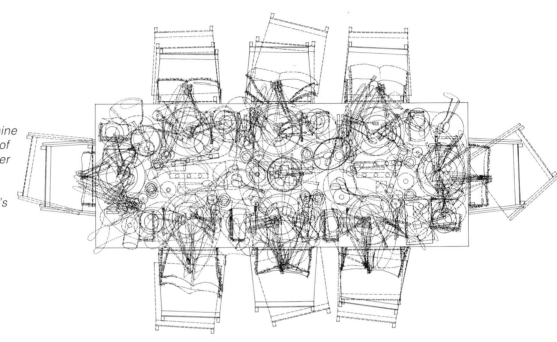

The Trace

The dirty tablecloth, witness of disorder
Between space and time
The palimpsest.

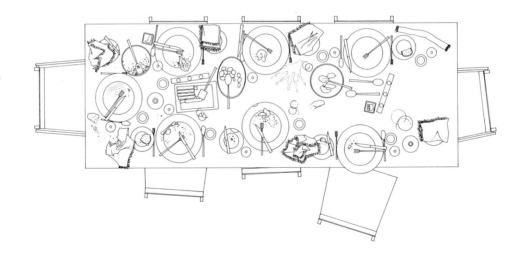

The Lay of the Plan

Recognition of an/other system of order
Domestic clutter filling the plan(e).

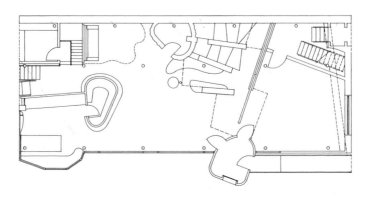

These four drawings are an exploration of the idea of order in architecture. They document the transformation of the plane of the ordered dining table into the plan of the house. The sequence begins with the table in readiness for an evening meal.

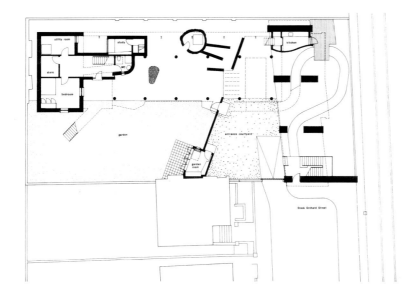

Ground Floor Plan

Open space under the floor plan of the house. Chickens foraging in the bark chips. Rude nature and a pile of compost amongst a grid of columns. The rhythm of residual party walls held captive in wire cages. A ramp which pauses to register the 10.05 to Edinburgh as it passes the trembling train spotting terrace. Bike sheds and back doors.

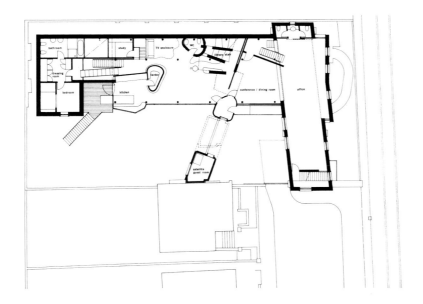

First Floor Plan

Bürolandschaft for the home. Attic loft for the office. Dining/Conference room as hall. Shiny columns against furry blobs and hairy walls. Cooling larder and warming hearth. A sandbag wall peels away to give momentary glimpses of whistling trains. Narnian wardrobe as a place of transition. The plan comes to rest as we go to bed. Guests docking with the lobby Mir-style; sliding like a snail back along the garden wall. No slimy trails.

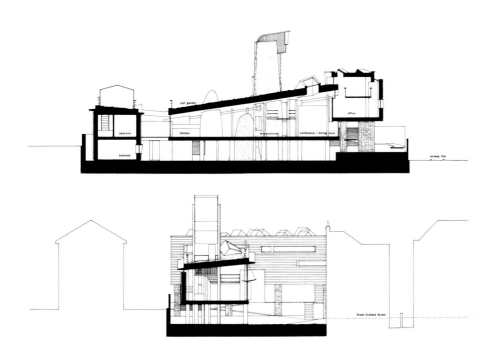

Section

A bed inside a cupboard. Planes punctured by projections. Wild strawberries growing on a tilted roof. A tower whose bricks are books, demanding exertion. A lookout post, a signal box, whose roof slips away under starry skies. A ramp climbing through ruined walls.

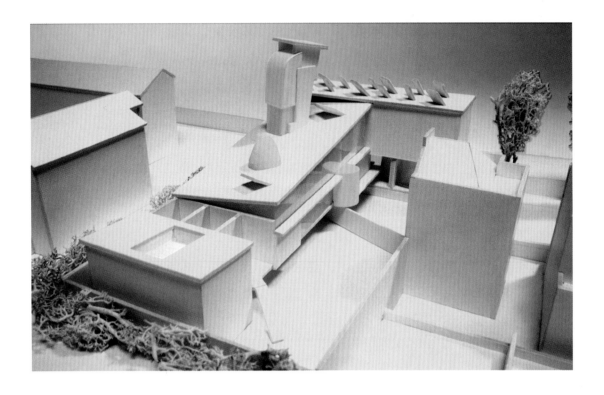

Story 2. Technologies of the Everyday

The technology of building is assumed to 'progress' towards increasing sophistication. The meaning of sophistication is: greater reliance on Western, energy-rich, complex, industrialised processes. It is not considered progressive to use resource-spare, readily-available by-products from existing industries. Technology transfer is alright as long as it is a transfer to architecture from industries like aeronautical engineering, boat building or nanotechnology: cutting-edge manufacturing to which earthbound architecture aspires.

In contrast, all the innovative forms of building used in the house and office come under the category we have named 'reverse technology transfer'. In this transaction we adopt deliberately simple technologies to show how architecture has locked itself into patterns of thinking which are inscribed into its ideology and its legal codes (building regulations, for example). Our technologies are obvious and easy to construct; they can be performed by people without great prior knowledge and they make use of existing and ready-at-hand materials. They are even fun.

Gabions The Office is a narrow strip of floorspace which sits on four thick walls made of gabions. Gabions are normally used as retaining walls alongside river banks or motorways, cages of galvanised steel wire into which are packed stones, rocks or, in our case, lumps of concrete recycled from the site. They are physically too big for their job but why should engineering always be about the minimal? Why shouldn't it be about excess?

Sandbags The Office faces a main-line railway. The wall fronting the line is defended from this aural invasion, just as we did in wartime, by stacking sandbags against the force of the intruder. Civil defence authority hessian bags are filled with a mix of sand and a small amount of cement. After some months and some rain, the cement goes off. Later, when the hessian rots and falls away in shreds the form of the bag, complete with the imprint of the weave on its surface, remains.

Strawbales Thick, insulating and light to handle, straw bales are the perfect material with which to make a north wall. Strawbales wrap the house on these faces, coddling the bedroom wing from head to foot like a feather-filled coverlet. While they can be used as a load-bearing system, we are using them as infill between timber trusses. Both walling material and insulation rolled into one, the bales are clad in a rainscreen made of transparent polycarbonate, celebrating the beauty of the natural product. The tension between the roughness of the bales and the sleek exterior of the cling-film sheathing disturbs the normal architectural categories, uniting the slick with the hairy and the fetishised with the repressed.

The Duvet A cloth covering upholsters the office like a chair, reuniting the domestic artefact with the place of work. Puckered and buttoned, the external and internal are elided. Non-stick cloth. Silicone implanted fibres. Behind its apparent fluidity and weightlessness, the solid walls of the office resist the vibration of the trains passing by.

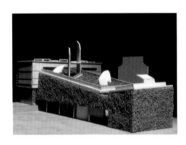

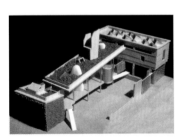

FROM ABOVE: View of model showing building in context; view of model with strawbale wall; view of model

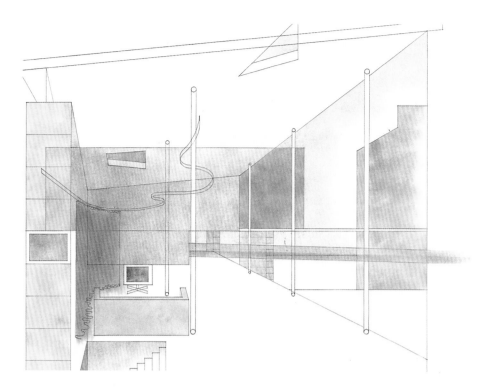

Story 3. Watching the World Go By

We are already living in the house we have yet to build. Constructed only through drawings, space and events compacted in our head. Straight ahead a television, that old 'window to the world'. But the velvet curtain is pulled back, so attention is distracted, views shifted. To the left, a housing estate caught in the deep reveal; he's doing his hair again, silhouetted against bobbly glass. To the right, picture windows picture the street; the new milkman looking for a doorstep. Ahead the office is suspended, waiting. Escape its presence upwards, through the rooflight and join the passing plane on its way to holiday romance. And through it all a train passes. It is the 10.05, the Edinburgh one.

Story 4. Scaling the Library

Stack of books. Worry about how to order them. Chronologically? Oldest at the bottom, like archaeology? Alphabetically? But Zola is a favourite and too long a climb. Thematically? But what is to be at the top, floating us heavenward, books of dreams or books of thoughts?

Start to climb, past the rude green lump, lights caught in its rough surface. The window salesman is in there, panicking at the waterless loo, confronting his own shit. Up past the balcony, cello waiting to learn to play. On up perforated stairs, criss-crossing between work and play. Through the roof, head level with the meadow, scorched in the sun. Room at the top still looks funny, leaning towards the trains. We have the timetables up there, a little joke. And at night, the roof draws back and we lie on the single bed, starwards.

Scaling the library

KOLATAN/MACDONALD STUDIO
OST/KUTTNER APARTMENTS
Vienna

This interior project (1997) was conceived as a form of miniature urbanisation. It consisted of three phases: identification of 'sites' within the existing space to act as locations for new structures; generation of these structures through cross-profiling; mapping of similarities using a method akin to co-citation mapping.

For the generation of the new structures on each site, section profiles of everyday domestic objects and furnishings were cross-referenced electronically, regardless of original scale and category, with an interest in registering the formal and operational similarities between them. Based on this information, they were then organised spatially and resurfaced.

The resulting structures are chimerical: the initial profiles as indexes of particular identities (bed, sink, sofa, etc) are now inextricably embedded within an entirely new entity, which they have helped produce. We will loosely refer to this new entity as a 'domestic scape', or synthetic topography.

The domestic scape, unlike the domestic space (the room), or the domestic object (the furniture), cannot be identified by categoric classification. Rather, like a particular landscape, its identification is contingent on the presence of a set of idiosyncratic features. As the discussion of identity is linked here to programmatic performance, it is useful to continue the landscape analogy in evaluating the synthetic topography. In the case of the bed, this would mean that a 'plateau' of

a certain measurement can be indentified as, but would not be limited to, a potential sleeping area. This is very different from the concept of a 'bed' or a 'bedroom', which are both categoric designations of identity, and therefore fixed in their programmatic associations.

The formal and programmatic conditions thus obtained are unknown and impossible to preconceive or predict. This excess of information poses an interesting problem in as much as it is ambiguous and therefore open to interpretation on many levels. The resulting synthetic topographies, unlike conventional subdivisions by rooms, do not register legible distinctions between spaces or programmes. The domestic scapes are always situated across the boundaries of the existing domestic spaces. The bed/bath scape, for example, forms a continuous surface within its own limits, a seamless transition between the space shaped by the 'bathtub' and the bedroom floor/wall. (A door into the 'bathtub' is sealed as the water level rises and presses against it.)

While the topographic model is useful in understanding certain aspects of these structures, it is important to note that the surface in this case is not just terrain, a top layer with a fairly shallow sectional relief, but deep – both conceptually and literally. Conceptually, this term is used to denote the possibility of an increased range. The surface is not exclusively thought of as thin, shallow, external etc,

but as capable of incorporating degrees of cavitation, thickness, interiority, three-dimensional space and so on. Considered in this way, the relationship between deep and shallow, space and surface, is not defined as a dichotomy, but within the terms of transformation. It is this capacity of the scape to change incrementally and continously that produces a chimerical condition between furniture, space and surface.

Conventional assumptions about the codification of the interior surfaces as floors, walls and ceilings do not always hold here. At the very least, the place and manner in which these elements meet is redefined.

In the final phase of the project, these individual scapes are interconnected across the space of the apartment in a manner similar to co-citation mapping (electronic literary indexing). This kind of similarity mapping yields both an analysis of already existing relationships by indicating the co-presence of certain idiosyncracies across, or regardless of, type, as well as a relational method of production that produces simultaneous effects across an established network.

An electronic web of second-iteration sites is constructed with the intention of mapping similarities and differences between previously unrelated entities. The individual sites are bound together as a system in which small-scale manipulations affect changes throughout varying scales and locales.

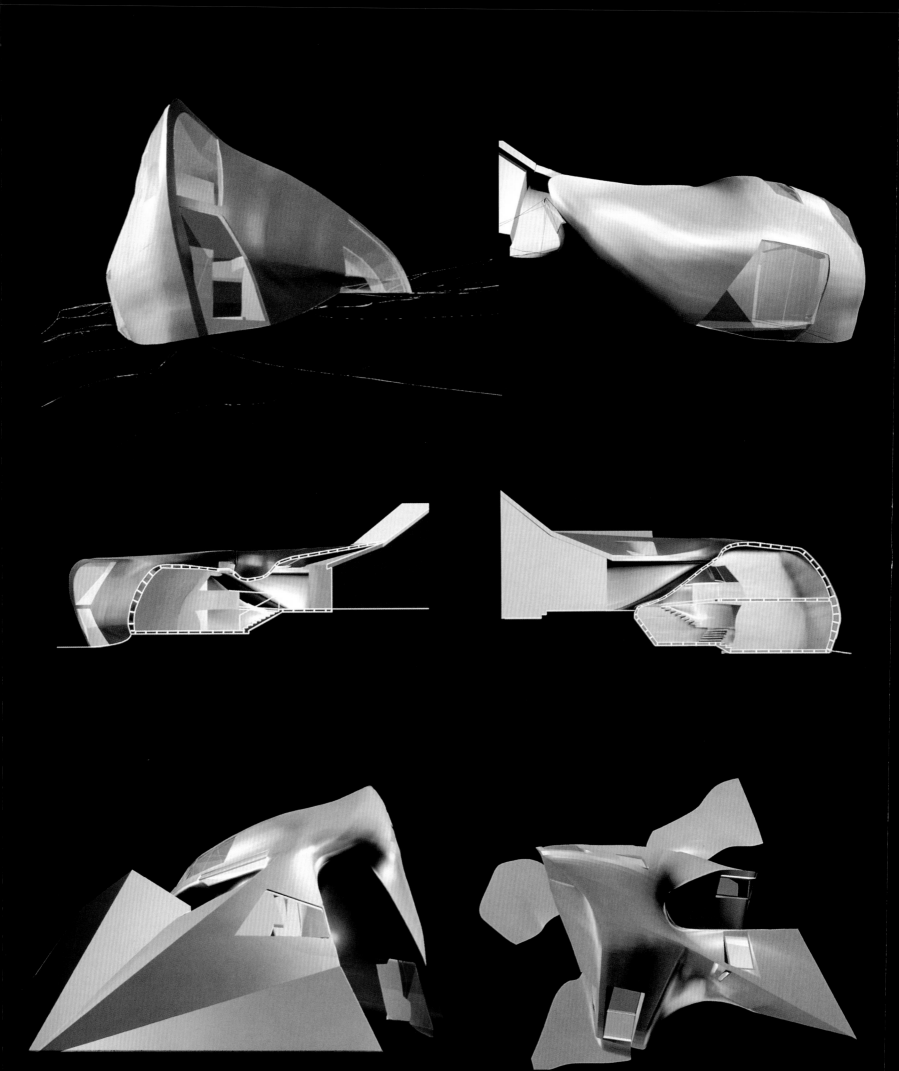

KOLATAN/MACDONALD STUDIO

RAYBOULD HOUSE ADDITION

Sherman, Connecticut

This project explores the potential of a hybrid architecture. The computer's specific capacity to map similarities across different categories while performing transformative operations is crucial to its conceptual and physical production.

For the design of this 'weekend home' addition, completed in 1998, information has been culled from the existing house, the landscape and the car. Their respective protocols and structural and spatial identities were electronically cross-referenced and systemically transformed into the new house.

The brief was to provide a 150-square-metre addition to the existing house, primarily used by the New York-based client to entertain guests. The new extension consists of two adjoining living areas, two bathrooms, and two bedrooms.

The 5.5 acre site is a gently sloping, 'pie-shaped', wooded parcel of land adjacent to an intersection on the south, a roadway on the east and farmlands to the west and north. The area of the compound includes a stream (with dam), which splits the site nearly in half along its longitudinal axis; two existing 17th-century structures (a 150-square-metre house and a 370-square-metre barn); a kidney-shaped, 1950s swimming pool and a small entry bridge.

The entry drive is on the eastern-most boundary of the site, running perpendicular to the stream. The immediate site of the addition is on the north-eastern side of the existing house. In this area, the landscape slopes some 30 per cent from west to east. The site drops sharply at the rear of the existing house, creating a 2.5-metre differential between the plateau on which the existing house rests and the lowest ground level of the new addition on its most eastern facade.

As a result of the project's proximity to a wetlands area, the addition had to be located no less than 23 metres from the top of the stream's bank. The structure's entire height could not exceed 10.5 metres.

The three-dimensional geometry of the building has been developed as an 'open-net shell'. This faceted structure is comprised of varying lengths and thicknesses of wood, which were calculated and designed by consulting engineers through structural analysis on a computer. The joinery of the wood members utilises a metal box that typically receives four struts in each of the intersection points of the faceted structure (not unlike a geodetic system). The double membrane panels are sheathed by rubber-cored plywood, which allows for the double-curving surface.

Most of the interior of the shell is finished in Philippine mahogany-veneered, rubber-cored plywood. The bathroom walls and floors are mainly tiled. The exterior, waterproof membrane is covered in a custom-tailored, reinforced-thermoplastic membrane with hot-air welded seams. The window mullions continue the faceted structure.

For drainage purposes the window and door openings (along with their deflector and gutter systems) are strategically placed in the flattest surfaces of the structure. The mechanical systems are central air-conditioning and radiant-slab heating. All other flooring is carpeted.

OPPOSITE: Computer-generated images of exterior and sections; BELOW: Site plan

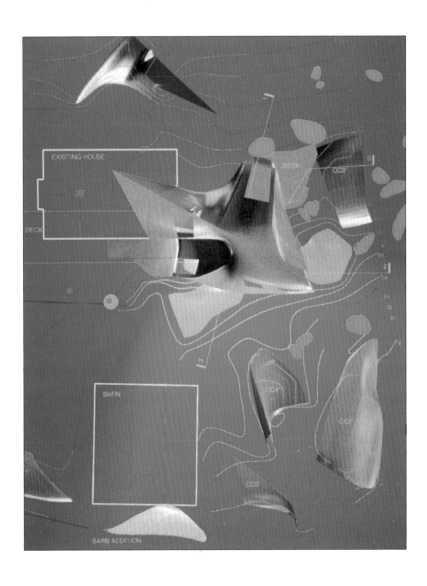

1

2

Living, 1990

Archigram Group

The intention of this exhibit, sponsored by the *Weekend Telegraph* on show this month at Harrods in Knightsbridge, is to demonstrate how computer technology and concepts of expendability and personal leisure might influence the form of future homes.

The living space **1, 4**, is intended to be in a space frame **2** or suspended within a tensegrity structure. Enclosure is created by skins which close together or separate electronically. The floor and ceiling can be transformed from hard to soft as acoustic/space/light regulators or inflated in certain areas as required for reclining and sleeping. The adjustable screens of the robot towers (robots Fred and James) **8**, define smaller areas within the main volume where one can be totally enclosed—enveloped in an event generated by the projection of films, light, sound and smellies. The push of a button or a spoken command, a bat of an eyelid will set these transformations in motion—providing what you want where and when you need it **10–16**. Each member of a family will choose what they want—the shape and layout of their spaces, their activities or what have you. The hover chairs **1, 9**, will provide an instant link-up with local amenities or access to the nearest transit interchange. A fully integrated systems approach to domestic bliss.

SECONDARY STRUCTURE PYLONS [REMOVABLE]

ROBOT

ROBOT

INFLATABLE SKIN

UP TO UPPER LEVELS

SOFT POTENTIAL

SOFT

SOFT

ROBOT

SOFT

SOFT

INTO LIFT

NEXT DOOR NEIGHBOUR PREFERS COOL ARRANGEMENT [ALL PART OF THE SERVICE]

SOFT

SOFT

BED-CAPSULE CAN BECOME HOVERCRAFT & TRIP OFF

SOFT

covered free area

SOFT

ROBOT

SOFT

ROBOT-MAD SPACE FOR MUSIC-NUT

ROBOT

CLIP-ON ORCHESTRA

ROBOT

SOFT

ROBOT

UP & DOWN BY ANTI-GRAVITY PADS

ROBOT

SOFT

INFLATABLE SKIN

OPEN

GUIDED MOVEMENT ROUTE

MEGA-STRUCTURE

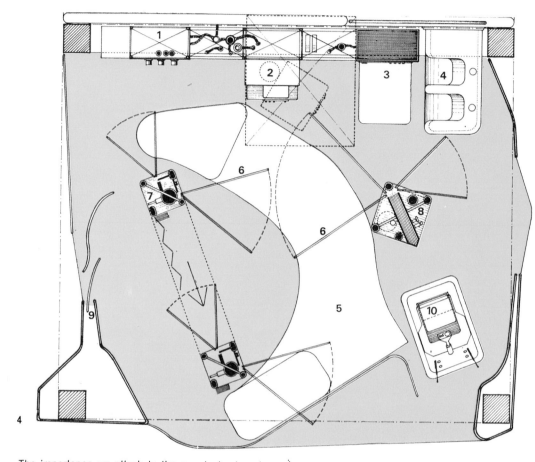

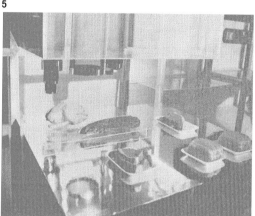

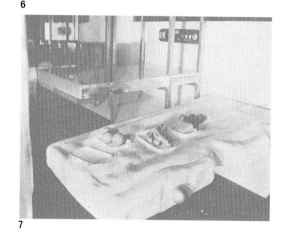

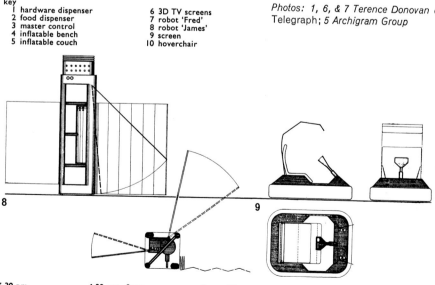

The importance we attach to the new technology is quite clear. To say that electronics is important to the future of architecture is a truism—something to talk about and discuss, yet feel unable to produce constructive and significant propositions about. This vision of the dwelling of the future takes an elementary and popularized form, but it is not a compromise. It makes clear, without any falsification of our beliefs, ideas that are otherwise difficult to grasp. Participation in an event such as this helps to redefine the problems we recognize to be important; clarifies our position before another step is taken. It might enable all of us to endure better the crisis we live in. Architecture remains well outside the orbit of technological forecasting—the ability to look ahead further than you can see—but inevitably and eventually it will be pressurized into a more receptive position. The public is not interested in the current betrayal of the Bauhaus achievement; it is equally, reluctant to suffer the inefficiencies of Welfare State housing. The only way to involve the public in architecture is to give them what they want. We see self-selection as the obvious solution.

Warren Chalk

key
1 hardware dispenser
2 food dispenser
3 master control
4 inflatable bench
5 inflatable couch
6 3D TV screens
7 robot 'Fred'
8 robot 'James'
9 screen
10 hoverchair

Photos: 1, 6, & 7 Terence Donovan courtesy Weekend Telegraph; 5 Archigram Group

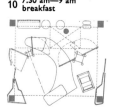
10 7.30 am—9 am breakfast

11 9 am—4 pm individual activities

12 4 pm—6.30 pm children tea/TV

13 6.30 pm—8 pm teens/adults activities

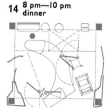
14 8 pm—10 pm dinner

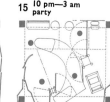
15 10 pm—3 am party

16 3 am—7.30 am sleep

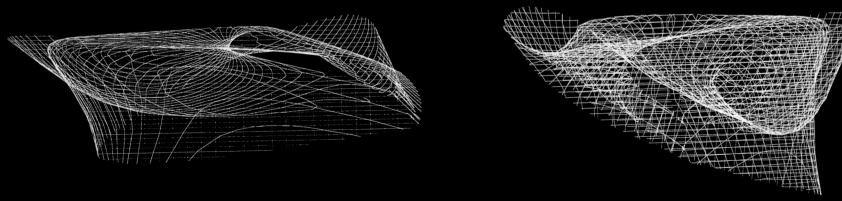

STEPHEN PERRELLA WITH REBECCA CARPENTER
THE MÖBIUS HOUSE STUDY

This study (1997-98) is an investigation into contemporary domesticity to reconsider dwelling for the new millennium. A preliminary analysis revealed that the pervasive use of technology in the home presents an ontological dilemma. Current house formats are no longer tenable because space and time are reconfigured by a lived informational geometry. Dwelling has become problematic solely in terms of Euclidean space as a result of media infiltrations – a force that implodes distance and then perplicates subjectivity as it enfolds viewer perception into an endless barrage of electronic images. This occurs in combination with, and yet is dissimilar to, the dynamics of teletechnology and computer-to-Internet connectivity. As home-viewing narrows onto the TV surface, it fuses with an image-blitz into a perpetual present.[1] Teletechnology contributes to a burrowing effect, altering the home as an exclusively interior condition. This battlefield of intersubjectivity problematises the dweller-consumer as an ego-construct-identity, traditionally based upon an interiority divided from an exteriority and governed by an ideality.

The Möbius House study diagram for post-Cartesian dwelling is thus neither an interior space nor an exterior form. It is a transversal membrane that reconfigures

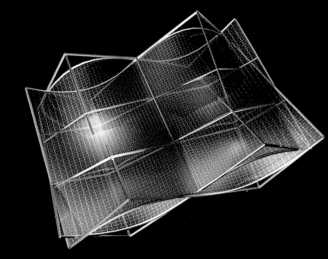

binary notions of interior/exterior into a continuous, interwrapping median – it is a hypersurface. The current phase of the study presents a fluxing diagram-membrane generated by an animated inflection. It is a hypersurface generated by first deconstructing the supporting geometry of a NURB (non-uniform rational B-spline) curve in the animation software by Microsoft/Softimage. Each singular control point that governs a five-point NURB was animated along the path of a Möbius surface, generating a topology that cannot be understood by either Euclidean or Cartesian geometry. Within the animation sequences, temporal delays are programmed to avoid determinate, linear form: what is otherwise known as 'the stopping problem'.[2] The Möbius House study is thus irreducible, rendering it open to complex, temporal experience: it is architecture that is not based upon fundamental form or space and therefore, in part, constitutive of experience; not an attempt to contain or act as a plane of reference. It is a transversal construct.[3] A domestic hypersurface program thus emerges immanently from the diagram-substrate, facilitating proprioceptive experience, a radical empiricism more commensurate with the complexities of new-millennial modes of inhabitation.[4]

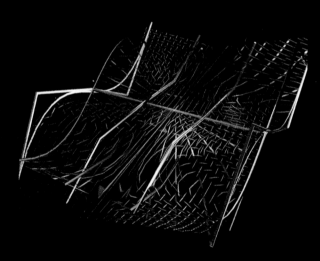

Notes

1   In *Blue Sky* (Verso, 1997) Paul Virilio discusses the notion of pyknoleptic from pyknolepsy, a medical term denoting childhood avsence epilepsy.
2   In the 'Emerging Complexities' Symposium at Columbia University GSAP, Spring 1997, theorist-economist Akira Asada raised the issue of whay he called the 'stopping problem' – a way of describing work that attempts to bring temporality into architectural form. He noted that at a certain phase of design development, the form must be frozen and then conceivably built as such. Hypersurface theory and the Möbius House study

argue that if the constituting or governing structures of form are considered separately from a lived program, then 'animate' form will exist only in the realm of materiality. What is most significant about the work of Deleuze and Guattari is that they ofer a means to evacuate such dualities.
3   See Gary Genosko's essay in this volume, pp32-37.
4   See Brian Massumi's essay in this volume, pp16-25. His thesis on proprioperception entails an enrichment of experience that embraces but reworks the impoverishing dynamics within the schizophrenia that stems from capitalism.

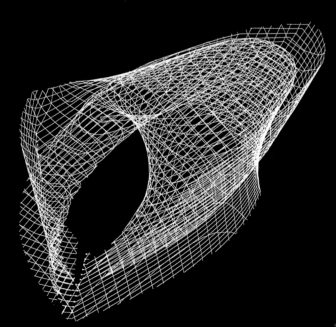

OPPOSITE: X, Y, Z sections; FROM ABOVE: Hypersurface panel studies 1 and 2; X, Y Z axonometric

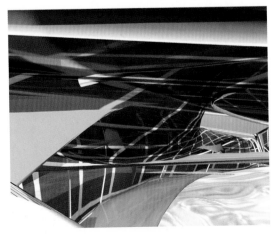

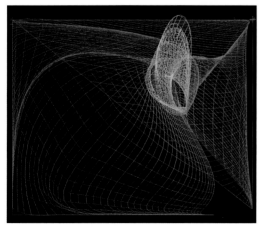

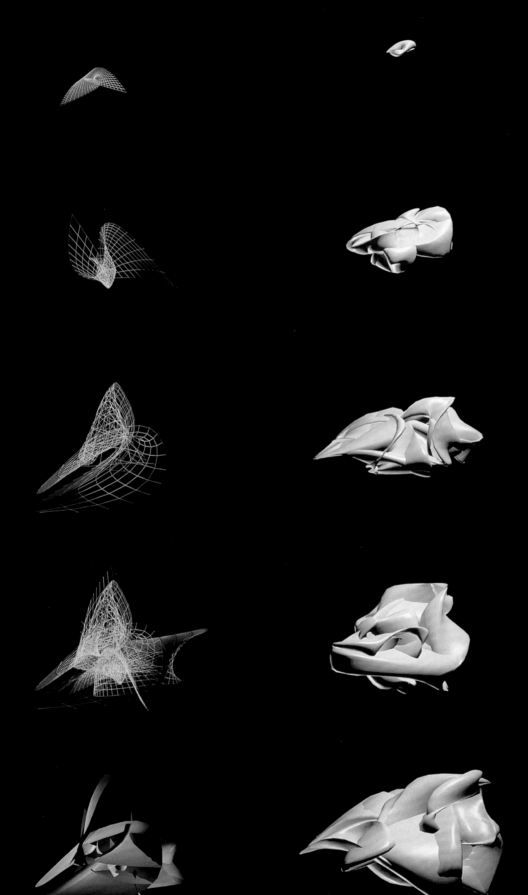

FROM ABOVE LEFT: Evolving virtual environment: *A prototype sequence testing the development, evolution and mapping of an experiment in the collaborative evolution of a virtual environment by global participation on the Internet; FROM ABOVE RIGHT:* An experiment in global cooperation to evolve a virtual environment on the Internet

JOHN H FRAZER, MANIT RASTOGI, PETER GRAHAM
THE INTERACTIVATOR

Evolutionary cellular model

The model is based on the sequential evolution of a family of cellular structures in an environment. Each structure begins development from a single cell inheriting genetic information from its ancestors and from a central gene pool. The same chromosomes are contained in each cell, and make up the genetic code. The cells divide and multiply, based on the genetic code script and the environment, with each new cell given the same genetic information. The development process of each member of the family consists of three parts – cellular growth, materialisation and the genetic search landscape. A genetic algorithm ensures that future generations of the model learn from the previous ones as well as providing for biodiversity during the evolutionary process.

Data structure of the model

The data structure of the model is based on a universal-state space or isospatial model where each cell in the world has a maximum of 12 equidistant neighbours and can exist in one of 4,096 states, this state being determined by the number and spatial arrangement of its neighbours.

The local environment of a cell in the world can thus be coded in a 12 bit binary string. The growth and development of the cellular structure is controlled by chromosomes. For example, a string of the type (110110000110) would spatially represent the following configuration: A typical chromosome consisting of four parts – condition, action, flag, strength – corresponding to the following order: (10xxx10x11xx) (000011011010) 1 192.5) condition: the local environment of a cell

(X being a don't care situation)
action: the state of the cell in the next generation
flag: whether a chromosome is dominant or passive
strength: fitness of the chromosome with respect to the environment

Cellular growth

Chromosomes are generated by either being sent in by any remote user, an active site or as a function of selection, crossover and mutation within cellular activity and are maintained in a main chromosomal pool. The physical environment determines which part of this pool becomes dominant. The local environment of each cell determines which part of the genetic code switches on, and the cell then multiplies and divides accordingly.

As cellular division takes place, unstable cells are generated. In the next generation this leftover material creates a space of exclusion within the cellular space, which in turn interacts with the physical environment to create a materialisation of the model. Boundary layers are identified in the unstable cells as part of their state information and an optimised surface is generated to skin the structure. This material continues to exist throughout the evolution of the model and will initially affect the cellular growth of future generations.

Genetic search landscape

The selection criteria in the model is not defined but is an emergent property of the evolution of the model itself. A genetic search landscape is generated for each member; graphically representing

the evolving selection criteria based on the relationship between the chromosomes, cellular structure and the environment over time. Form, or the logic of form, emerges as a result of travelling through this search space.

Once chromosomal stability has been achieved, the parent cellular activity is terminated. The final cellular structure, the materialisation and the genetic search space are posted out. A daughter cellular activity is then initiated from a single cell. The fittest chromosomes from the parent generation are bred using selection, crossover and mutation and combined with the newly dominant chromosomes from the main pool to form a new chromosome set for the daughter generation. This generation then repeats the development process.

Current state of the model

In the first two weeks of the model being launched on the Internet, it evolved four family members based on chromosomes received and those bred internally, each member achieving chromosomal stability in about 120 generations. It is impossible to predict the nature of the model yet, or its internal logic, but there seems to be a pattern emerging towards its selective and hence, evolutionary process.

The next step is to recode the model so that it can evolve on any computer platform, eventually making it completely autonomous on the Internet. The model could then evolve indefinitely by allowing itself to replicate on to any host computer.

*Internet: http://www.gold.net/ellipsis/
evolutionary/evolutionary.html
e-mail: 100415.1704@compuserve.com*

Bibliography

JH Frazer and JM Connor, 'A Conceptual Seeding Technique for Architectural Design', PArC 79 International Conference on the Application of Computers in Architectural Design, Berlin, 1979. Proceedings, PArC 79 Online Conferences with AMK, pp 425-434.

JH Frazer, 'Datastructures for rule-based and genetic design', *Visual Computing - Integrating Computer Graphics with Computer Vision*, Springer-Verlag,

June 1992, pp 731-744.

PC Graham, JH Frazer and MEC Hull, 'The Application of Genetic Algorithms to Design Problems with Ill-defined or Conflicting Criteria', Conference on Values and (In)Variants, Amsterdam, 1993, Systemica, vol 10, 1995, pp61-76.

JH Frazer, 'The Architectural Relevance of Cybernetics', *Systems Research*, vol 10 No 3, 1993, pp43-47.

Brian Hatton, Interview with John Frazer, *Lotus 79*,

Electra, Rome, 1993, pp15-25.

JH Frazer, 'The Genetic Language of Design', in *Textiles and New Technology: 2010*, S Braddock & M O'Mahony (ed) Artemis, London, 1994, pp77-79.

JH Frazer, PC Graham and M Rastogi, 'Biodiversity in Design via Internet', Proceedings of conference Digital Creativity, Brighton, April 1995, publication pending.

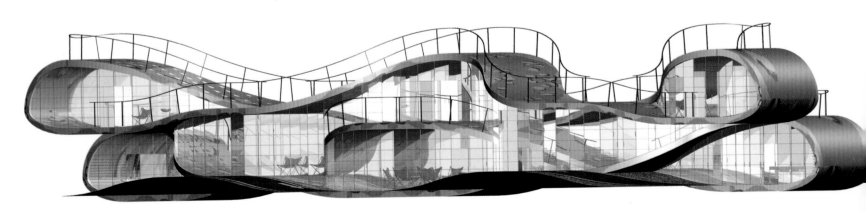

FROM ABOVE: Rendering of interior and exterior view

FOREIGN OFFICE ARCHITECTS
VIRTUAL HOUSE: POTENTIAL BEYOND THE FUTURE

Traditionally, innovative and visionary architectures have been associated with the invention of the future. However, FOA is not interested in the future, but in the virtual, as a source of new architectural possibilities. The idea of the future implies an expressed recognition of the discontinuity of time into fixed frames, as if the process of actualisation of a certain reality were independent of a continuous process of change. FOA sees the future, the past, the present as static, believing that only the virtual is able to capture the dynamic nature of a situation or organisation by extending the real towards the potentials and the memories that it contains.

The Virtual House was commissioned by Any Corporation/FSB Brackel in 1997 in order to explore the idea of the virtual in a domestic project. It researched a form of habitation in order to unfold potentials beyond the given identities of form, function and place. But it is impossible to produce the virtual unless it is seen as a changing system of relationships, triggered by a certain process. The virtual will always move systematically out of one's grasp just as it becomes actualised. It is not possible to produce the virtual itself, only its potential actualisations, or a process that will trigger them.

FOA's attempt in this project was to unfold the effects that a physical structural system would produce in the given identities and forms of the dwelling. Its strategy to produce the virtual was not to replace the real with a sophisticated surrogate, as in 'virtual reality', but rather to dismantle the complex assemblage of social uses, organisations of space and material qualities that have come to constitute what we generally understand as a house. The architects believe that the virtual is not the better, the future or the past, but what may unfold or inherit a series of lineages.

In this search for potentials, FOA focused first on the ground. The Virtual House would not become a figure imposed onto the ground, but would construct it. This virtual ground would not be an abstract and generic platform, a pedestal, but rather, concrete and specific. This virtual groundlessness would not have the verticality of the *Poeme de L'Angle Droit*, for it would no longer be in dimensional opposition to the ground. The construction of the Virtual House would no longer be an act of domination over matter and nature, but rather the act by which an artificial nature is produced, as an extension of singularities rather than as a field of resemblance.

The project emerged from a piece of artificial matter with indeterminate structural strength in terms of compression and tension, supplied with water and energy, and characterised phenomenally as a visually differentiated field. This field of visual singularity was made using Disruptive Pattern Material. DPM is produced by abstracting a given visual field into a differentiated distribution of colour on the surface of an object. It is specific not only in terms of its relation to a given visual field, but also in terms of its scale, dependent on the distance at which it is perceived.

FOA's new matter provided its Virtual House with a broad palette of abstracted regions, a collection of synthetic landscapes. The architects could now explore the groundlessness of the house by producing different models of ground, to proliferate the house into a series: the Arizona model, the Kwai model, the Steppe model, the Schwarzwald model and so forth.

This band of synthetic ground could be manipulated to produce the coding of space in a similar form in which a protein band folds to produce a DNA code: the organisation of matter would have precedence over the coding. It was manipulated in order to further challenge other categories that have been characteristic of the domestic spatial phenomenology, such as the opposition between inside/outside, front/back, up/down, and other cultural constructions of the dwelling.

In order to challenge the conventional categories of inhabitation, each face of the folded DPM surface would shift from a lining condition to a wrapping condition, disrupting the orientation of the relationships between the enveloping surface and the inside/outside opposition. Interior spaces would be generated by topological handles in the surface band. Each room would then combine with another to form a double-sided, double-used band. Each composite band would be combined with other composite bands to produce a more complex organisation of rooms, in which the folding bands would also grow three-dimensionally, as a pile of wafer matter. The rooms would not be segmented parts of the structure, but, conversely, singular points in a continuous space.

In order to explore the gradients of different conditions occurring on the folded surface, preceding the coding of inhabitation, the different areas were classified into three possible qualities of surface: wrapping/lining, inside/outside, and gravity in/gravity out. The superposition of the gradients of these three different categorisations would produce the instructions for the use of this topography of inhabitation. The distribution of supplies from the surface would be made not in respect to functional spaces, but as an overall act dependent on the specificity of the topography.

The system could now proliferate the body of the house *ad infinitum*, like a deep, inhabited, hollow ground, from the room to the city. Or it could perhaps deform itself into variations of the basic room. The Virtual House is not an organic, finished body, but a proliferating structure where the rooms are not functionally determined, and yet are specific.

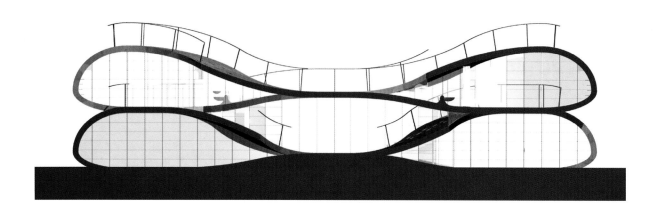

*FROM ABOVE: Front elevation; Collection of
landscapes; Elevation*

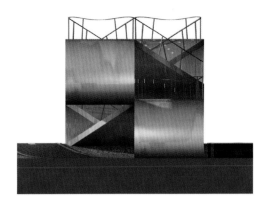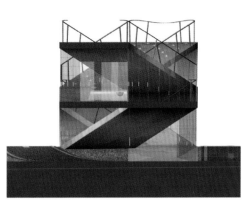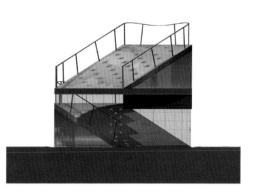

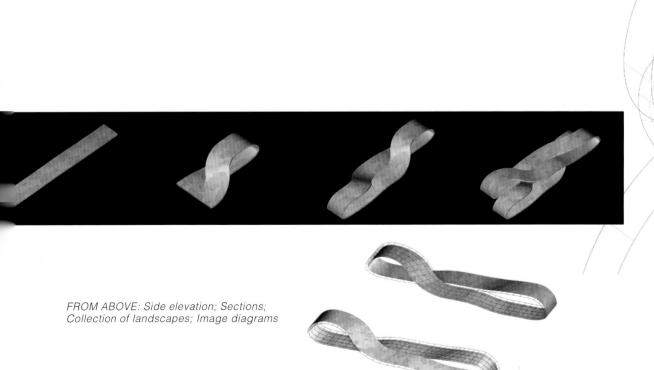

*FROM ABOVE: Side elevation; Sections;
Collection of landscapes; Image diagrams*

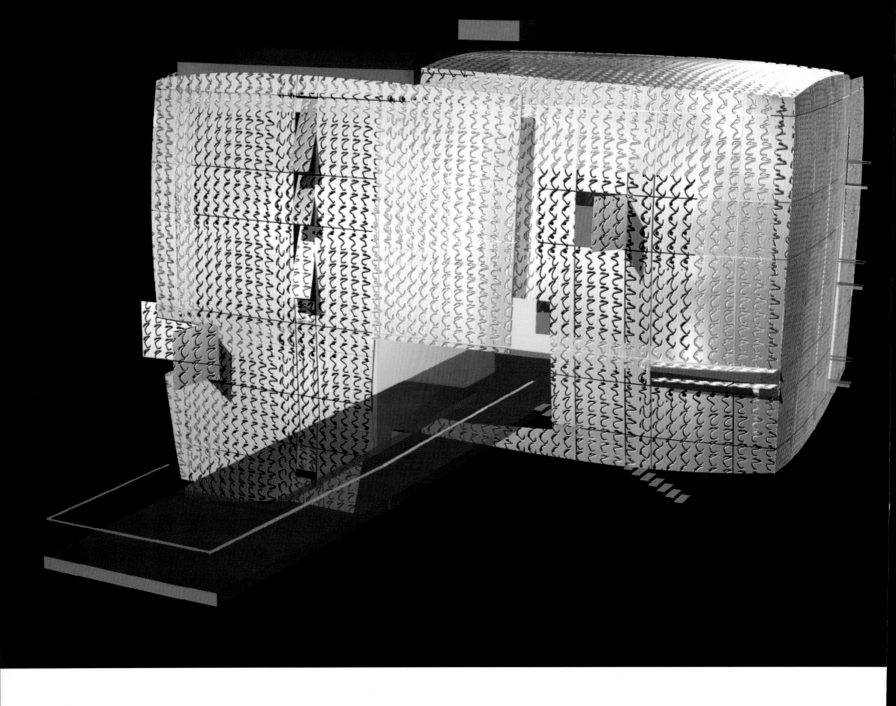

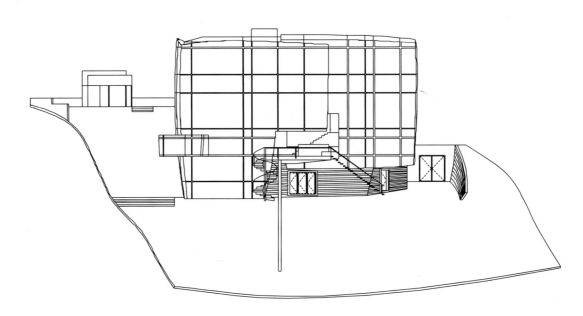

DECOI ARCHITECTS (WITH OBJECTILE)
PALLAS HOUSE

The Pallas House (1996) is a subtly amorphous form, whose embedded structure emerges from the ground as a restrained, mute shrouding, a curvilinear, metallic filter, which obscures the translucent house within. This 'light positive' – an arabesque carved delicately from the air – is held against the sculptural, languid forms of the landscape – a 'heavy negative' carved from the fluid earth.

One enters through a dark vortex, (the massive walls levitating sinuously), to a luminous void – a suspension of chiselled tracery that envelops the house, filtering the harsh environment.

The forms are at once simple and complex. A subtle deformation of surface is achieved through the use of sophisticated software. The warped stone walls of the landscape and the complex, curved shells of the carapace quietly distort the logics of industrial production to hint at a non-standard, post-industrial form. From the perforations of the metallic skin (trappings of movement), to the flutter and swell of the landscape, the project is generated numerically: chance-calculus imaginings of precise indeterminacy. Expressivity seems to implode, both in the generative process and in the final form, which have in any case fused as process.

The metallic filter was fabricated directly by numeric command machine, the linkage of creative machine and manufacturing machine opening up the field to non-standard complexity, to new numeric genres of decoration and organicism.

The Pallas House seems to be caught between logics, as if it were the reflection of a change-of-state, a mirror-image of representative collapse. The name Pallas refers to the twin sister murdered by the enigmatic and eidetic goddess, Helen. Here, the original sin at the root of all representative structure is exposed as the image becomes primary.[1]

Internally, the house is organised around a central void as a series of rectilinear boxes of translucent glass, which catch the patterns of light falling through the filtering screen and shroud the bodies moving within. These, too, seem to have undergone a formal glaciation, the cuts and abrasions in the crystalline surfaces quietly marking traces of slippage and movement, as if they were scars of emergence.

The spaces are translucent chambers of light-patterning (above), or voluptuous heavyweight wrappings (below) – forms of mute antithesis. But there is a sixth sense in the swelling shapes, as in the enigmatic calligraphy, of an imminent formal release, a potential for decorative excess. This rebirth of organic and decorative form within the interstices of a proliferating numeric capacity marks a new form of post-industrial profligacy.

Note

1 Working on the house with Bernard Cache, we were conscious of a profound shift in the manner of representation, whose temporal logics seem curiously suspended by CAD logic. The image is primary (a formulation from Cache's *Earth Moves: The Furnishing of Territories, Writing Architecture Series*, MIT Press (London), 1995) in the sense that it is a manipulable matrix of possibility, a form that at any moment is subject to change in response to any number of impinging criteria (client, budget, climatic data, etc). The image in no way re-presents something that is prior to it, but is the active generator of form. In this case we generated six different facade solutions in wood, metal, plastic, etc, perforated with morse code, calligraphic runes and electronic hieroglyphs.

OPPOSITE: Elevation; RIGHT, FROM ABOVE: Objectile prototype panel; motif

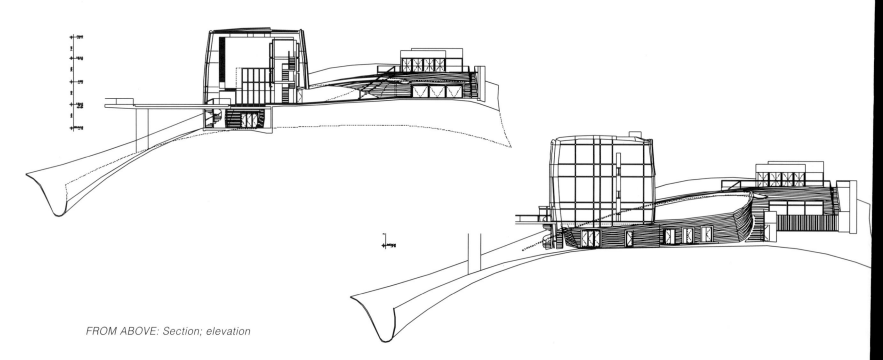

FROM ABOVE: Section; elevation

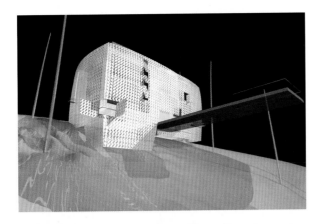

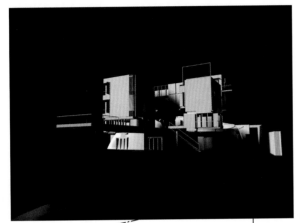

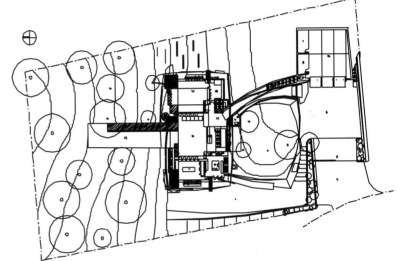

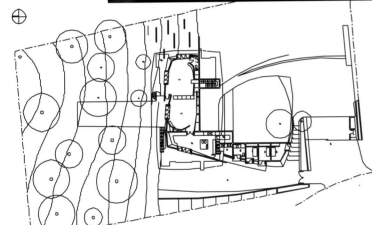

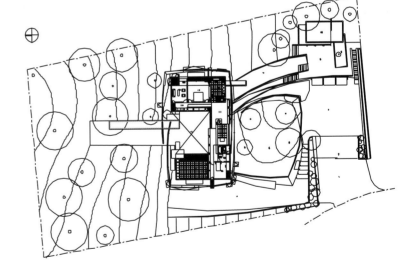

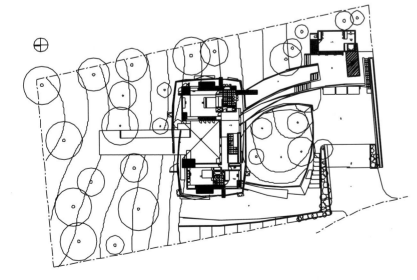

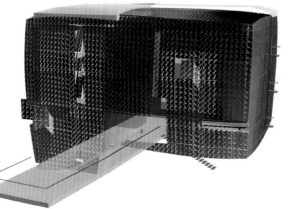

Plans

87

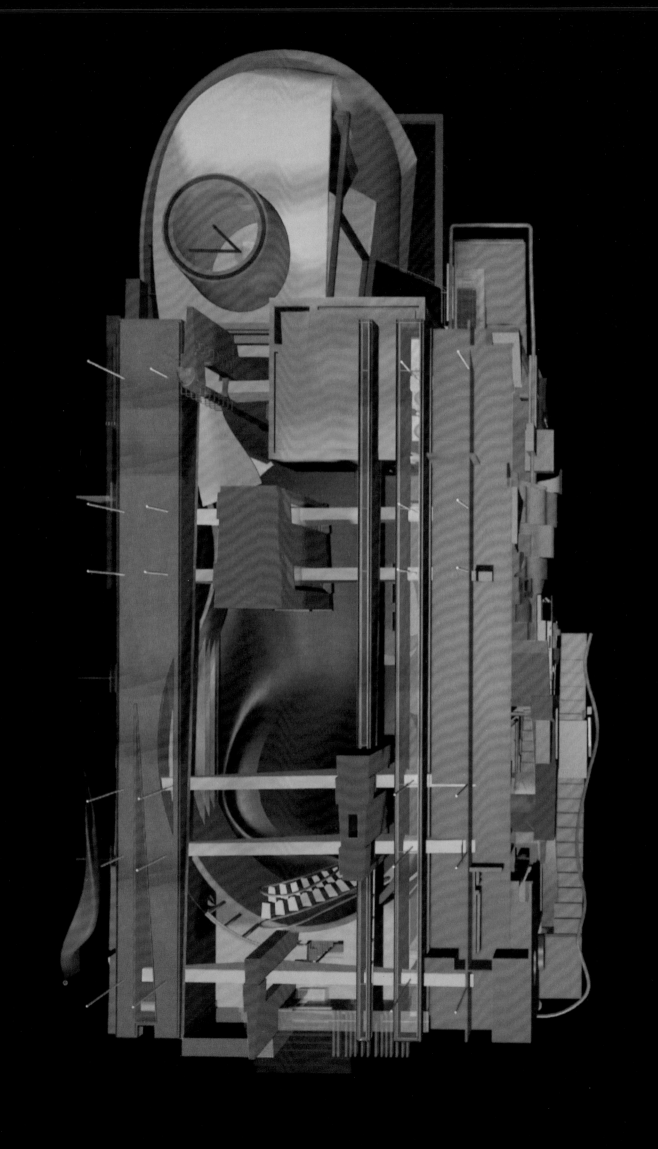

BEN NICHOLSON

WAR AND PEACEFARE AT THE LOAF HOUSE

An American nuclear family, the Loafers, has constructed a three-bedroom home within the city limits of Chicago. It is designed for a standard, homely interpretation of everyday activities, but is a place where the uncanny foibles of human nature have plenty of room to move. The rooms are configured to permit the many components of domestic life to drift across each others' paths with impunity. The parts are encouraged to form a spatial collage between the empirical and propositional aspects of home life.

The Loaf House exists in a number of forms, each a slightly different version of the same, and each requiring a different discipline to make the concept of homeliness complete. A series of drawings and collages work as multi-layered maps and, like all maps, suggest ways to locate the spaces in the house. The mahogany model functions as the palimpsest for the Loaf House, yet is restrained from committing to the actualities of the programme. The text 'The Loaf Notes' is a sequence of vignettes and propositions that form an apparition of life for the inhabitants. These three aspects of the Loaf House are then consummated in the virtual space of the computer, giving rise to a minutely described and fully programmed home, detailed to include everything from its overall structure to the form of the doorknobs.

In the context of computer design, the fiscal limits of actual construction have evaporated in the face of a raw determination to conceive a place that responds more accurately to the complexities of domestic intrigue. The computer allows the Loafers to wander at will in a place that is well beyond the pocket book of the average family. The Loaf House, as CD-ROM or on the Internet, could become a fully animated place for the domestic traveller to test life (without having to foot the bills) in a place that comes face to face with the modern daylight nightmare of irresolvable complexity and intrigue – laced with liberal doses of the ordinary.

The design has been undertaken by a team of over 30 people, working in relays of between two and eight, over a period of five years at the Illinois Institute of Technology. At each stage of its development, the Loaf House represents a discrete entity, be it in drawing, modelling, animation or construction. The intricate process of programming and three-dimensional computer design has created a very tempting apparition.

Were it to be built, the multi-storeyed house would take on the full spectrum of architectural method – of which the animated realm would then be its shadow. Every step of the design has been done to serve the worldly desire of construction and bodily intervention, where the virtual becomes actual, and where the Loafer comes to the giddy realisation that life itself is more potent than virtuality. Yet, as the poets have always told us, unless the virtual is experienced, the proposition of the actual might just pass by unnoticed.

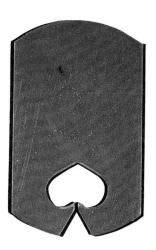

OPPOSITE: Loaf House, upper plan, 1996; FROM ABOVE: Chocolate bar, for mold and smell; Bread tag, for plan-shape and iconography, 1989: B-52 wheel well flap for technique and door, 1995

THE LOAF NOTES (EXCERPTED)

Addiction
What is so reassuring about the artistic temperament is that when the artist does not work, extraordinary melancholia sets in – which can be remedied by working again. The craving and ranting of the addicted draughtsman is reduced by the drug of drawing. Is addiction necessarily bad? Cigarettes or drawing both take you away from what you ought to love, to the same degree.

Animals
Should a house have insect screens on the windows? Differentiate between butterflies and mosquitoes. Is the discomfort to the eye, in seeing the world through a wire screen, greater or lesser than the discomfort to the ear caused by the noise of buzzing flies bumping into light bulbs? See Gardens.

Architecture
Architecture stretches the faculties in every

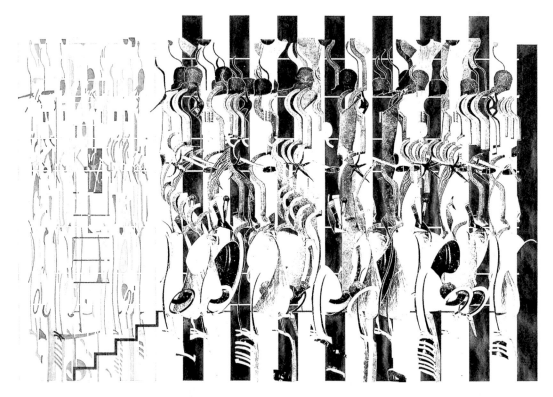

direction. It could be large as a Parthenon or as small as a garden shed, for architecture comes to any maker who is willing to go to the wall to make ideas fully blown. The great works are those that employ the emotive and fiscal reserves of a nation: the Space Shuttle might have laid claim to this definition of architecture, but it missed whole parts of the cultural spectrum – the scratchy metallic beast was just too useful to be any good for the Spirit of Mankind.

Beach Flotsam

On the beach I picked up a white rocket cone made of plastic, measuring 2 centimetres across its head. It fits perfectly on the end of my finger. It has lived in my pocket for quite a while, now being the inverted receptacle that my finger tip invariably seems to find. This morning I was walking around the kitchen, trying to throw it out, to part with it by slipping it into the recycling bin. But the object had served its apprenticeship in my pocket and became part of me; it received a stay of execution and instead entered my collection of plastic bits.

Birds

Pirates have parrots on their shoulders and scholars like to keep a perched bird nearby their desk. The antics of birds keep the workaholic sober: they bite, shit on your books and squawk at random. They prick hubris and make the only intelligible conversation when concentration is called for. When not nibbling the pirate-scholar's ear, the favourite perch of an imprisoned bird is to sit on the outside of its cage. Yet cages provide safe refuge from domesticated cats: cats turn cages from prisons into havens, they confuse what is considered inside and outside.

Breezeway

A wind catcher, made to know the shape and hardness of air. Running passages of air take away smells, moisture and excess heat or cold. Winds blow predictably and those of Chicago are subject to the Lake Effect: easterly to the lake in morning and westerly to the hinterland in the afternoon. 'Air can be funnelled into a jet or broken down and diffused' [Alberti, I.3].

Cabins

When we retire to rest, our bodies hardly move; we occupy as small a space as our species is able to. What size of room is right for our still and shared bodies? Is a bed a room within a room, much like the curtained four-poster bed used to be? See the cabins in the U-boat at Chicago's Museum of Science and Industry.

Curtains

Curtains fill the emptiness of the night window, and are spread across with a map of expectation. The morning after, they fold into the window's edge, presenting a semiliterate curvaceous blur of the night's openness, and make a perfect home for children to secret themselves.

Defeat in War and Peace

Saint-Exupéry tells how an army, close to defeat, becomes obsessed with the nurturing of simple tasks, such as the changing of a wheel, or the polishing of a gun stock. Contemporary suburbanites, at the brink of their follies, do the same; a whole afternoon is spent trolling around the malls, in search of the perfect T-shirt, and when found, the search continues to locate the same shirt, but at a lower price. This trivial human activity may well be our saviour, the hunt has become more valuable than the quarry and it indicates a weaning away from materialistic culture. If revolution is to happen in the first world, it will be characterised by consuman beings suddenly being no longer interested in shopping, and there will little anybody could do about it. (Imagine being forced to shop at gun point, in order to make the system work!)

Electrical Cords

Plugging extension cords into themselves is odd: apparently it is not good for an electric cord to be subjected to this; perhaps the residual electricity accelerates around the loop formed by the incestuous plugging.

Faults

'Faults are due either to intellect and sense, such as judgement and selection, or to the hand, such as committed to the craftsman. Errors and faults of intellect and judgement . . . are less easy to rectify than the rest' [Alberti, IX.8]. A fault is a capital moment: it makes apparent the need for change. A fault is easy to see and, even if it is an act of carelessness, it is always potent.

Flag Pole

A place to put things for public visibility: a flag pole is a vertical clothes line.

Garden

Tending plants (and animals) provides a direct link with the humility and force of the natural world. It is a form of measure that sets in context the political discombobulations of daily life. Bee keeping permits the eating of the hinterland by way of pollen from flowers set in the most abrasive landscapes in the city. (The poppy was the first flower to bloom on the nature neutered battlefield of the Somme). See Animals.

Graffiti

Nearly every day there is new graffiti on the walls and billboards of the local subway stop. Dutifully, the City Transit Authority paints it out in the morning, preparing the fresh white surfaces to be resprayed the next night. The diurnal and nocturnal cat and mouse game is reminiscent of the ways of warfare conducted in Vietnam. Now would it not be interesting to play a different game with the graffiti artists? Everyday the CTA could make a photograph of the former night's activity on a particular billboard and then glue the photograph onto the billboard. Would the graffiti writer graffiti the graffiti? Is it enough for the CTA to laminate the work/cry of the graffiti maker between the layers of CTA paint? The result is that our subways are decorated with Ply-paint, a layer of CTA paint and then a layer of graffiti – *ad infinitum*.

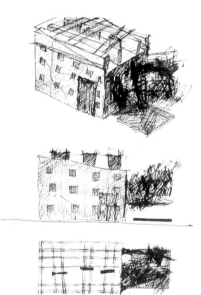

The Back will Blow Out onto slab+over

OPPOSITE FROM ABOVE: Kleptoman cell, north facade, 1989; Loaf House, view from north-east; FROM ABOVE: Fruit House, 1978; Pavement geometry #8, Laurentian Library, 1530-50s, possibly Michelangelo. Reconstruction, Minju Lee, J Kappraff, B Nicholson, B Summers 1986-96; Loaf House vacates itself, 1995

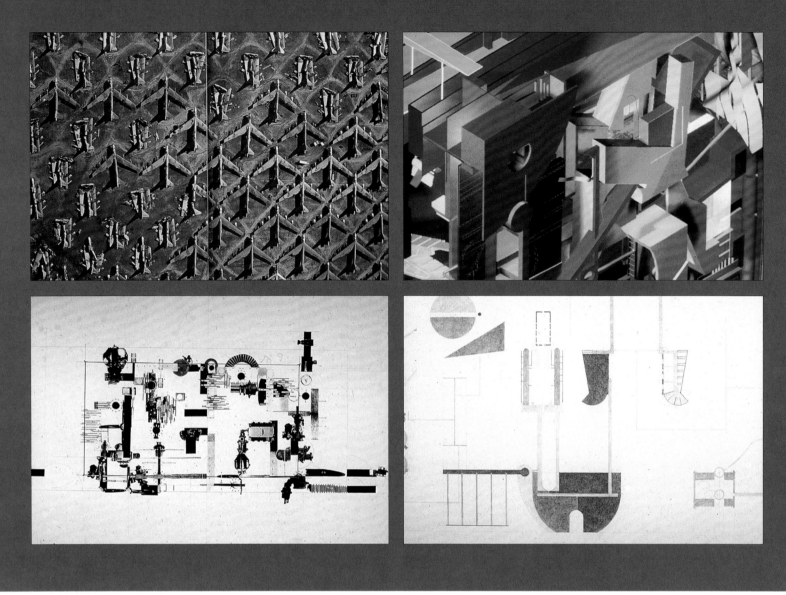

FROM ABOVE, L to R: B-52s at David Monthan AFB, Arizona; Loaf House – north wall, 1996; collage plan, 1991; Loaf House – non-specific section, 1991

Interiority

A burden of living in America, having lived in Second and Third World countries, is being condemned to use the last 5 per cent of bars of soap, tubes of toothpaste and bottles of shampoo, that regular citizens think of as finished. Packaging has a way of extending materialism, by offering up its hidden interior surface areas – to which much sticks. During the eking out of stubborn goods, the packaging can sometimes be discovered to be more useful than the packaged goods. This might induce a developed shopper to throw away the contents and get at what is useful.

Kitchen

Grind, cut, squeeze, liquefy, heat, cool, store, display.

Lost Voices

This morning I woke up, not knowing if I still had lost my voice. I did not know if I had a voice until I had spoken. What words do you utter to test if you have a voice, first thing in the morning? Surely not 'Testing, Testing, Testing'?

Magnets

Large magnets set behind sheet rock enable metal objects to adhere to walls without hooks. Set a grid of 12 magnets into a wall.

Messages

On the outside of a Hallmark Christmas card are the words 'Printed on Recycled Paper, including minimum of 10% post consumer and 40% pre consumer fibre'. On the inside of the same card are the words, 'May we always remember that Christ is the reason for Christmas'.

Model Aircraft

Building model aircraft gives one access, through three dimensionality, to the substance of the subject. The task becomes a cenotaph to three-dimensional consideration. By allowing the hands to glue for hours, there is the chance to think about the same for hours too. Craft is a word used by makers to hide the fact that they have the opportunity for hands-on thinking.

Money

Some spend their lives as if money had changed hands.

Nomads

Whose address is worth writing down in ink in America?

Notebooks

Many pages of the notebook are done against the will, a reluctant few hours each day, but it accumulates up to something. The notebook drains the head of stubborn little things that, if not reported, change themselves into leather beaded nuts the size of grains of sand and imbed themselves under the surface of consciousness.

Pit

The house stands in a pit (basement): the entire basement is a pit – a saw pit.

Possessions

Possessed by possessions.

Quilts

The Amish tuck themselves up at night beneath a quilt pieced together with shards of cloth from their own backs. The coloured fragments assemble into an eight pointed star, out-stretched across the counterpane, stitched

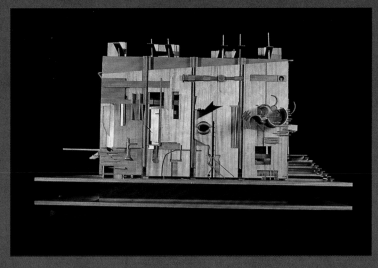
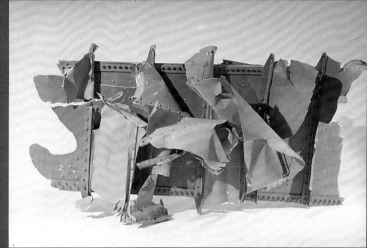
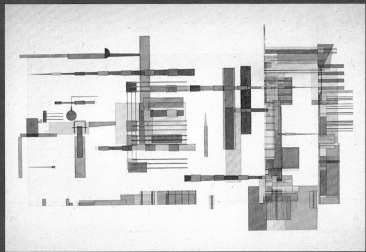
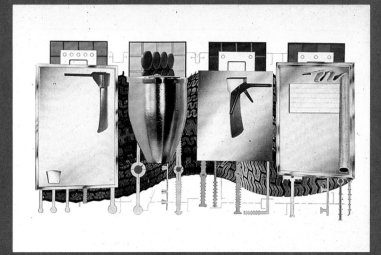

FROM ABOVE, L to R: Loaf House, south facade, 1994; B52, fragment of stabiliser, 1995; X-ray plan, 1992; Appliance House, collage, 1987

from edge to edge to form the Sign of Resurrection. As they sleep beneath the spread octagon, they restore the death of Christ and, upon waking, the quilt is folded and readied for another cycle of day and night.

Remodelling the House
Some homes are an endless site of construction. A family adjusts to the piles of intentions that block passages, and when the lumber evaporates in a frenzy of construction, it goes with a huge sigh of relief. The project of adjustment never finishes: it gets a temporary stay here and there, but then curiosity demands another alignment to life. The most stultifying houses are those that are finished – as if conditions had been found that permitted a state of perpetual satisfaction – but how we crave to be stultified.

Revolving Doors
A man and a woman come to a revolving door from opposite directions, he going into the subway and she going out to City Hall. Through the greenish wind-milled surfaces of glass, they make eye contact: they ask each other who will be the first to push the rail, to make time pass.

Sundial
A sundial can be set into a bedroom, guarding time on sunny days when there is nobody present, casting a temporal shadow that exists in a quiet vacuum.

Tape Decks and Record Players
Remember that recorded music comes from an electrical box and is not the same as music made from a hand-held instrument.

The Big Country
If you wade across the Rio Grande to Mexico, it is possible to hurl all the rocks you wish at America – and hit it every time.

Tub and Tubroom
One of the two worthwhile legacies of the Yuppie movement (the other being the awareness of good food). A tub that is in the sun: bathing should never be done in the dark during daylight hours. Tubs need access to

outside air and a terrace: sunshine for the naked body to bathe in, and remember that people using hot saunas are always rolling in the snow! The combination of steaming hot water, flame light from candles and cold champagne is inimical.

Vault
A strong safe in which to keep valuable things like gold, money, papers, heirlooms etc. The vault is to be cast into the concrete foundations. The door leading to the vault is smaller than the vault itself, preventing the vault from being wholly stolen away. Pyramids.

Wrecking Ball
A house could be provided with its own means of end. A wrecking ball could be deliberately hung from the upper reaches of the building fabric, held back from its slow swing during its life, but always cocked to render the place into a blaze of poetic subsummation. The Swiss have grasped this concept for they build explosives into their mountain-pass bridges.

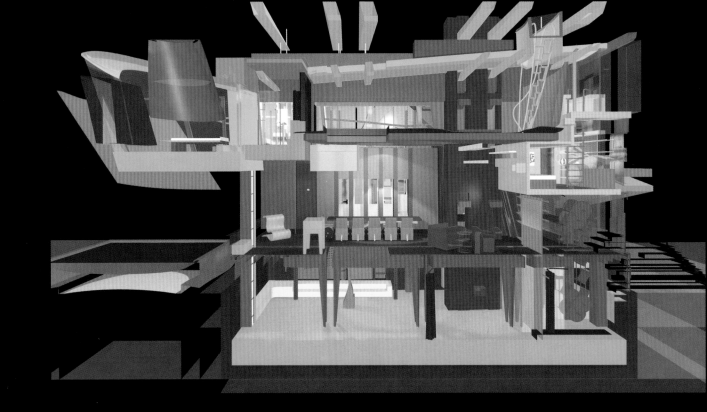

FROM ABOVE: Section; view from north east

BEN NICHOLSON
LOAF HOUSE

The Loaf House was originally planned for a site at 31st and Prairie Avenue in Chicago, where there had once been a turreted Victorian mini-mansion. Deflected by a technological squall, the house retrenched itself into the maybe world of cyberspace. Today, it is entirely digital and beneath its surface is a hypertext that leads into the quandaries and preoccupations of contemporary American domestic life.

Viewed within cyberspace, the Loaf House appears to be a brightly glowing, vapid nonentity. As one gets closer, it gathers focus to resemble a squared-off peg, hammered deep into the ground. Its ethereal appearance soon materialises into an accretion of gravity-bound things – some hanging, others thrusting upwards, and all inextricably linked.

Four looming, 10.5-metre towers, dedicated respectively to liquid, power-source, dirt and micro-airwave, push up through the innards of the building, extending citrus-yellow beams. These hover in the air, dangling rods from their tips, which support the facades like marionettes.

The facades
The end facades of the house 'fill-in' this dangling structure, giving the building the appearance of a tightly plugged tunnel. It is a tense structure, the perfect antidote to the weekly juggle of Saturday-morning soccer and after-school piano lessons for the kids. The east facade is a diaphragm of glassy shards, like a curtain of splinters. At the west end, a full protuberance pokes out of the glassy wall to form a well-rounded nose. And whenever a 'nose' makes itself felt, the spectre of a head is always suggested.

Viewing the south facade, overlooking the street, the observer's eyes must work fast, nipping about from place to place, roaming over the full panorama of the wall, finding clues about the experience of a day spent in the Loaf House.

In times gone by, such a facade might have sported an ornamental splendour of carved-stone *putti*, perched upon the leading edge of the wall. But this one opens itself to mechanical intervention: it is a spectrum of overt and latent forces, linked to the raw elements and to the activity of people within the house. It is criss-crossed with signs of movement, each caused by an activity known only to those inside.

Throughout the year, a substantial concrete cylinder moves sporadically up and down the wall. Sometimes it is wound tight against the supporting pulley, set high in the wall, at others it dangles low in its basket near the ground. Mostly, it slides back and forth against the markings, taking the temperature of some unknown virus inside the house. No one outside is privy to the logic of this public oscillation.

Above the house, a dull, flapping noise emanates from a crimson flag, billowing out from the edge of the roof. The flag flies only on certain days, no doubt when something worth celebrating is happening inside the house. Just below it are the blades of a windmill. When the actions of a windmill and a flag are seen side by side, the chore of one becomes the liberation of the other. The windmill appears to express curiosity as to why the flag is let loose to crack in the wind, doing nothing but announcing its freedom. The flag, in turn, seems surprised to see the hardened cycle of repetition reiterated over and again by the windmill. The sails of the windmill are mounted on a stumpy axle protruding from the facade. Its curvaceous blades flop round and round in the lake wind, turning an arbor connected to something deep within the house.

The entrance way
The front door and the postcard-sized kid's room are set into the east facade's sea of glass shards. The kid's room is at the nexus of the house, surveying the majority of the activities going on inside and out. A boxy hidey-hole sticks out in front of the glass facade, scaled to that famous space 'beneath the stairs' that shuts darkness in and grown-ups out. The front door is reached by a collection of steps that leads to a pivoted door, seemingly approaching and receding simultaneously. Its dense weight makes it look as if it is stranded in the glass facade. It is not so much an entrance to the house, as a weighted impediment to match the gravity of the place. Once through the door, the visitor is led into a tiny vestibule, lorded over by a caged balcony that is part of the kid's room.

Conglomeroom
Beyond the vestibule is a tall, compressed space called the Conglomeroom, a grand admixture of kitchen, dining room, living room and study. It is punctuated by the four towers that sustain the house and is lit by a trickling of lights, to which the eyes need time to adjust. One's fingers skirt over every surface, stopping to extract the secrets of the house by tapping into the hypertext lurking beneath its patina.

The kitchen is wrapped in a veneer of hyperlinked websites, probing the American preoccupation with food, drink and sanitation. Not only does a monitor above the stove offer up thousands of recipes from around the world, but virtual bacteria can be inspected when a fly lands on the plates drying above the sink. Nearby, the dining table is set for ten people culled from the nation's suburbs, selected for their normality. Behind the dining table is a shelved library, jammed with stacks of websites revealing metasystems, generic information, and the classical categories of knowledge established by Aristotle.

Basement
The basement is a collection of subterranean adventures that are best not spoken about too much, but are always loved and remembered. Down here is the pool-table, sauna box, and a repository for books – attached by a book wheel to the study above.

Angst Collector

The Angst Collector is a thin, undulating copper plate that forms the upper floor of the Loaf House, the sound-board for the cathartic life within the house, where the Loafers put up their feet and relax. It is drenched in history: its metal is taken from the copper wiring pulled from a B-52 bomber, which formerly conducted the millions of messages that kept the craft afloat. The metal is beaten flat by the collective memory of a whole city, replacing the brittle angst of citizens with the ring of a million hammer blows, a metallic choir for militaristic endeavour.

Vertical garden

The upper floor is accessed either via a staircase set into the south

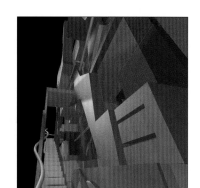

choreographed by the constant adjustments of the manipulatory webmasters around the world.

When the bedroom is vacant, a sundial pin, set into the conical funnel above the bed, guards time on sunny days, casting a temporal shadow that exists in a quiet vacuum.

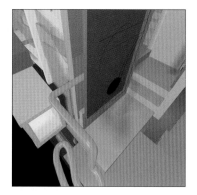

wall, or by way of a compound stairway embedded in the north wall. This wall is a vertical upended garden, a 2-metre-thick band of materiality, threaded with every sort of step and fireman's pole to give a sense of the true grace and vertigo experienced when going up and down.

An orange handrail winds its way between the structure, lancing the house as it passes the children's room and the Angst Collector and peeking into the fleshy sweetness of the bathroom. It then goes on through a portal to the outside, to an upper balcony that overlooks the bedroom.

Bedroom

The bedroom, which shares a peek-a-boo glass wall with the shower-stall next door in the bathroom, is a place that enhances the realm of horizontality. Above the queen-sized bed (a 4:3 ratio celebrated in antiquity) hovers a conic funnel leading to the sky. In here bodies can knot themselves in a frenzy or lay out flat to snag dreams, restore health and defragment their brains in readiness for the next day's onslaught. The mouse can scurry about the bedroom, peering into cupboards that are pregnant with the stuff of adornment: mysteries

The views beyond

The views from the Loaf House windows lead out to all manner of contextual websites. Worldwide weather can be tapped; cameras on sites across the world can be peered through, and the terra firma of Indian Country beneath the house can be prodded for content. Up above the house is an extensive roof terrace. Chicago takes special pleasure in its summer evenings, and there is no better place to gaze across the even landscape than from the flat rooftops of its housing stock. The roof is designed for spectator sport, and has all manner of appendages to view the streetscape below and the incoming clouds above. Running the entire length of the house are five skinny skylights that reveal slices of the life inside the house. Residents can climb up onto a tractor seat, set onto the top of the western tower, and gaze across the prairie and the scorched-earth city

lots. Peering out from this perch provides the opportunity to put things in perspective. The view below offers a seamless grid of houses, each bursting with life and seemingly placed there to provide one with the outlook beyond one's own domain. Above, passing aircraft smear contrails across the sky, triggering our desire to be somewhere new and leaving us with just a thread of smoke to remind us where we stand.

The CD-Rom of the Loaf House is available to the savvy digital traveller and the voyeurist couch potato alike; it even provides a degree of handicap access for the digitally challenged. It is a cheap way for a thousand owners to roam about in an alternative realm, waving to their neighbours as they groan under the weight of the million-dollar mortgages that encapsulate the stuff of reality.

OPPOSITE AND ABOVE:
Walk-through vertical
garden of north wall;
RIGHT, FROM ABOVE:
South facade; kid's
room; CD-Rom pages

GIFU – REVERSIBLE DESTINY
CRITICAL RESEMBLANCE HOUSE AND ELLIPTICAL FIELD

The critical, ironic stance requires the taking of things to heart as much as does any other stance; it requires perhaps a double taking of things to heart. God (ungendered)

So that life might be ample, take things to heart as much as possible, but remember that taking things too much to heart will destroy you. God (androgynous)

The fate of each 'I' is sealed by that which surrounds it. In the sentence 'I am a person', it is not only the word 'I', but all four words or concepts of the sentence taken together that give 'I' its meaning. In addition to this, the 'I' receives support from all sentences and concepts within which the speaker/reader has found 'I' to be active or has believed it to be embedded. Embedding (words infiltrating each other), the division of linguistic labour (language not as the possession of a single speaker but as a co-operative activity; terms cannot be defined in isolation, each word holds a part of the meaning) and holism (all sentences have a say in the resultant meaning) as working principles of language bolster the stand-up sliver or slip of an 'I'.

Despite massive shoring up, the 'I' can readily be undermined, as Arthur Rimbaud's amazing equation demonstrates in a flash: '*Je suis un autre.*'

'I have met the other and that other is myself of yesterday as well as the "me of today".'

'Do you wish to express an estrangement from the smell of your own intimate me?'

'Nothing is closer to my (that is the other's) heart!'

'Who or what is this other to which or to whom you impute your very self?'

'Any other will do.'

* * *

'What does the other want?'

'The other wants to persist as me!'

'Which me!'

'The other more expandable, less caved in me!'

The purpose of architecture is to sculpt the other, although most architects are unaware of this. Architecture exists to sculpt the other into a long and longer life. Architecture should provide circumstances that allow the other to sculpt the length of its own existence as an 'I'. Let architecture reek of the other.

What needs to be done to effect this?

Configure the landing sites in their mechanicalness to refurbish sensibility.

In the case of the first site of reversible destiny the other finds itself in central Japan. Here is the Japan of your otherness.
A 122m Japan outlined by cement and filled with sprawling herb gardens straddles the entire elliptical bowl. Nearby, at right angles to it, lies a 45m cement Japan painted silver. A 1.8m topographical map of Japan sits on a mound on the outer face of the steep slope at the bowl's edge. Underground within the bowl, far tinier Japans surface as nothing but light and air. Everywhere one looks Japan lies ready to be found. Japan, the island-chain nation, loses its singularity becoming instead only one of several similarly configured sets of landing sites, each of which readily accepts, even begs for, the designation Japan. The most 'real' of all the configurations of landing sites that add up to a 'Japan', the actual Japan, the land, the island-chain and the nation, upon and within which the whole slew of variously scaled other Japans sit, paradoxically enough turns out to be the one that is, at least in its contours, the most invisible of all!

One Japan subverts, or supplants, another and the co-ordinating of landing sites becomes discordant. Japan in profusion, a superabundance of references, threatens to erase position through over-determination.

Within these surroundings, the question 'Where are you?' readily translates into 'What goes into (or participates in) your determining of where you are?' A divided loyalty to position becomes thinkable, or at least noticeable, and the architecture motivates a complex response to a whole set of what were once, but no longer are, difficult-to-comprehend questions. As for what goes into the determining of where one is, the universal reply would more or less add up to: 'The group of everything that I hold in place is determinative of where I judge myself to be. For example, I form Japan out of all that I hold in place as Japan. Japan is/are a group.' Asked 'How is Japan sited' or 'How have you sited it?' or, more in keeping with the present terminology, 'Where have you landed' or 'Where are you landing?' the reply of virtually every visitor to the first site of reversible destiny would convey chiefly this: 'In part here, in part there, in part everywhere within my perceptual ken.'

Mounds like those situated within the elliptical bowl are placed both on the surrounding slopes at one end and atop the high wall at the other. These raised mounds mediate the distance. Visitors will associate them both with the rounded caps of Yoro mountain and the mounds sitting within the bowl. Artificially raised above the earth and positioned neither here nor there, even though they are certainly where they are, these mounds, in any event, belong to Japan and represent yet another degree of it. And the sky too at this juncture? – yet another degree of Japan?

Under investigation here is everything, every entity, event and site that goes into the determination of where one is. Holding open one's positioning of oneself, keeping it in abeyance, allows for regrouping. As demonstrated above, not only is/am 'I' an other, 'I' am/is/are also a group, with now this surfacing, now that surfacing as me, as my other.

Each neighbourhood is designed to redirect the co-ordinating of landing sites in a distinctive way, so as to be a unique approach to a holding open and re-distributing of the world as formed and forming. Streets within the section known as **Elsewhere** and **Not** are named contrary to that which is the case for those who traverse them. Named in contradistinction to where they are in relation to those setting foot on them and so never able to be successfully landed upon as what or where they purport to be, they propel whoever visits them constantly ever onward, always elsewhere. In a few cases, instead of presenting visitors with information not jibing with the facts, street names in this section serve up blatant non-truths. In the section known as the **Body Enclave**, street names appeal more directly to the body than to the person, but it is the other way around in the **Person Region**. Street names in the **Person as World Suffusion Zone** alert a visitor to how determinative – of the world in which she finds herself – is that which constitutes her as a person; the sum of each and every one of her actions. Street names within the **Neutralized and Neutralizing Delta** encourage a neutralizing of subjectivity. The above-mentioned areas and the following ones as well – **Landing Site Processing Zone, All Here and There Village,**

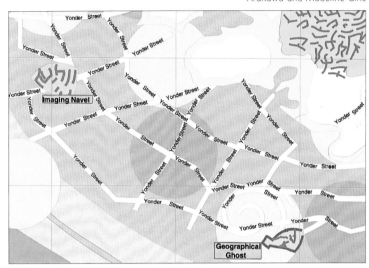

Voice Plaza, Scale Adjustment Zone and Reversible Destiny Re-doubled Effort Zone – help visitors elude the defeatism of a thus-far universal belief in the inevitability of death and guide them toward working out a viable reversible destiny.

Every one of our streets might have been named 'This Street' to a different effect. Where are you now? I am on 'This Street', but only a moment before I moved along a completely different 'This Street'; 'This' as a name affixed to a street derails the language-game of proper names. There might be a 'This or That Street' that could be taken either way depending on where one was situated, but failing that, if the rules of naming are to be followed, no 'This Street' can be correctly pointed out as a 'That Street' despite the urgent demand that grammar would seem to put on one to do so. What might be permissible would be to allude to a 'that "This Street"', as in, 'I was skipping along on that "This Street" prior to having arrived on "This Street".'

A thoroughgoing naming of streets with 'This' and only 'This' as a chosen name might lead to descriptive sequences such as the following: 'Here I am on 'This Street'. I'll turn off it at this point and go down 'This Street'. 'This Street', my third 'This Street' in this sequence, is far more demanding of my attention than the first two were.'

A name this general, applied ubiquitously, foregrounds the shape, angle and the position of what is being named (the paths). Naming in this way also highlights the body as it is experiencing the path, the forms the body assumes in response to what 'This Street' puts before it. Each 'This Street' has its own explanation.

Alternatively, all our streets marked 'This Street' might be taken as an all in one 'This Street' that, traversing the whole of the site, at times breaks off, but remains re-connectable, re-connecting, unitary. In this interpretation as well, the special features of each turn in the path would come to the fore, doing most of the 'talking' thanks to the self-effacing nature of the name.

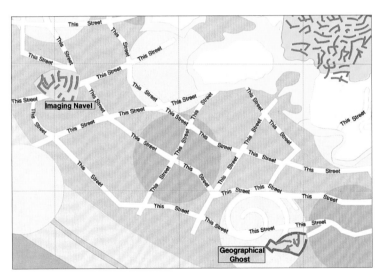

The above case of street naming exemplifies a refusal to use words to make distinctions even as the naming process continues. In the following example, along with a refusal to make distinctions, comes a stated contradiction scheduled to detonate each time the reader/walker sets foot on the street. The naming process permits, in some sense, a walker to tread where prior to such naming she never could; it enables her to stroll through the heretofore impossible region of the 'here yonder'.

But the avowed wish is to arrive at a reversing of destiny. How then to punch holes – black holes, writhing holes, source holes, Blake holes, replete holes – into mortality? Sieve mortality and stop it. Begin by punching holes in the referring process.

'Pardon me, what is it you are referring to?'

'I am not referring to how to live forever, only to come to a rude and abrupt end!'

* * *

Doom: the 'natural' conclusion of a 'real' life is said to be death. All death is mortal.

To be human is be mortal; to be human is to err. Death is a reference that flaps in the breeze. Next subject.

'Excuse me, I don't quite know where I am. Could you tell me what street I'm on?'

'Of course. You're on "Afar Street".'

'Really? Well, where does that get me? Or, what a relief not to have to be where I am. Or, I bite the distance.'

'And did you say you would wait for me on "Only Street"?'

'Granted it is not the only street in the vicinity and yet it is the only one on which I expect to meet you, never mind that it is only a street.'

Only: a jot of, a jutting out of, the stuff of, the only universe, holding its own as a landing site.

'All that you take to heart will be taken from you!'

The only streets worth standing on are those set up to guide the body to construct a world in different terms from this. The body in person is a co-ordinator of, a juggler of, landing sites. Moving along humble, little 'Only Street', the body will learn many of the intricacies involved in the co-ordinating of landing sites. Until one day, when strolling along another street, one that is also only what it is, one perhaps named, yes, for example, 'Anti-Cemetery Lane', the body as a person will in some definitive way be found to have at last escaped the wrath of God, that is 'God'. The universe could not ask for more, at least not prior to there having been such an escape.

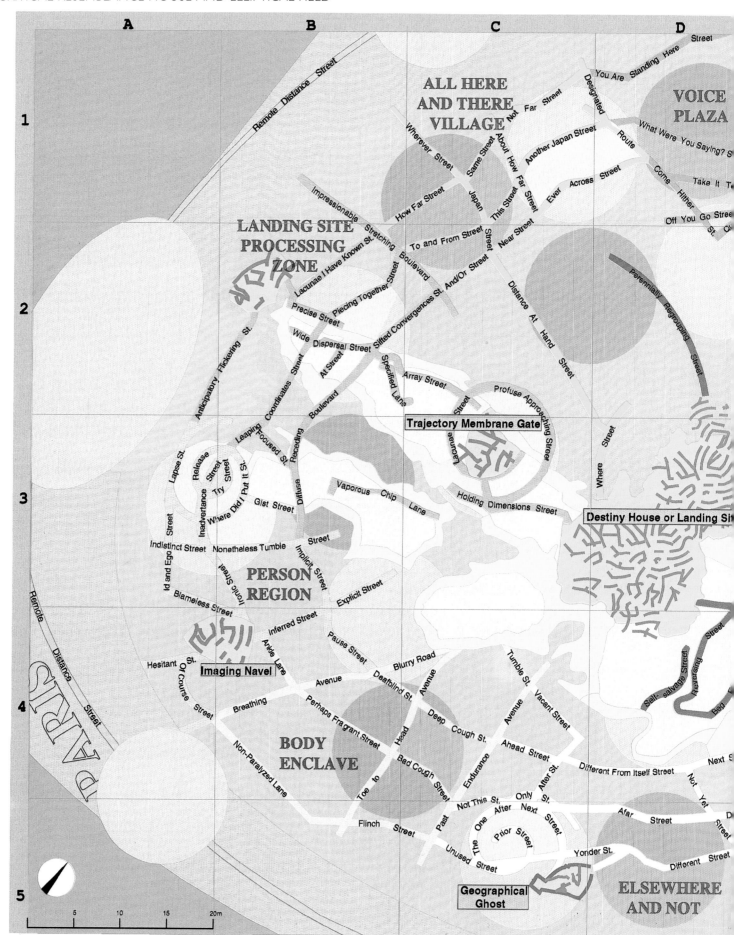

THE GAME BOTH BEGINS AND IS OVER, OR TRANSMUTES INTO A NON-GAME, ONCE THE RE◆

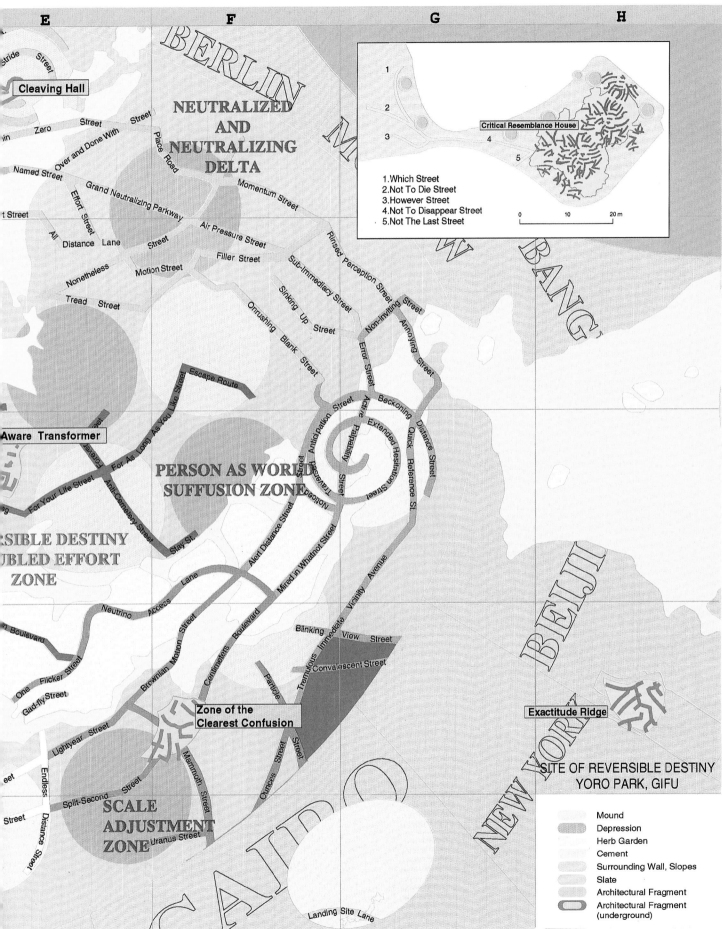

Critical Resemblance House

1. Which Street
2. Not To Die Street
3. However Street
4. Not To Disappear Street
5. Not The Last Street

0   10   20 m

Cleaving Hall

BERLIN

NEUTRALIZED
AND
NEUTRALIZING
DELTA

Stride Street
Zero Street   Street
Over and Done With
Named Street
Grand Neutralizing Parkway
Effort Street
All Distance Lane   Street
Nonetheless   Motion Street
Tread   Street
Place Road
Momentum Street
Air Pressure Street
Filler Street
Sub-Immediacy Street
Sinking Up Street
Onrushing Blank Street
Rinsed Perception Street
Non-inviting Street
Annoying Street
Error Street

Aware Transformer

PERSON AS WORLD
SUFFUSION ZONE

Escape Route
Tolerance
For As Long As You Like Street
Anti-Intensity Street
For Your Life Street
Stay St.
Anticipation Street
Active Palpability Street
Extended Hesitation Street
Beckoning
Quick Reference St.
Distance Street
Noticed
Traversed

RSIBLE DESTINY
UBLED EFFORT
ZONE

Neutrino Access
Boulevard
One Flicker Street
Gad-fly Street
Alert Distance Street
Lane
Mired in Whatnot Street
Brownian Motion Street
Centimeters Boulevard
Vicinity Avenue
Blinking Immediate View Street
Tremulous Immediate
Convalescent Street

Lightyear Street
Endless
Street
Distance Street
Split-Second Street
Mammoth Street
Particle
Street
Ounces Street
Uranus Street

Zone of the
Clearest Confusion

SCALE
ADJUSTMENT
ZONE

Exactitude Ridge

BANG
BELIII
NEW YORK
CAIIRO

SITE OF REVERSIBLE DESTINY
YORO PARK, GIFU

Landing Site Lane

Mound
Depression
Herb Garden
Cement
Surrounding Wall, Slopes
Slate
Architectural Fragment
Architectural Fragment
(underground)

ONAL APPROACHES TO (THE SECURING OF A) REVERSIBLE DESTINY HAVE BEEN DETERMINED

GIFU – CRITICAL RESEMBLANCE HOUSE AND ELLIPTICAL FIELD

TYPES OF FUNCTION:

FOR HUMAN (SUPER-)COMFORT
Le Corbusier . Villa Savoye . 1931

FOR THE SAKE OF UNIVERSAL SPACE-TIME
Mies van der Rohe . Farnsworth House . 1951

FOR THE SAKE OF THE BODY
FOR DETERMINING THE SITE OF A PERSON
Arakawa + Madeline Gins . Critical Resemblance House . 1995

Instructions for use (to be continued)

The Elliptical Field

• Instead of being fearful of losing your balance, look forward to it (as a desirable reordering of the landing sites, formerly known as the senses).

• When moving through the **Elliptical Field** remember as many views of the **Critical Resemblance House** as possible, and vice versa.

• Try to draw the sky down into the bowl of the field.

• Use each of the five Japans to locate, or compose, where you are.

• Always question where you are in relation to the visible and invisible chains of islands known as Japan.

To secure a sense of yourself as this site (the entire elliptical field):

• Vary the rate at which you move through it.

• Associate each of the extreme forms your body is forced to assume in traversing it with both a nearby and a distant form.

• If accidentally thrown completely off balance, try to note the number, and also the type and placement, of the landing sites essential to reconstituting a world.

• Frequently swing round to look behind you.

• Minimize the number of focal areas (perceptual landing sites) at any given moment.

• If an area or a landing site catches your eye and attracts your interest to the same degree as the area through which you are actually moving, take it up on the spot, pursuing it as best you can as a parallel zone of activity.

• Make use of the **Exactitude Ridge** to register each measured sequence of events that makes up the distance.

• Within the **Zone of the Clearest Confusion** always try to be more body and less person.

• To make a decision or to become more subtle or daring, or both, in regard to a previous decision, use the **Mono no Aware Transformer**.

• Inside the **Geographical Ghost** renege on all geographically related pledges of allegiance.

• Wander through the ruin known as the **Destiny House** or the **Landing Site Depot** as though you were an extraterrestrial.

• Move in slow measured steps through the **Cleaving Hall** and, with each arm at a distinctly different height, hold both arms out in front of you as sleepwalkers purportedly do.

• Close your eyes when moving through and around the **Trajectory Membrane Gate**.

• In and about the **Kinesthetic Pass**, repeat every action two or three times, once in slow motion.

• Walk backwards in and near the **Imaging Navel**.

The Critical Resemblance House

• Enter the house several times, each time through a different entrance.

• If thrown off balance when entering the house, call out your name or, if you prefer, someone else's.

• Strive to find a marked resemblance between yourself and the house. If by chance you fail to do so, proceed as if the house were your identical twin.

• Move through the house as though you were presently living in it, or as though you were its next resident.

• Should an unexpected event occur, freeze in place for as long as you see fit. Then adopt a more suitable (or more thought out) position for an additional 20 seconds or so.

    Perceptual Landing Site: any discerning of any event whatsoever.
    Imaging Landing Site: any filling in of the gaps between/among perceptual landing sites.
    Architectural Landing Site: any registering of dimension/position.

• Try to incorporate two or more horizons into every view.

• Use each set of furniture as a concrete reference for the other sets.

• Search out identical moments in segments of the house that are remote from one another. Attempt this initially with strikingly similar configurations, and eventually with widely divergent ones.

Key words : judgement . no-place . place . without judgement

ABOVE:Ad9GrBel5[7]. 0Sa314; BELOW: Ad9RdSpRo5[7].0Sa615

MODAL SPACE: THE VIRTUAL ANATOMY OF HYPERSTRUCTURES
Karl S Chu

(The Philosopher must be) like a child begging for 'both,' he must declare that reality or the sum of things is both at once – all that is unchangeable and all that is in change. Plato, *The Sophist.*

Ever since Anaximander speculated on the substance of the cosmos by the non-limited, *apeiron,* our perception of reality is determined, to a great extent, by the conceptual models we have of it. This was true in the past and is still true for us now. Reality is a concept that is limited by the nature of our conceptual models. Anaximander believed in a circular conception of time and the eternal recurrence of the same. The Judaeo-Christian legacy of linear time, however, has prevailed at least for the history of mankind so far. Perhaps, from a science fictional standpoint, the era of civilisations may be measured, someday, by the forms of global temporalisations that are every bit as spatial as they are eventual. Universal history, wrote Borges in his essay on the 'Fearful sphere of Pascal' may be the history of a handful of metaphors. It is a history of displacement and condensation that maps out a manifold trajectory of involution and evolution, of endophysics and exophysics, and, most significantly, of the collapse of the closed world towards the infinite universe. The projection of universal narratives, each with a claim to being absolute, is, no doubt, over. The 20th century will probably be known, among other things, as the century that suspended the quest for metaphysics as part of the fulfilment of the programme of the Enlightenment.

With only a few years left towards the end of the second millennium of the Christian era, there is a glimmer of realisation that metaphysics is a necessity if we are to make any sense of the ubiquitous state of affairs to which we are thrown into. To say that metaphysics is nonsense, as we now realise, is either ludicrous, since there is no statement devoid of presuppositions that are fully accounted for, or, itself a metaphysical

statement. One of the sources of traditional metaphysics, claimed the logical positivists, is in the misuse of language. Ironically, the attempt to demystify its use, to establish a clear and distinct specification of its structure and meaning, has invariably led to meta-linguistics and genealogies that are, more often than not, deeply tainted with speculative logic that characterises some of the best metaphysicians of the past. As Levinas stated, when commenting on Derrida: attempting to deconstruct metaphysics is more metaphysical than metaphysics itself.

The meaning of the prefix meta- points to a conjunction of two terms, about and beyond. Every theory of information carries with it this twin desideratum. Semantic holism states that the meaning of 'Q' word cannot be reduced solely to its atomic definition, but must be accessed as a function within the field of state space semantics. By extension, it is inferred that there is no discourse that is not already implicated within the conceptual space of some meta-discourse even if the nature of that association is yet to be explored or established. Gregory Chaltin, the metamathematician from IBM, remarked, during the 'On Limits' conference, that the theory of incompleteness and undecidability, as discovered by Godel, developed by Turing and further extended into an effective theory of algorithmic complexity by him, is only the tip of an iceberg of an underlying mathematical reality.

The number of mathematical objects is much larger than the number of atoms in the universe, and the universe of mathematics is much more extensive than the physical universe which physics is concerned with. Steven Smale, a chaos mathematician from Berkeley, during the *'Chaos'* conference, facetiously pointed out that the physical universe is not large enough to hold all the fractals there are in fractal geometry. The tacit awareness of this mathematical state of affairs has led some mathematicians to assert the existence of an archaic mathematical

reality that is, essentially, invisible but real. This is a principle of existential generalisation, the resolution of which, in the foundations of mathematics, is far from over.

'When God calculates and exercises his thought, the world is created' says a marginal annotation to the *Dialogue on the Connection Between Things and Words* of 1677 by Leibniz, one of the first rationalist philosophers to work out the properties of the binary number system, which of course has turned out to be fundamental for computer science. Unaware of the limits of computability at the time, but fully aware of the combinatorial exhaustion of knowledge in calculating the size of a book that would contain all true, false and meaningless propositions, Leibniz proposed a universal calculus in *De Arte Combinatoria* that could compute, or, rather, calculate every set of relationships based on a system of combinations by means of *characteristica universalis.* With regard to the architectonics of geometrical harmony, Leibniz, however, relies on the principle of continuity, a *principe de l'ordre general,* which he developed as a calculus of indiscernibles. It requires that the lawfulness of phenomena be conceived as expressing a systematic integration of individual real elements beyond the level of empirical sequences. He transforms the method of calculus *de maximis et minimis* into a method *de formis optimis* applicable to the real world, a form of geometrical teleology that optimises and reveals the internal laws as sufficient reasons that regulate the harmony throughout nature.

Cassirer pointed out that nothing characterises more the shift from the substance of things to the substance of relations as in the calculus of indiscernibles proposed by Leibniz. Whilst, as John Wheeler, an American scientist, remarked, nothing so much distinguishes physics as conceived today from mathematics as the difference between the continuum based formulations of the one and the discrete character of the other. In the article entitled 'It from Bit', Wheeler also suggests that it from bit symbolises the idea that the physical world has an immaterial source and explanation that is information-theoretic in origin. Nothing characterises more the implementation of discrete logic than in the determinate state transitions produced by the emergent computations of Cellular Automata (CA). Steven Wolfram, a computational physicist, introduced a dynamical classification of CA behaviour, and, speculated that one of his four classes supports universal computation. Instead of relying on differential equations, a mathematics of continuity, to describe the behaviour of nature, Wolfram investigates into the dynamics of CA, discrete state transitions, that behave similarly to the dynamics of physical systems. The field of Artificial Life, triggered by emergent properties of CA behaviour, has produced concepts of phase transitions that are computations at the edge of chaos. The guiding hypothesis is that life emerges at this periphery in the second order phase transition, referred to as the liquid regime poised between the solid and the gaseous regimes.

Every paradigm has a set of governing metaphors that compress and express its meaning, and the Information Paradigm, as an emergent phenomenon, is no exception. The emerging consensus is that nature/reality is a function of some form of computation even though there is no evidence that nature computes algorithmically. The Universal Turing Machine (UTM), named after Alan Turing, its inventor, has become the *de facto* standard by which computability is measured. It is an abstract machine developed from the serial act of counting and is looked upon as an anthropomorphic model of computation that is perfectly suited for a number theorist. Every modern computer is a technological embodiment of the UTM. According to the Turing/Church thesis, everything that is computable, in principle, is UTM computable. This is an extraordinary thesis that,

if proven true, will have implications in every field of endeavour. There are logical as well as physical limits to computation as in the class of intractable problems known as NP completeness. The travelling salesman and the four-colour problems are in this category. However not all problems are so readily decidable and many are undecidable in relation to the halting problem.

A crucial development in the theory of computation is the complexity of a minimal string necessary to generate or solve a problem as formulated by Chaitin. Algorithmic information theory states that compression is a function of recursion and is limited by the amount of random information present within any system. One of the profound insights discovered by Chaitin is that the field of arithmetic is random; it is not compressible, and that there are mathematical truths that are true for no reason – a remark made during the 'On Limits' conference. No amount of human reasoning will ever solve some of these mathematical problems, and Leibniz's notion of the principle of sufficient reason has proven to be inadequate. As grim as this may seem, fundamental insight in physics and mathematics does not involve yes-no answers to algorithms, but rather a search for structures and the relationships between them. This has led to research into new forms of computational models, such as CA based dynamical systems. Some of the developments in emergent computations have shown that Byzantine complexity, as displayed by nature, contains archetypal features which surface in many disciplines in disguised forms – a reflection of the same phenomena in different mirrors. The configuration of these generic classes of self-organisations are, however, exponentially rare.

Even before the discovery of these emergent phenomena, Ed Fredkin, a computer scientist, had proposed the provocative idea that the universe may be a form of cellular automaton; a computational system that computes itself into

existence. If the laws themselves evolve and radically change over time, then, there has to be a meta-space of competing laws that somehow engender the various stages of evolutionary development. This metaphor of universal cellularity however is a falsification, offering an effective symbol that displaces the universal clockwork of mechanism and the Industrial Revolution.

These are issues not without implications or relationship to architecture, yet architecture, has always been, slow to express the prevailing paradigms of knowledge and organisation. If there is 'Q' forgetfulness, an unequivocal suspension of the epistemic fields and hierarchies outside of the typographical language of architecture, it most probably originates from ignorance of the meaning of the actual term itself. The coupling of the two Greek terms, *arche* and *techne*, which establishes the conditions for the possibility of a worldly constructivism is intrinsically metaphysical in orientation. Even in the most limiting of cases, as in naive realism, the definability and qualification of architecture can no longer simply be attributable to the empirical logic of buildability, but needs to be extended into the sphere of constructibility in modal space. The internal logic of modal constructivism would include the notion of complementarity, forms of computation, generative systems, self-organisations, ensemble theories, non-linear dynamics, morphogenetic potentials, statistical models of configuration space at different regimes of reality, combinatorials, artificial life, complexity, mereology, theory of limits and category and set theory at the very least.

It is not generally apparent that reality has a modal structure to it. Since much of the imperative of worldly affairs is driven by the obvious identification of the real with the actual, it is assumed that the counterfactual universe of modal space is nothing but a plausible speculation at best. The universe of modal space, which includes the domain of the possible and the actual, is much larger than the logic of implication derived from subjunctive conditionals such as 'if, then' situations in modal semantics. Modal logic, as practised by philosophers, is based on two concepts, necessity and possibility. Modal constructivism, as a theory of architecture, would have to be conceptualised, along with the criteria of necessity and possibility, within the emerging framework of the so-called Information Paradigm inclusive of morphogenetic principles of dependent co-origination. The possible, from the standpoint of modal constructivism, must be given a systematic logic of embodiment and can only be effectively delineated by viable theories of morphogenesis. It is now obvious that the dynamics of information has overtaken the dynamics of energy in the modelling of physical systems. Therefore, it has become evident that the notion of buildability based on material systems is only a subset of the logic of constructability within generative systems. In fact, it would not be unreasonable to suggest that the universe of mathematics is the counterpart of the universe of modal space. Without having to invoke, the status of transworld identity and individuation as explored by some modal logicians, a modal version of monadology where the logic of beings is not identical to the logic of bodies, the conceptual efficacy of modal constructivism can be developed and applied as an extended form of architectural praxis.

With the emergence of cyberspace, we are witnessing the advent of a second order phase transition in our global culture, unprecedented in its scope as well as in its transformative power, it will radically alter our perceptions of reality, and the terms of engagement will be unimaginably rich and treacherous. If we generalised the era of the first order phase transition as spanning from the time of primitive forms of economy and exchange to the time of telepresence, the second order phase transition appears with the emergence of virtual worlds – a

parallel universe instantiated by massive clusters of abstract machines in the interactive dominion of cyberspace. We are, without exaggeration, on the verge of a possible world that we cannot even begin to imagine except through the emerging paradigms of artificial world. Virtual entities are, no doubt, present and embedded within semiological systems of the first order regimes, however the radicality of the second order regimes lies in their capacity for the co-evolution of hyperstructures – higher forms of self-organisations, in the virtual sphere of artificial ecologies. The separation of the imaginary and the real, the factual and the counterfactual, the actual and the potential can no longer be clearly demarcated in this profusion of virtual worlds. The significance of this lies not only in the representational power of simulation but also, and to a greater extent, in the interactive arena of self-organising systems that will have a reciprocal influence on the two levels of reality, the physical and the virtual.

Within the sphere of virtuality, the transaction of value will be tied to organisational depth and the cost necessary to generate self-reproducing systems. The political ecology of hyper-structures will be measured in relation to the cost curtailed in the emergence of different levels of complexity. Entropy, formulated in terms of the second law of thermodynamics, is a mathematical expression of the amount of disorder in any system and as such it is an inverse expression of the amount of organisations within the universe. The shift from energy to information is now conceptualised as the capacity for algorithmic compression relative to the amount of random information present within any system. Therefore, the production of artificial beings and entities has an information-theoretic cost that is as real as energy and material costs. Information is the currency of nature, and as Seth Lloyd, a physicist from Cal Tech, suggested, its value depends not only on the amount of information, but on how diffi-

cult that information was to produce. This transvaluation is most succinctly expressed, again, by Lloyd: 'any species stumped by an intractable problem does not cease to compute, but it would cease to exist.' Existence is an emergent form of computations in cybernetic space. The genetic make-up of a species registers all the exchanges and interaction from the tracks of the epigenetic landscape. The evolution of massive interaction over time within cyberspace will no doubt register a complex set of virtual history and genealogy that will surely become the archeological site for cryptographers and, most uncannily, artificial beings. It would be a virtual topography of the sublime and the tragic.

What will architecture be in this sphere of virtuality? No one knows for sure, however one thing is certain, traditional conceptions of territory, of dwelling, of identity, of the phenomenology of existence and being will no longer be the same. This domain will be the arena of complex adaptive systems at the global level of the mechanosphere, accommodating a collective co-evolution of models that converge towards the virtual anatomy of hyper-structures. It is very likely that some form of modal constructivism will emerge, allowing architecture to address a multitude of emergent phenomena at different levels of scalar and specification regimes, and opening up a universe of possibility for architectural invention. Shakespeare once remarked that we are the stuff from which dreams are made of, and nothing characterises this more than the coming era of hyper-reality in modal space. This brave new world, a spectral fusion of neural-networks-in-action, filled with hope and danger, will be the future horizon that must be measured by the collective space of experience without falling into a massive state of amnesia. This will, no doubt, be one of many ethical challenges for life and architecture in virtual reality. Cyberspace, ultimately, may be the entry level simulation of artificial worlds within modal space.

GIOVANNA BORRADORI
AGAINST THE TECHNOLOGICAL INTERPRETATION OF VIRTUALITY

An image, for Bergson, is 'a certain existence which is more than that which an idealist calls a representation, *but less than what a realist calls a* thing *– an existence placed halfway between the "thing" and the "representation."'*

Matter is not out there, in the world, but a mix of self and world, perception and memory.

For the majority of theorists, virtuality describes the totality of effects and mutations brought about by the information and communication network.[1] Virtuality designates not only whatever happens on, or is generated by, the Internet but includes the impact of the media on the way in which we apprehend, represent and consequently build the world around us. By this definition, virtuality concerns the blurring of the distinction between perception and representation, original and copy.

How does such blurring occur? For many, the explanation lies in the fact that in virtual space objects do not appear as self-contained entities, accessible via sensory perception; rather, mediatised technology fabricates objects as irreducibly represented and reproduced. This irreducibility is the characteristic of virtual space, where objects become 'simulacra'.[2]

I believe this definition of virtuality to rely on a reductionist assumption: if virtuality amounts to a technologically generated set of events, it is in fact reduced to physical states of affairs. I want to call this reductionist standpoint 'representationalist'. By contrast, I see the possibility of developing a nonreductive concept of virtuality, in which it reflects technologically generated events, phenomenologically understood as an aspect of our experience of the world. With reference to Nietzsche's definition of perspectivism as the doctrine for which there are no uninterpreted facts or truth, I shall call this nonreductive alternative 'perspectivist'.

These two definitions, the representationalist and the perspectivist, are based on fundamentally different conceptions of space. In my reading, the representationalist understanding of virtuality heavily depends upon the rationalist notion of space, whose origins are to be found in Descartes' mind–body dualism. The perspectivist alternative is, instead, a critique of the rationalist notion of space in terms of what I name 'virtual spatiality'.[3] Diametrically opposed to the objectification of space as alienated and homogeneous 'outside', this kind of spatiality has as its chief features heterogeneity and movement.[4]

Drawing from the philosophical insights of Nietzsche and Bergson, I shall unfold a heterogeneous and dynamic concept of virtual spatiality in which tensions and qualia override oppositional pairs: in virtual spatiality, direction and movement cut transversally across the distinction between subjective and objective; density and rarity replace the opposition between material and immaterial; latency and expression take predominance over presence and absence.

Virtuality De-Technologised

How does the concept of virtuality intersect with the fields of philosophy and architecture? Is virtuality a contingent or a necessary link between these two disciplines? Most architectural theorists interpret virtuality as a change of technological paradigm and in so doing opt for the thematic type of connection. At a determinate point in time, so their claim goes, architecture begins to be reshaped digitally, in terms of both its technology and its object. Since the paradigm-shift has occurred, architectural design has been increasingly produced through digital means; the spaces architecture has been called to design are themselves virtual; and, even more importantly, architecture has been put face to face with a different spatial sensibility, derived and constantly enriched by the experience of cruising the digital highways. This different spatial sensibility goes together with a new range of spatial needs, the identification of which is still under way, as ever-larger portions of our existence are being conducted on line. The role of philosophy is restricted to helping architecture demarcate this sensibility.

While I am by no means attempting to deny the compelling aspect of technological virtuality, I dissent from reducing it to a contingent historical occurrence, both in the architectural and philosophical sense. To me, virtuality designates a necessary connection between architecture and philosophy, provided that virtuality be de-technologised.

The nontechnological interpretation of virtuality concerns, both etymologically and metaphysically, the Latin notion of *vis* (force), which is a *leitmotif* in Nietzsche's philosophy. Diametrically opposed to the rationalist conception of space, as the container of entities and forms, Nietzsche's idea of space is that of an immanent field of forces. If space is conceived as a field, entities and forms are not simply 'contained' by it but produced by the very differential that constitutes the relation between them.[5] If we understand the nature of these forces to be discursive, virtual spatiality will emerge as the experience of a nomadic discursivity that, because it is yet unexpressed, is virtual.[6] If this de-technologisation of virtuality is indeed pursued in the direction of a new phenomenological definition of the virtual, what will an architecture of virtuality look like?

As the de-technologisation of virtuality should not imply, I believe, an opposition or denial of technological virtuality, but an attempt at interpreting it as a specific mode amongst a larger phenomenological spectrum, the architecture of virtuality should be viewed as intertwined with its metonymical correlative: the virtuality of architecture. By this, I mean the constitutive role that architecture plays in the creation of the human subject, which is what makes virtuality a necessary rather than a contingent link between architecture and philosophy.

The virtuality of architecture suggests that the individual is not just 'always already thrown' into existence, as Heidegger would have put it, but 'always already built'.[7] Architecture, from this

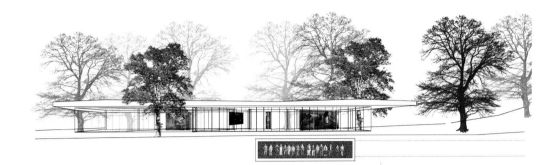

point of view, does not elaborate theoretical, aesthetic, functional propositions 'in' space but becomes the condition of possibility for the primary hermeneutical exchange between the individual self, others and the environment. It is this exchange that makes the human subject a being-in-the-world. The virtuality of architecture relies on the premise that, if we come across ourselves as 'thrown' into the world, we do so in the face of the fact that such a world is built or constructed spatially, as well as socially, historically and culturally. From the standpoint of the virtuality of architecture, architecture builds us as much as we build it.

Why is 'Virtual Space' a Representationalist Concept?

Why is the reductionist interpretation of virtuality also representationalist? What is the coincidence between reduction and representation? If an entity can be reduced to its physical and quantifiable components, it can also be faithfully 'represented' in terms of those components. Since the Renaissance, perspective has been the science of representation, the technique used to rationalise, quantify, order and control spatial relationships.[8]

The role of representation in the rationalist lineage is one of the central themes of Heidegger's later philosophy. According to Heidegger, representation can be minimally understood as the relation to a primitive 'presence': the substantial rather than accidental features of an entity.[9] The more representation is granted epistemological transparency, the more the presence of which it is a representation is presumed to be stable, permanent, self-identical. However, stability, permanence and identity cannot exist without that which allows the object to be present: space. Neither reduction nor representation could happen without the homogeneity of the Newtonian and Cartesian space.

Both a reductive and a representationalist apparatus is at work whenever virtuality is understood as the host dimension for simulacra or for effects of simulation. Whenever the blurring of the distinction between perception and representation is justified in technological terms, not only a reductivist but a representationalist position is being offered.

Most of the representationalist positions have a semiological foundation. Simulacra are conceived as infinitely layered compounds of mediated information whose object or reference, assumed as self-contained presence, is ultimately irretrievable. In the vocabulary of poststructuralism, largely influenced by Saussure's linguistics, such an infinite layering of mediated information without a definite object or reference is translated as the endless deferral from signifier to signifier. Whether only simulacra are available, which are neither copies nor originals, or only signifiers are available, which are pointing to each other rather than to a transcendental signified, the categorial framework seems to remain essentially representational.

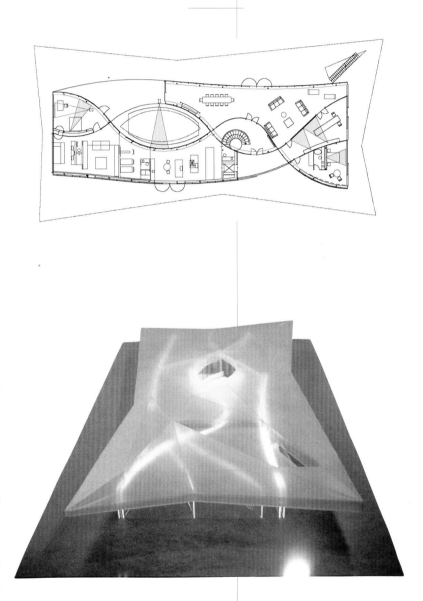

Herzog & De Meuron, Kramlich Residence and Media Collection, *California, 1997-2000. FROM ABOVE: elevation; site plan; model.*

The Cartesian Theorem

Cartesian theorem about space could be called the underlying sense of space shared by such different architectural experiences as 19th-century historicism and large sections of the Modern Movement. Descartes' conception of space revolves around the central opposition between the empirical dimension, defined as having spatial features, and the transcendent or spiritual dimension, which characterises mental features. We can doubt everything, he writes in the *Meditations*, except that we are thinking beings, because, even if we think that we are not thinking, we are still thinking. Assumed as self-reflection, thought is freestanding, internally justified, autonomous from all sorts of empirical support. In fact, the inescapability of thinking does not prove at all that we are awake or completely sober. All it proves is that thought is absolutely primary and independent of anything that is extended in space.

To make the transition from philosophy to architecture, let us pair what Descartes calls thinking with the notion of form. The Cartesian theorem entails the mutual exclusion between form and space. Any thinking being – or, in our parallel, any form – exists in its own perfection and balance, completely independently from space. The mind injects space with forms and, in turn, the absolute emptiness of space does nothing but receive them.

The extreme polarisation of activity and passivity, in terms of mind and body, form and space, is essential in the history of representationalist architecture.[10] This polarisation is at the root of the obsession with novelty so crucial to the high-modernist visual avant gardes and made programmatic by architectural modernism. The fact that form is located completely beyond space, as well as the empirical sphere, protects it from any mediation, change, obsolescence and fallibility. Conceived in this way, radical novelty can exist only on the condition that it be transcendent. The new is whatever is possible, and therefore not real (otherwise it would no longer be a possibility). As in the Cartesian theorem, form is not immanent to space but transcends it; it is form that represents the possibility of an installation in space from an ageless and mental 'inside'. Such an inside is purely transcendental and spaceless. In this sense, form is structurally utopian. Descartes is the philosophical ancestor of the modernist conception of the new as necessarily utopian. Utopia, however, only in its literal meaning of nonplace, because the modernist utopia is a political project of social emancipation. The modernist utopia is a nonplace in the sense that it is not-yet real but may become so on the basis of conditions found in the real. The utopian side of modernism coincides with a foreseeable possibility; otherwise it could not encompass an emancipatory project, which is one of its essential components.

Two Conceptions of the New

Both in architecture and philosophy, the representationalist approach entails a conception of the new as foreseeable possibility. By contrast, from a perspectivist angle, novelty corresponds to the actualisation of virtual presences: presences virtually contained in the real but not yet actualised. A representationalist notion of novelty is based on the category of possibility: on what is not-yet real but may become so on the basis of conditions found in the real. Perspectivist novelty is the affirmation of submerged and unexpressed forces, virtually contained in the real but not yet actualised. In other words: while representationalism moves within a system of oppositions based on two classical modalities, reality and possibility, the perspectivist

set-up is based on the nonoppositional pair constituted by actuality and virtuality. Moreover, while possibility is larger than reality because it contains whatever could become real on the basis of the conditions found in the real; virtuality is co-extensive with the real, for virtuality is already real, inclusive of the yet unexpressed or non-actualised portion of the real.

Virtual spatiality does not perform the function of space, insofar as it does not provide forms with material and objective stability. While space is the receptor of forms, virtual spatiality is the generator of forms. Virtual spatiality is an active and differentiating dimension rather than a homogenising or alienating one. Forms are not injected into space as if from the outside, but generated within it. While the notion of space implies the installation of the radically new into reality, virtual spatiality implies the affirmation of the yet unexpressed, silent, discursive forces by which reality is constituted. What are these discursive forces? Let us turn to Nietzsche for the answer.

Perspectivism and Force

In Nietzsche's analysis, representation has historically implied the suppression of the notion of force and the dynamics between forces, producing hegemonic outcomes. Instead, representation needs to be looked at as just one of many 'perspectival' alternatives. Perspectivism is the name Nietzsche gives as an alternative to representationalism, that is, to the dogmatic and totalising aspiration of traditional philosophical systems. Why does Nietzsche pick out perspective for this scope? And how does his perspectivism affect architecture?

Perspectivism is laid out as the doctrine according to which there are no uninterpreted facts or truths. Perspective seems thus both a synonym of interpretation and distinguished from knowledge, where knowledge is clearly identified with the detection and rationalisation of some objective dimension. Despite Nietzsche himself using perspective and interpretation interchangeably more than once, there is a subtle difference between them that should not be overlooked by those interested in the contrast between space and virtual spatiality, both from a philosophical and architectural standpoint.[11] While perspective indicates the relativity and uniqueness of our spatial and sensory location within the world, interpretation is an intellectual organisation of perspectives. This is because the juxtaposition of perspectives can be apprehended only at an abstract, intellectual level. Thus, perspective, not interpretation, is the primitive unit of Nietzsche's discourse. Perspectivism reveals the determinacy of our sensory presence within space, assumed by Nietzsche as incompatible with any other. Interpretation is a more constructivist concept, made out of a plurality of perspectives.

Far from naturalising perspective in the representationalist way, as the transparent means of rationalising spatial relationships, Nietzsche attributes to perspective an existential and thoroughly materialistic meaning. In Nietzsche's perspectivist approach, there are as many foci as there are eyes in the world. Perspective is not a technique of representation but the affirmation of one's own actualisation as well as the intuition of the virtual spatiality of others. Perspectivism is both a critical project of displacement of the focus, and an affirmative project consisting in the actualisation of other foci, an actualisation whose scope is to give the undecidable, enigmatic, unpredictable features of existence a new legitimacy. Nietzschean affirmation injects ambiguity into the apparent unity of the actual, opening up fissures of virtuality and becoming.[12] To affirm means to experience the multiplicity of 'perspectives' virtually contained by a present state or form. These perspectives are the virtual lines along which becoming unfolds.

For Nietzsche, becoming affects all facts in the world, whether material, mental or formal. This becoming is the virtual aspect of experience. While form is necessarily actualised, becoming is yet-unformed. The challenge of the architecture of virtuality is diametrically opposed to any formalism. For architecture to be able to connect with perspectivist virtuality, it needs to abandon all formalism, since its challenge would no longer be to simulate or represent existing forms and events but to respond to the yet-unformed. The yet-unformed is pure movement, the movement produced by the pushing of the forces against each other. A movement that, in Nietzsche's philosophy of force, comes before space in the sense that it constitutes spatiality.

The Unformed and the Untimely
The primacy of movement makes perspectivist virtuality available to a thoroughly material, sensory type of experience. But what is movement? How can we 'represent' movement? Can the monumental, archival, memorialising function traditionally attributed to architecture be reconciled with it? The Nietzschean answer would be yes, provided that we shy away from all forms of historicism, including, I suggest, postmodern neo-historicism. Historicism kills movement. History is the first area that architecture has to rethink in its meaning. Next to it, as I shall indicate in relation to Bergson, is memory.

According to Nietzsche, there are two possible connections to history: one is authentic and life-enhancing, and the other is inauthentic and destructive. Inauthentic historiography imposes itself whenever history is taken as a given, as the historicists do by monumentalising and revering it indiscriminately. History has neither determinate meanings nor a unifying scope. Since it is not a self-contained presence, it must be challenged rather than religiously respected. By contrast, authentic historiography depends on the ability to 'make history', which Nietzsche distinguishes from simply 'being in it'. This ability hinges on what Nietzsche names 'plastic power'. Life *is* plastic power, the power to shape new perspectives without becoming self-defensive or losing oneself. Only if this power is affirmed and cultivated, rather than suppressed, will history serve movement and life.

The authentic understanding of history, and of human existence within history, is contingent upon what Nietzsche describes as stepping into the 'Unhistorical'. Such a leap consists in a type of 'creative forgetting', disengaged from the normative power of history, and it is necessary for one's plastic power to strengthen. 'It is possible to live almost without memory, and to live happily moreover, as the animal demonstrates; but it is altogether impossible to live at all without forgetting'.[13] Forgetting means disconnecting from a linear sense of time, described as a series of punctual 'nows', some of which are no-more and some of which are not-yet. This linear description represents selves and cultures as located in time, rather than constituted by it and becoming with it. Switching between the Historical and the Unhistorical, making the present part of becoming, is what secures a healthy, constructive relationship with history, for both philosophy and architecture. What is no-more cannot be objectified as something without an active influence on the present, but needs to be reactivated precisely in terms of these influences. This is the transformative function of time that the Unhistorical is supposed to introduce into the present. Implementing the role

that time, in its transformative function, plays in existence means to implement the contact with a specific ontological modality that is located in reality but is not actualised: virtuality.

The relationship with history opened up by contact with the virtual dimension of experience is neither the radical rejection of the past promulgated by architectural high modernism and the International Style, nor the reverence for the past adopted by the postmodernist appropriation of historical styles. Nietzsche's perspectivist history is not, as it is often all too simplistically interpreted, the generating matrix of an unqualified relativism, that both in architecture and philosophy translates in a neohistoricist kind of sensibility. Perspectivist history presents both the philosopher and the architect with the question of how to interpret the yet-unformed, whether conceptually or spatially. Sensing becoming, responding to movement: these are the new challenges that need to be faced by attempting to capture form as it emerges from the process of its own formation and deformation.

The Tensions of Memory and Perception
Is there a technique of capturing movement, or more precisely, the movement of forms and forces, before their expression? For some, the answer is topology, the digital animation of form, which could lead to 'topological turn'.[14] In contrast to the formalistic orientation promoted by the evolution of modernism into the International Style, topology has pushed architecture to stop viewing form as its ultimate scope but as a by-product of the design process. Topological design no longer consists of a highly polarised activity where the architect injects form and meaning onto an inert, white surface representing space. It has transformed into the interactive experience between a mind and a form, which is interactive because the form emerges from its own generative process. Movement, in other words, exceeds form.

For Bergson, virtuality is the ontological modality of consciousness, or duration. Duration roughly corresponds to what William James, with a famous aquatic metaphor, called the 'stream'. As James's conscious stream is continuous, forward-moving and in constant change, Bergson's duration is the succession of qualitative states of mind, indiscernible as atomic units but only feasible in their interconnectedness and passing. The passing-character is the result of deeper currents that, while remaining submerged, push water towards the surface. Both the deep currents and the superficial motion of the water that they create are real components of our experience. But while the motion on the surface is actual, the submerged currents are virtual.

What does this virtual modality entail? In a word: memory, which Bergson discusses in opposition to perception. Perception and memory are tendencies along which experience 'tends' to organise itself, but do not constitute independent kinds of experience, available separately from one another. Bergson defines perception as the 'abstract' tendency of our experience, referring to what our experience would be like if extrapolated from the effects of time. To stay with the Jamesian metaphor, abstract experience would mean to take the layer of moving water at the surface separately from the deeper currents beneath. This is the kind of experience we tend to produce artificially, when we look at the world objectively, with causal, quantitative, or geometrical models in mind. By contrast, memory embodies the 'concrete' tendency to experience the world as a constant becoming-other than itself. It is experience in terms of the effects of time on it.

 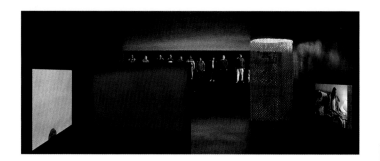

Herzog & De Meuron, Kramlich Residence, *California, 1997-2000. Interior perspectives.*

Here, we need to put aside the aquatic metaphor because Bergson indicates these two tendencies as radically heterogeneous to one another. It is as if deep and superficial could not be measured against each other.[15]

> Whenever we are trying to recover a recollection, to call up some period of our history, we become conscious of an act *sui generis* by which we detach ourselves from the present in order to replace ourselves, first, in the past in general, then, in a certain region of the past – a work of adjustment, something like the focusing of a camera. But our recollection still remains virtual; we simply prepare ourselves to receive it by adopting the appropriate attitude. Little by little it comes into view like a condensing cloud; from the virtual state, it passes into the actual; and as its outlines become more distinct and its surface takes on colour, it tends to imitate perception. But it remains attached to the past by its deepest roots, and if, being a present state, it were not also something that stands out distinct from the present, we should never know it for a memory.[16]

Either we are 'in' memory or 'in' perception. We don't reach the past from the present via the extension of the representational model. Quite the opposite. As we intentionally try to recollect something, we step into the past and its virtuality, and we navigate it, not rationally but intuitively, until we meet the virtual current pushing along the memory we are looking for. In order for us to individuate it and recollect it, that specific memory needs to be actualised and transformed in a perception. But, as Bergson warns in the last sentence of the quotation, part of the memory still remains attached to the past, otherwise we would not be able to discern it is a memory. This explains the sense of uncanniness, otherness, vagueness and suspension that memory entails.

The co-existence rather than integration of perception and memory is key to Bergson's relevance to my discussion of space, virtual spatiality and architecture. Bergson articulates such a co-existence within a peculiar conception of matter defined as the fullest aggregate of images, the sum total of all the past, present and future images available. An image for Bergson is 'a certain existence which is more than that which an idealist calls a *representation*, but less than what a realist calls a *thing* – an existence placed halfway between the "thing" and the "representation."'[17] Matter is not out there, in the world, but a mix of self and world, perception and memory. An example can clarify this point.

Even the most simple perception, like feeling cold or hot, takes time. When I analyse perception and quantify it according to objective scales of measurement, I act as if this time, indispensable to experience, did not exist. In the same way, as I try to recapture a memory long past, I won't be able to revive it without transforming it into a perception. The interesting feature of the differential relationship of memory and perception, virtual and actual, is that perception of actuality is arrived at, according to Bergson, from memory or virtuality. The present is accessed from the past, and not the reverse, so that experience is the constant reassessment of the present in terms of the past.

In concrete experience, as Bergson calls it, form is not injected into space as if from some otherworldly, timeless, geometrical outside, but emerges from the generative process of its own formation and deformation. What contemporary theorists identify as the animation of form, via topological techniques, Bergson illustrated as the infiltration of memory in perception. Such an infiltration provides experience with what Bergson names its 'pictorial' character, which indicates the process-like nature of the world. Paradoxically, it is time itself that constitutes experience pictorially, as a cinematic sequence. Thinking in objective terms implies a conception of matter and space as empty, homogeneous and passive, rather than full, heterogeneous and in constant motion: namely, as an aggregate of images in endless tension and becoming.

Let us go back one more time to the metaphor of virtuality as a range of deep currents that, while remaining submerged, push water to the surface. These submerged currents are virtually present to the stream. It is these virtual movements of duration that determine the emergence, or actualisation, of whatever stretch of the stream of consciousness reaches the surface. Bergson's suggestion is that the virtual currents correspond to what the pure past would be like if it were accessible. The emerged stream taken in isolation from the deep currents corresponds, instead, to what the pure present would be like as a self-contained discrete dimension. However, what is true for the dynamics of aquatic currents is true for perception and memory, present and past, actual and virtual. Experience is the theatre of these dynamics, where the invisible, or deeper layer, is always responsible for the emergence of whatever comes into view.

In contrast to the representationalist interpretation of virtuality, according to which virtuality can be 'represented' as the sum total of the effects of communication and information technology on how we know and build the world around us, I have been trying to elucidate an alternative concept of the virtual by phenomenologically understanding it as an expression of intentionality. My perspectivist definition of virtuality describes a constitutive component of experience, irreducible to physical processes as well as to quantification and formalisation. If this phenomenological interpretation is viable, experience contains a virtual dimension that calls into question a whole range of philosophical categorisations and architectural presuppositions. First of these is the Cartesian notion of space as passive receptor of forms, installed by an active and independent mind. If the hypothesis of a stable and controlled space fails, one of the most enduring bridges between philosophy and architecture is swept away. On its remains, a new concept of virtual spatiality emerges.

The relevance of Nieztsche and Bergson for my project lies in their insistence on the irreducibly passing character of our experience: this is what makes them champions of philosophical anti-Cartesianism and architectural anti-formalism. Cartesian space is incompatible with this passing and becoming feature, which is the greatest challenge of the architecture of virtuality.

Notes

1 I shall limit myself to a few references to indicate different tendencies in recent cybertheory. A utopianist, science fiction-type analysis is represented by Howard Rheingold's *Virtual Reality*, Summit Books (New York), 1991. A more scholarly approach, attempting to bind cybertheory to classical philosophical sources, is Michael Heim's *The Metaphysics of Virtual Reality*, Oxford University Press (Oxford), 1997. A comprehensive theoretical account is Pierre Lévy's *Becoming Virtual: Reality in the Digital Age*, Robert Bononno (trans.), Plenum Trade (New York), 1998. John Beckmann's *The Virtual Dimension: Architecture, Representation, and Crash Culture*, Princeton Architectural Press (Princeton), 1998, is an anthology of essays from a variety of disciplines including architecture.

2 The term was first introduced by Jean Baudrillard. See his *In the Shadow of The Silent Majorities*, Semiotext(e) (New York), 1983; *Fatal Strategies*, Semiotext(e) (New York), 1990; *The Gulf War Did Not Take Place*, Indiana University Press (Bloomington), 1995. In the context of this essay, I use it as emblematic of the 'technological' conception of the virtual, which I critique as 'representational'. Greg Lynn has similar views: 'The term "virtual" has been so debased that it often simply refers to the digital space of computer-aided design. It is often used interchangeably with the term simulation. Simulation, unlike virtuality, is not intended as a diagram for a future possible concrete assemblage but is instead a visual substitute'. *Animate Form*, Princeton Architectural Press (Princeton), 1999, p10.

3 I coin this expression in order to mark the difference between the rationalist concept of 'space' and my nonreductive perspective. In my analysis, the notion of 'space' coincides with the idea of a mutual exclusivity between *res cogitans* and *res extensa*, inaugurated by Descartes. The expression 'virtual spatiality' echoes the Heideggerian 'spatiality', which together with 'temporality' and 'historicity', is at the centre of his phenomenonological and existentialist project as laid out in *Being and Time*. These terms imply a critique of the way in which the tradition of Western metaphysics has 'objectified' space, time and history, which amounts to the inability to posit the meaning of these concepts beyond the oppositional framework set up by the subject-object distinction.

4 The critique of the rationalist concept of space as an alienated and inert 'outside' is one of the steadier themes in Heidegger's philosophy, spanning *Being and Time* to 'Building Dwelling Thinking', 1952. Section III of Part I of *Being and Time*, contains the kernel of his treatment of space. The discussion of spatiality is conducted as a critique of what Heidegger calls 'the Cartesian ontology of the world'. If my perspectivist conception of virtual spatiality draws from Heidegger the opposition to spatial inertia, it draws from Bergson and Nietzsche the further characterisation in terms of movement and heterogeneity.

5 It is difficult to locate a single definition of force in Nietzsche's work, since force is one of the most deeply embedded concepts in his philosophy. In this text, I discuss the idea of force as it is developed in the second of the *Untimely Meditations*, 'On the Uses and Disadvantages of History For Life'.

6 The discursive nature of forces cannot be pursued here. I define discursivity in relation to the all-encompassing notion of textuality assumed as a background for both deconstruction and hermeneutics. Since I derive the notion of force directly from Nietzsche, and the question of the nature of those forces remains problematic in Nietzsche's own writings, I prefer 'discourse' over 'text' because it describes more pertinently what would be the nature of those forces according to a distinctly Nietzschean line of argument. It is no coincidence that Michel Foucault, who coined the term in the mid-1960s and launched it in the postmodernist and poststructuralist context, did so around the time when Nietzsche appeared on the French scene. Deconstruction was not yet born and Heidegger, along with hermeneutics, was still to make his impact on French philosophy. I wish to anchor the term to that context, in which it meant the implicit knowledge that underlies and makes possible specific social practice, institutions or theories.

7 One of the fundamental notions in *Being and Time* is 'thrownness' (*Geworfenheit*), which refers to the way in which we find ourselves always already 'placed' in our existence – we are not objectively present in it, but have to make it our own place,

to appropriate it, give it meaning. It seems to me that within this, architecture plays a major role. The world in which we find ourselves thrown is a 'built' world, which has constituted us as what we are in many substantial ways. Some studies have tried to unravel the constitutive role of architecture along Heideggerian lines. A lucid analysis of this theoretical knot is provided by Karsten Harries in his *The Ethical Function of Architecture*, MIT Press (Cambridge, MA), 1997. See also David Farrell Krell, *Architecture: Ecstasies of Space, Time, and the Human Body*, SUNY Press (Albany), 1997 and Edward C Casey, *Getting Back Into Place: Toward a Renewed Understanding of the Place-World*, Indiana University Press (Bloomington), 1993.

8 See Erwin Panofsky, *Perspective as Symbolic Form*, Zone Books (New York), 1991; Hubert Damisch, *The Origin of Perspective*, MIT Press (Cambridge, Mass.); Alberto Perez-Gomez, *Architectural Representation and the Perspective Hinge*, MIT Press (Cambridge, Mass.), 1997.

9 In the Introduction to *Being and Time*, Heidegger first raises the question of presence (*Anwesenheit*) in conjunction with the Greek interpretation of being in relation to time. Assumed as *parousia* or *ousia*, the Being of beings is both ontologically and temporally understood as presence: a definite mode of time (the present). The identification of a specific temporal modality with the way in which beings are, is for Heidegger a meaningful move on the part of Greek thought, since it indicates a fundamental 'repression' of time's becoming quality. Western thought seeks to confirm being in terms of eternal stability (the notion of presence), which is but the abstraction of a specific modality of time: the present.

10 In the history of architectural theory, the concept of 'space' becomes central only from the late 18th century, as the issue of canonical authority, previously identified solely with Vitruvius, is raised in connection with a universal definition of authority, established on human rationality rather than canonical sources. This question is deeply intertwined with the interdependence of the Enlightenment categories of fraternity, humanity and freedom. The paradigmatic example of the role of space in the Enlightenment debate on the foundation of rationality can be found in Siegfried Giedion, *Space, Time and Architecture*, Harvard University Press (Cambridge, Mass.), 1974.

11 A thorough discussion of this point can be found in the excellent chapter on 'Perspectivism, Philology, Truth', in Alan D Schrift, *Nietzsche and the Question of Interpretation: Between Hermeneutics and Deconstruction*, Routledge (London, New York), 1990, pp144–68.

12 On this issue of ambiguity, I disagree with Brian Massumi in 'Sensing the Virtual, Building the Insensible', in Stephen Perrella (ed) *AD: Hypersurface Architecture*, vol 68, no 5/6, Academy Editions (London), 1998, who sees virtuality and ambiguity as incompatible: 'Ambiguity . . . belongs to signifying structure. It is nothing new for architects to build-in ambiguity in order to make an event of standing form, but ambiguity still addresses the conventional function of the sign-form'. I don't see why ambiguity needs to be interpreted in terms of the 'signifying structure'. Why can't it be felt or sensed? Bergson's definition of memory against perception touches exactly on this point. In order for a memory to emerge at the surface of consciousness, it needs to become a perception. However, there is a fraction of memory that remains attached to the past. This is how we know it is a memory and not a perception. Such attachment to the past gives to memory an aura of uncanniness, otherness, and, I claim, ambiguity.

13 Friedrich Nietzsche, *Untimely Meditations*, Daniel Breaseale (ed), trans RJ Hollingdale, Cambridge University Press (Cambridge, Mass.), 1997, p62.

14 See Perrella, *Hypersurface Architecture*, op cit; Lynn, *Animate Form*, op cit.

15 'Deep' and 'superficial' are typical examples of vague predicates and as such, are unmeasurable. I cannot tell, for example, whether 6 feet of water are deep or not, as I cannot tell whether a 3-millimetre cut in my skin is superficial or not. No amount of conceptual analysis or empirical investigation can settle these matters. See, Timothy Williamson, *Vagueness*, Routledge (London), 1994.

16 Henri Bergson, *Matter and Memory*, trans Nancy Margaret Paul and W Scott Palmer, Zone Books (New York), 1988, pp133–4.

17 Ibid, p9.

THE GREEN APOCALYPSE
THE PRAGMATISTS VERSUS THE IDEALISTS

An important issue that was routinely ignored in economics text books until very recently is the issue of ecological capital. The problem of unsustainability in economic terms is that we are not reinvesting in ecological capital in order to make good the various depredations that our activities and our consumption reek upon it . . . The government's role is to get the accounting system straight, to incorporate green accounts within the national accounts, to engage in the strategic planning of resources, the setting of targets, time scales and budgets to come within these kinds of sustainability conditions. Also to start incorporating in the prices of those goods and services that use environmental resources, a realistic estimate of the real cost of those environmental resources.

Paul Ekins, Economist

In many ways we must have both the idealism and the pragmatism. We know very broadly what to do for the first few steps towards sustainability and it is not impossibly costly. But one of the reasons that we don't do it is that we're not clear enough about its implications, about what it will actually mean in daily life and about the ultimate destination of 'the sustainable society sustainable economy to which we might be heading'. So how does this relate to architecture? . . . We know that buildings use for example 40% of our energy. Much of that is a legacy of the past when people didn't know that this was an important consideration. We know that the way we build has fundamental implications for land use, for transportation, countryside, community and aesthetics. This is a pretty important part of the sustainability agenda. I know that architects aren't responsible for a lot of it. Yet on the other hand architects have an expert role to play in talking about it, in formulating policies about it, and in helping to show society what is possible.

Paul Ekins

Sustainable development also needs idealism. It needs people who can show where it is we might be going, who can create experiments and pilot projects, sometimes on a small and sometimes on a large scale, which will overcome peoples' fear of the unknown and which will enable them to loosen their hold on the habits of a lifetime, of a generation, and indeed the habits of the Industrial Revolution as a whole. That will give them the confidence to look forward to a millennium which we can be certain will be a millennium of ecological scarcity. Much of the planet is already populated and towards the middle of the next century there will be ten billion people, twice today's number, whom that planet is expected to sustain. It is only conceivable that it can do that if we utilise both our vision and our pragmatism.

Paul Ekins

It is still possible to produce a very low energy design and not be truly sustainable for a number of reasons. The most obvious would be that so much energy has been invested in the construction that the building only just manages to harvest enough ambient energy to repay this initial debt before it starts falling apart. The other is more subjective and begins with the concern that the quality of life within the building is so claustrophobic, stuffy and unpleasant, with poor daylight and little visual contact with the outside world, that nobody will want to live in it and the proposal will be a social failure. However, we must take the debate beyond mere kilowatt hours. There is a long history of rural exiles from the city, and we, the former hi-tech offices, have been left alone to apply sustainable principles to inner-city briefs without really having any contact with these people working in more remote areas.

Bill Dunster, Michael Hopkins & Partners

Just as this century has been the century of electricity and nuclear energy, the next century is the century of the sun; we have a new beginning. We're just in the early days, if I was a millionaire I would invest very, very heavily in solar technologies.

Susan Roaf, Lecturer Oxford Brookes University

The house is no longer just a site anymore, it must be seen in the local, environmental and global context.

Susan Roaf

A second point is the degree to which the ecological movement and architects have a community of interest: that architects might be useful to the ecological movement – for at least symbolic gestures - as to what might be achieved and what aspirations might be set. Of course ecology and ecological thinking can offer architects some sort of legitimisation which is the underlying feeling of what we are discussing.

Jeremy Melvin, Building Design

We have not even begun to win the argument. I mean this whole area is still considered as an eccentric minority view by the media, by central government particularly, partly by local government, by most institutions and, as you quite rightly said, by architects – which is sad but true. People recognise that there may be right in it, but it has not entered the bloodstream of political debate and until it does we've got a real problem.

Mark Fisher, Member of Parliament, Labour Party, Stoke-on-Trent Central

Firstly, in terms of the urban issue of energy, which is what a lot of you are talking about, the solution that you must accept is solar power. You need things like Susan Roaf going on 'News at Ten', and the supplement of The Times showing a picture of her house, very normal, very mainstream. Now architects come up to me and say, well it's a bit ugly and I'd rather have it this, this, this and this, and have lots of quibbles about it. But she's done it, she paid for it out of her own pocket and it's in the national media, and we're getting calls from people at Greenpeace saying 'I want a solar home, how do I get one ?' . . . So that's the issue about how to champion the cause with good practice. Then you need political signals from industry. Remember you need to crystallise your view in order to instigate change.

Colin Millais

We only talk about one half of the problem which is the cost side – reducing costs. Everything is reducing costs, but you need to spend money and spend costs to obtain benefits. You can never obtain something for nothing, so it is not just the question of cost that we should be talking about, we should ask what costs will ultimately benefit us.

Marcial Echnique, ME & P Architects

It's not just the architect alone in these considerations: a consultant team is required to work together to produce an energy efficient building. I would also say that there is a risk in all this, in as much as every building is a prototype, and that a lot of clients aren't prepared to put their money into a risk element. To that extent I admire the architects who have actually produced their own houses and in a sense participated in that experiment.

Richard Brearley, John Miller + Partners

Without defending the Treasury, the interesting thing that has happened recently is that all of a sudden we have got contractors coming to us who are doing PFI [Private Finance Initiative] proposals, for many public sector buildings, and they're being forced financially to have to think about the building over a two-year life span. Consequently, the questions being asked are: how long will it last, how easy is it to maintain, and can we look at green environmental concerns .

Mark Fisher

Even in a small building it really makes sense to allow the building to take over the intelligence and to run efficiently. On a domestic, and much more on a public scale, people just don't have time to constantly turn on lights and control the heating, particularly in such institutions as a hospital. Lights are left on all the time, the same with heating, doctors are busy saving lives rather than worrying over the building's performance and I think it's one aspect where architects can really make huge input in specifying building management systems.

Gabriele Bramante, Bramante Associates

If we actually set quite modest, but exciting, targets for a 25-30% reduction in energy usage we would buy ourselves time to look at the long term solutions. We would have a huge impact, both short and long term, and we would begin to demonstrate good practice. The normality of this would then get it onto the political agenda . . . Maybe the best approach would be to reconcile short term problems, to give us a chance to look at better solutions for the future.

Mark Fisher

Quotes are taken from the Academy International Symposium, The Green Apocalypse, The Royal Academy of Arts, 23rd April 1996

EXEDRA ds
ENVIRONMENTALLY FRIENDLY HOUSES: THE REALITY

There is more to designing an ecologically friendly, speculative house than having a developer who is convinced of its virtues. Typically, he is more than willing to accommodate passive design solutions and environmental ideals, provided it can be done economically. One difficulty stems from the process of developing ecological architecture when compromises to the basic design criteria are needed to entice the consumer. Whilst the purchasing public may be educated in environmental issues and their benefits, the problem is convincing a mortgage lender that a property which, for example, does not have a conventional central heating system may be better, not worse, than a standard speculative house.

Treating the building as a speculative house, with minimising cost being the ultimate criteria, is still viable and pragmatic if the architect avoids hi-tech solutions and returns to basic passive design principles. The integration of solar collection, distribution and storage, together with ventilation and auxiliary heating, can be simple and economic to achieve.

All of these factors have been realised in the following residential design in Bristol. The site is a redundant piece of urban land formerly occupied by a substation, surrounded by roads at the brow of a hill. The design is based upon solar path orientation, and luckily this best suited the views across the city. A mature horse chestnut tree located at the western end of the site was exploited to provide solar shading in the summer, while not inhibiting what solar energy is available in winter. The occupants of the house will live with the seasons.

To facilitate these aims the house was constructed using only simple building techniques and holistic materials: a criterion based on the natural resource of the raw material, the energy used in harvesting and refinement, and the long-term effect on the environment, including recyclability. This can all be achieved without reducing profit margins.

Designing against the norm, the building is turned on its head with the bedrooms on the ground floor, surrounded by thermally massive stone walls. These absorb heat passively during the day and release it at night. The heavily insulated areas on the first floor provide splendid views from the common rooms, while conveying the feeling of living within the branches of a mature tree. Similarly, whereas standard speculative houses utilise the 'condom' approach to building – using plastic vapour checks to prevent moisture entering the fabric – this house uses breathable walls to control moisture migration through the construction.

A built-in conservatory rises through the southern elevation to maximise solar gain. This punctuates the main roof and provides a heat collector. As hot air rises through the building it passes through a simple heat exchanger, warming the incoming fresh air. This supply air is distributed to the ground floor bedrooms to provide heating and ventilation. The passive heat sources are backed up by a solid fuel stove, whose output is capable of maintaining the whole house at a comfortable temperature even during the winter. To achieve the speculative appeal of a family home, night storage heaters have been included even though they will never be used.

The market for speculatively built, energy efficient and ecologically friendly homes, whilst small, has the potential to develop rapidly. The problem is mortgage lenders who are unsure of the market and reluctant to add any premiums to their valuations for energy efficiency.

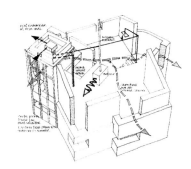

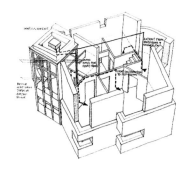

OPPOSITE, FROM ABOVE: Rendered elevation; site plan; FROM ABOVE: First floor environmental strategy; ground floor environmental strategy

BILL DUNSTER
HOPE HOUSE
East Molesey, England

The largely self-built Hope House establishes a coherent relationship with the landscape by maximising views of the river, despite coping with a very tight site, changes in the level and the privacy of neighbouring plots. All available south-facing apertures are designed to maximise solar energy and daylight. These sustainable resources are used for space heating, food cultivation, illumination and as a source of electricity. Additionally, the domestic sunspace provides a thermal buffer zone which, occupied seasonally, provides extra living space. This feature is a development of the self-irrigating, self-ventilating and self-shading conservatory built by the architects as an extension to an existing suburban house.

In response to emerging socioeconomic trends, especially large-scale unemployment and changes in employment patterns caused by information technology, this house effectively merges the traditional allotment with the leisure generated conservatory. In fact, it uses these two ingredients, already essential to a typical suburban lifestyle, to create a more sustainable urban typology. Despite using materials with a low embodied energy content, the house was built on a very low budget and 95% financed through the local building society. Active water-cooled photovoltaic solar systems and a rainwater thermal store will be added to the scheme when the client has the available funds. The architects have incorporated elements of this house into a higher density urban terrace which is part of the Hopetown sustainable city environment.

FROM ABOVE: Conservatory, 6 Hurst Road, Molesey, England; model, Hopetown
Photographs: Dennis Gilbert

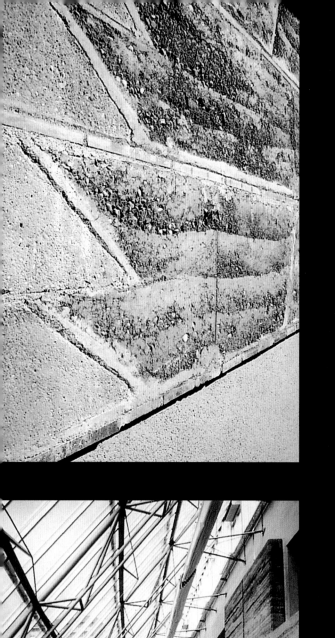

LINDA WATSON
EARTH AS A BRITISH BUILDING MATERIAL

Earth is no longer regarded as a major building material despite the fact that it continues to leave an undeniable and distinctive imprint on the architectural landscapes, both rural and urban, of many countries.

Hugo Houben's statement would probably be dismissed by people as having no relevance to Britain. Few realise that we are a country that has inherited a rich and varied legacy of earth buildings. Whilst the quantity, geographical distribution and regional variation is not yet fully known, new examples are being discovered everyday as it is recognised that earth was a viable, British building material. The vast inheritance of earth (cob) buildings in Devon alone, suggests that the material was used continuously for several centuries, refining a body of knowledge past through generations of builders, to not only produce utilitarian farm buildings and simple cottages but fine gentry houses in town and country and some public buildings including, early 19th-century Sandford School.

Whilst the past use of earth presents a conservation issue to the guardians of our heritage, a more current and broader conservation issue considers the viability of using earth to build today's architecture.

A few enlightened British designers are beginning to recognise that earth has great potential, and that the modern building construction industry, which made this ancestral technique obsolete, may well experience a paradigm shift in the light of the need to produce sustainable development and relearn the skills of building from earth. Britain is not unique in this reawakening. Many countries have already made considerable advances in the use of earth. Some have over two decades of experience in achieving contemporary forms. Others never forgot this timeless material, continuing to create appropriate buildings in the most hostile of climates. This list is endless, but it is sufficient to state that an international network exists, utilising communication technology to share experiences, disseminate research findings and give advice. This support is very reassuring in our current rediscovery of the material.

But why reintroduce what many cynics believe to be an inferior material best left in the past? The material when used in building is recognised as having a number of remarkable characteristics important for the realisation of sustainable development. Its considered inferiority is irrational when the numerous ruins from the past are considered. The Great Wall of China and the Alhambra in Granada are testimony to the longevity of earth in building.

On purchasing a site, earth is one of the few building materials which comes free, and there is no financial premium put upon the suitability of the earth underfoot for building. Using this material, or at least the subsoil, for walling avoids costly and time consuming transportation, which increases environmental pollution. Generally landscaping, engineering and excavation on site provides sufficient surplus material for building purposes. The use of earth avoids the large scale, centralised extraction of alternative materials which contribute to landscape degradation and ecological imbalance.

Whilst it is likely that many of the British soils can be used in building, not every site can claim such opportunities. Where the surroundings are rich in earth building it is very likely the site materials will be suitable. The character of the soil available can determine the building technique utilised. These broadly follow either a monolithic load-bearing construction such as rammed earth or cob; a block load-bearing construction such as adobe or compressed block; or an infill such as wattle and daub. Where the soil does not suit the chosen technique it can be modified by additives or sieving. Stabilisers, such as lime or cement, may be added, posing philosophical, environmental, aesthetic and practical questions which may be difficult to resolve. For instance, laboratory testing has shown that cement improves some properties of earth and reduces others, but its addition may negate any environmental benefit.

Simple field and laboratory tests exist to analyse the soil, allowing architects to understand its suitability for the various construction techniques and the appropriateness of its modification through additives.

The preparation of the material and the manufacture of the building components require 'low technology' and little energy. Architect Gernot Minke, researching at the University of Kassel, Germany, through his tabulation of the amount of energy required in the manufacture of building products, shows earth to require only 1% of that of burnt brick or concrete elements. The recyclable characteristic of the material – the reaction earth undergoes when transformed into a building product is reversible – means there is no industrial waste. This is very important today with our problems of waste disposal and the relatively high percentage produced by the building industry. Neither does the process produce any toxic chemicals or gases assisting in the build-up of acid rain.

Financial investment in manufacturing equipment is low and this, together with the simplicity of production, makes the material very accessible. There is no mystery involved and the process is delightfully described by Alfred Howard, who equates building cob in Devon with the swallows building their nests. But time has to be invested in the relearning of old skills, and, if the contemporary techniques utilised overseas are to have an impact on British architecture, new research must be undertaken. These skills are appropriate across-the-board, from the mass building industry through to the do it yourself enthusiasts, as can be demonstrated by current earth building in Australia and southern states of North America. But should the local traditional techniques be continued? It may represent the most suitable building method in material terms, yet is it appropriate for the current construction industry and if facsimiles of the past are created as a consequence, are these appropriate to our current culture?

Glossy collections of international earth building photographs show there to be endless possibilities in formal and textural terms from the organic cob cottage to the classical linear houses of rammed earth, the flat surfaces of lime renders to textured and profiled decoration incised into forms. All appears possible with this versatile material. The designer is not restricted to 'brown bread' architecture.

Finding out exactly how to achieve earth buildings presents a problem for the British designer today. Although internationally there is a wealth of knowledge, much of which is documented, its accessibility can be frustrating. Fortunately the United States, Australia and India have produced informative literature in English, but a great deal exists in other languages. Until there is a much greater demand for the information, it is unlikely that the British publishers will be persuaded to translate this for an English speaking market. And also the question must be asked how transferable is this information, given the variation in subsoils, climates, architectural ambitions, lifestyles, labour forces etc. A good example of this is the wealth of excellent literature produced for 'developing' countries, where generally labour is cheap and materials relatively expensive. Very different circumstances exist currently in Britain.

However, a great deal of important work has been undertaken abroad which is vital to this British earth renaissance. At present in Britain the following apparatus exists to facilitate the construction of earth buildings: suitable field and laboratory testing techniques have been developed; programmes to predict the material's performance and the modifications achievable with various additives; plant to ensure rapid and efficient manufacture and erection; standards and codes for contemporary construction techniques, and the means of training specifiers and contractors. The proposed earth centre at Doncaster could provide the vehicle to transfer this knowledge to British soil.

And once an earth building is complete, what are its benefits? Available literature and laboratory testing supports the idea that earth walling, if designed and constructed correctly, will achieve the required structural performance required of a two-storey dwelling with more than adequate factors of safety. In fact multi-storey buildings, as found in countries such as the Yemen, could mean there is no need to be restricted to low-rise developments.

The longevity of surviving buildings demonstrates the durability of the material if appropriately detailed and well maintained. But standard tests have been developed to quantify this durability in countries such as Australia.

Its thermal performance is frequently questioned and, although there is much information on earth's capacity and its improvement through additives, no definitive documentation is available for use in Britain at this present time. However, this will be rectified as a consequence of current research. A recent house completed in Sweden to the design of Sverre Fehn, used clay/straw blocks to satisfy the rigorous thermal requirements by providing very high insulating properties (K=0.28). Gernot Minke is experimenting with porous mineral aggregates, such as expanded clay, expanded glass, expanded lava or pumice, added to earth to increase thermal insulation. In addition to this, he has found that this process also eliminates any shrinkage in the material.

Similarly, acoustic performance and fire resistance have also to be quantified for Britain. Again, work abroad is already under way. For instance, the Australian research states that any earth construction will have at least a two hour resistance to fire.

However, the variation in subsoils, the numerous natural and artificial additives, the variation in construction techniques and the degree of quality control means that several thousands of tests are necessary to numerically quantify the material's performance. Fortunately many have already been undertaken, especially overseas, so in many instances it is a matter of transference and modification of existing data.

And what of the 'feel good factor' many inhabitants of earth buildings claim to be one of their greatest assets? Gernot Minke, believes this to be related to the constant relative humidity of 50% within earth buildings, the optimum level for a healthy respiratory system. Over eight years, measurement of Minke's own house were shown to vary only 5% throughout the year. Others claim there is great satisfaction gained from the occupation of a building erected from natural material taken from beneath the ground upon which your home rests. And rests is just what it does, when there is no longer any need for the building, the earth walls will return to the ground from which they came and the cycle is complete. The reaction which cause subsoil to change into a suitable building material is reversible, creating no redundant material to be disposed. What better credentials for a sustainable building material.

Linda Watson is the co-ordinator of the Centre for Earthen Architecture, University of Plymouth.

PAGE 86, FROM ABOVE: Church, Arse, near Lyon, France; Martin Rauch, rammed earth spine wall, Feldkirch, Austria; FROM ABOVE: Cob tholos, under construction, Tricombe Cottage, Tricombe, Devon; new earth building in progress, Attricombe Cottage, Devon

SUMITA SINHA
DOWN TO EARTH BUILDINGS

arth is one of the most cost-effective building materials available. Almost 33% of the world's population, mostly in the developing countries, live in earthen homes due to its availability. Although local climate, environment and culture, as well as the physical limitations of the material itself, have contributed to distinct vernacular traditions, earth has been used as a building material in three basic ways. The first, is as masonry where it is shaped and compressed into bricks or blocks, and occasionally even balls as it is in East Anglia, England. These are then bonded together using a mortar which is very similar in composition to the basic building block itself. The second method involves pouring earth into formwork and compressing, or ramming it so that it sets into strong monolithic walls. The ramming is carried out in stages known as lifts. The third way is to use earth in conjunction with another material, as in wattle and daub.

The main problems associated with earth structures are water protection, durability and stringent building regulations that demand quality control in manufacture and functionability. Unfortunately, the communal, small scale of earth construction, combined with its spontaneity, means that it cannot be standardised. Furthermore, the favoured modern architectural image, with its open-plan spaces, expansive glazed planes and orthogonal aesthetic has eliminated the use of earth in contemporary projects. The existing palette of earth building does not allow large openings or even straight walls. Traditional earthen architecture is soft edged, thick walled and large massed, more like an elephant than the gazelle-like sleekness that contemporary design demands.

Why use earth?

Earth is defined as the accumulation of uncemented, or weakly cemented, particulate material, often of variable character and thickness, on relatively unweathered bedrock. The top portion of the soil, commonly referred to as topsoil, can support vegetation and is often not more than 0.5 metres thick. The underlying material is engineering soil and is used for construction purposes.

Excavated earth from building, landscaping or engineering works near the site can be used for construction purposes, saving on transportation, labour and processing costs which also have a high proportion of hidden, embodied energy. Similarly, unburnt earth does not create pollution, utilise great amounts of energy during its manufacture, or require extensive maintenance following its construction (see table). As earth is a non-toxic it is safe to use as a building material, and after demolition, simply melts back into the landscape without creating environmental problems. Earth walls are also highly insulative, thus lowering the need tor heating or cooling: 600 millimetres of cob walling has a superior U-value to the same width of brick wall. Finally, because earth has been used as a constructional material for centuries throughout the world, it can consequently offer an extensive tradition that can be experimented and expanded upon.

Materials	Energy content kWh/Kg	Rating
Soil/earth	0.01	very low
Bricks (fletton)	0.86	medium
Concrete 1:3:6	0.28	low
Aluminium	27	very high
Timber (local)	0.2	low
Timber (imported)	1.4	low
Glass	9.2	medium
Plastics	45	very high

In 1986, realising the unique advantages of the medium and wishing to exploit the rich Gallic tradition of earth construction, the French Housing Ministry invited architects, including Jourda and Perraudin, to design a scheme which would fuse earthen and modern architectural styles, and techniques, into a coherent whole. As a result of this foresight, the housing at Isle d'Abeau, near Lyon, stands as an inspiration for what architectural inventiveness, combined with a respect for tradition, can actually accomplish. The wide breadth and scope of this ground breaking development is quite breathtaking and manages to incorporate rammed earth and concrete houses, timber-sheathed earth walls, earth and brick architecture and a five-storey earthen tower standing defiantly over the landscape.

There is also support available too in France for architects who wish to work with these versatile mediums. These include Craterre, an independent French research organisation, the architecture school at Grenoble, which runs courses on earth construction, and numerous other smaller architectural practices like Centre de Terre, which offer invaluable expertise in the full variety of techniques that are available. Other countries in Europe, like Germany, Denmark and Finland all have examples of contemporary earth architecture and there is renewed interest and research in this field world-wide.

Types of contemporary earth construction

In order to ensure compliance with modern constructional requirements, various techniques have been developed to make the material more durable and water-resistant. For instance, earth is usually tested under laboratory conditions, prior to construction, to determine its composition, especially its water and clay content: the properties that determine its overall strength. If required, strengthening agents called stabilisers – typically lime, pozzolanas, bitumen or cement – are added. The following types of contemporary earth construction are utilised regularly:

Blockwork: In this type of construction earth is formed into blocks or bricks mechanically, and then laid like masonry. The mortar used is made from mud, lime or various mixes of the two combined with cement. The required strength of the mortar depends upon the type of block used. The main disadvantage with this method is the slowness and expense of buying or hiring the necessary plant.

Monolithic: Here earth is poured between vertical shuttering, like concrete, and then compacted mechanically. Although this form of construction is quick and needs very basic equipment, it is inflexible and cannot be altered once built. Both rammed earth and earth block construction require a similar composition of soil, containing clay, silt and gravel in varying proportions.

Secondary: In this type of construction, earth is used in conjunction with other materials like timber, brick or even concrete. Soils that cannot be used for the previous two methods, for instance those containing too much sand or clay, can be used in this way.

Earth building today

Although earth buildings are now generally associated with the vernacular architecture of developing countries, the work of modern architects like Jourda and Perraudin, Mike Reynolds, Nader Khalili, Robert Vint and Glen Murcutt have given this material a new meaning and lease of life. On the continents of North America and Australia, the use of earth has taken on the dimensions of an industrialised building material.

Adobe or unburnt earth brick architecture was imported by the Spanish to the southwestern states of the United States. Today, adobe contractors can be found in the telephone directory as well as in specialised directories and journals. This aesthetic is so popular, that if an individual cannot afford a real adobe construction, a number of firms will dress up an ordinary concrete block house to look like one. However, in the midst of all this, some architects have taken on the task of keeping traditional earth building alive and are currently developing a number of exciting experimental projects.

Mike Reynolds, based near Taos, New Mexico, has been working on 'Earthships': subterranean homes made from used tyres, and other waste materials, filled and plastered with earth. The finished aesthetic is very much inspired by organic architects such as Bruce Goff. The residences recycle water and use electricity from photovoltaic panels making them self-sufficient – hence the generic term Earthship. Clients wishing to live in these houses, enrol in Reynolds' courses and then design and build the majority of the house themselves. While these can be really inexpensive to finish, celebrities such as Dennis Weaver have spent as much as $1,100 per square metre to decorate theirs.

A few hundred miles away in the state of California, Nader Khalili, an Iranian born architect, has transported his native ceramic architecture to the earthquake prone state. He builds domes of earth bricks and then fires them so that the whole structure fuses together like ceramic. These buildings have proved earthquake resistant and been used by the government for emergency shelters. NASA are even developing a project to use this technique on the moon. They are intending to construct domes made of moon dust and then fuse the structure using

solar power – a cost-effective and innovative solution for a site where building materials cannot be imported. Robert Vint, an architect based in Arizona, has formulated a more traditional approach, using lime based mortars and finishes. He learnt his craft from old Native American and Mexican builders, and prides himself on a craft based, meticulously detailed, neo-vernacular style. He has designed residences for celebrities such as Linda Rondstat as well as homes and churches for Native Americans.

Australian builders, on the other hand, have concentrated on rammed earth buildings. Peter Mold, an expatriate builder from Devon who worked on the Globe Theatre in London, has been working with Ramtec, a Melbourne based company. They have been building extensively in Australia, experimenting with different types of earth mixes, limes and incised shuttering; while Glen Murcutt has recently unveiled plans for a building that uses rammed earth walls. Unlike Britain, Australia and the United States have earth building codes.

In Britain, the Plymouth School of Architecture and the Devon Earth Building Association, have started running courses and arranging international conferences aimed at not only reviving the earthen tradition, but also to generate interest in new build. Most of today's contemporary earth architecture appears to have been carried out by designers who have transported, or improvised, building techniques from other places after realising a need. To achieve a popular contemporary architectural style using this traditional material there needs to be more dissemination and sharing of knowledge, more experimentation and, above all, a realisation that earth is not a material of the past.

Sumita Sinha is a chartered architect working and teaching in the field of environmental design, who received the UIA:UNESCO award in 1987 for her work on earthen architecture. She has lived and worked in India, France and the UK, and has contributed to many conferences and publications world-wide.

PAGE 90: The sensuous curves of the Earthship's entrance, casting soft shadows, hide the rough and indelicate waste it is made from – used tyres and cans – under its coat of mud plaster; OPPOSITE, ABOVE: Nader Khalili designed these domed structures in earth bricks and fired them so that the whole structure fused together. The technique is known as geltaftan, the Iranian word that denotes ceramic architecture. They survived the double earthquake of 1992 in California; CENTRE: The earthships are designed to be self-sufficient with photovoltaic panels that generate electricity from solar power and a water and waste recycling system; BELOW: This structure made of used cans and bottles, held together by mud and designed by Mike Reynolds, will become the hub of the Earthship projects Visitors' Centre in Taos, New Mexico; ABOVE: This five-storey rammed earth tower in Isle d'Abeau, near Lyon, France, has looked defiantly over the countryside for more than ten years. The houses next to it are made of earth blocks; CENTRE: Jourda and Perraudin, the well known French practice, designed this dramatic studio house. The massiveness of the rammed earth walls is complemented by the thick concrete columns and contrasts with the delicate roof that sits on them; BELOW: Chalk, mud and even horse hair are used as infill in these timber framed houses situated in the wine producing regions of Dijon, central France

WHEN IS A DOOR NOT A DOOR?
NEIL SPILLER

Our self-satisfied attitude to the inertia of our buildings is becoming untenable. Architects building for the 21st century will have to smarten up. The idea that a new building must respect any urban context will become spurious faced with an architecture of motility. The purpose of this article is to swiftly chart the search for biological mimics and vitalistic architecture; to point out the ground breaking advances in smart material research and to guess some philosophical issues that may emerge.

Once architecture becomes buildable we are compromised by the ignorance of our materials. We have been conditioned by some foolish ideas about building buildings. Consider the brick, its merits, we are told, are its variety of colours, its human scale, its simple jointing methods and its procurement advantages; in fact its merits do not include a capacity to keep water out. The use of brick in building necessitates many preventative methods including damp proof courses and even the provision of another wall 75mm behind to stop water travelling to the inner face and allow space for insulation; a house within a house – a silly idea for the end of the 20th century.

One of the reasons for the proliferation of so called 'paper' architects is the inertia of the materiality of building compared to the dynamic of architectural theory and an ever evolving culture.

Perhaps, before describing two aspects of current technological theory, it might be beneficial to trace the infatuation man has had in trying to mimic biological systems. Some of the first recorded attempts involve the creation of automata. In the third century BC, a craftsman called Yen Shuh is supposed to have invented a mechanical man. This is the first record of the human quest to construct facsimiles of ourselves. Automata have a rich and surreal past. They become analogous to man's search for a mechanistic universe. Stories abound such as the tale of Jacques Vaucanson, who if the hand bills are to be believed, invented life in the guise of a mechanical duck which drank, ate, quacked, splashed about in water and even deposited duck droppings. The Japanese, who would sometimes refer to themselves as the *robotto okaku* (the kingdom of robots), have a distinguished history of automata research dating from the mid 16th century, including erotic automata for hire during the mid 1600s.

In alchemy automata have been used to symbolise man's reconciled existence within nature.

Some alchemic texts talk of the homunculus, an artificial man. The great alchemist philosopher Paracelsus wrote that the beginning of the process for creation of the homunculus is to develop a concoction which includes human semen. It is clear that by this time the creation of human facsimilies was seen, by the alchemists at least, as presenting special issues in relation to man and his integration with nature. The alchemists' homunculus was not intended to be mechanical but biological in some way. They were not interested in cogs, gears and so on but a state of oneness between man and his universe, whether that universe was cosmological or microscopic in scale.

In architecture during the 21st century, biological motifs and forms have been used, as they have in previous centuries, to symbolise an architecture close to and inspired by nature. This practice continued through Art Nouveau via the Bowellist adventures of the 1960s to the search for isotropic space and the movable pod idea, which still exists – all these notions were limited by inert materials.

The quest for biologically informed constructions, whether architecture or artificial intelligence, has a long and mixed history. It has been well known by some that intelligent materials, when they came, would totally alter our understanding of the word 'building' and have a far reaching effect on the human condition. We are on the threshold of this. Function will not be linked to materiality to the extent that it is now. The problem of mimicking large scale biological elements by purely mechanical means has forced experiments to adopt a microscopic scale. It is at this scale that truly responsive systems have to be developed, but adaptations and motions are impossible to control. Perhaps this blockage of thinking has been caused in part by the belief in a mechanised universe. Until recently, advances in material science had been conditioned by hard engineering to developing materials that rejoice in their capacity for inertia: low expansion; low

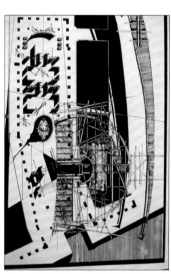

Spiller Farmer research project, 1993; OPPOSITE: Nigel Greenhill, Smart Skin

131

contraction; high impermeability – creating specific materials for different jobs whilst not recognising the multivalence of the biotic sphere as a worthy field of research.

Two recent breakthroughs in smart material technology, will prove to be crucial to architecture, these are Polymer Gels and Nano-Technology. Polymer Gels are less dramatic but definitely important in their consequence. The building industry likes to avoid 'wet' trades; however, in the future all building may well be wet. Gels consist of a series of long polymer molecules and a liquid. The molecular make-up of the liquid, or solvent as it is called, can cause the polymer molecules to expand or contract in a muscular way. Reactions can be caused by varying the levels of pH, intensity of an electric field or temperature, depending on the use of different types of gel and solvents. These gels could be the start of self-sensing and self-regulating 'soft' machines. Experiments have already been successfully conducted that have had gels striking small balls (gel golf or gelf), and edging along a rachetted beam.

The second and perhaps most astounding theoretical development in materials is that of Nano-technology. 'Nano' relies on the, at first amazing yet theoretically possible, idea of developing molecular sized 'factories' (replicators) that would include components such as assemblers, tape readers, chemical processors and a simple computer. In total, these replicator parts would number one billion atoms and be able to self copy itself in 15 minutes, the same rate as bacteria. At the end of ten hours of replicating, 68 billion nano machines could be developed, as the growth would be exponential. These machines could then be used to assemble or reassemble molecular structures, capable of developing any form of molecular arrangement and therefore any material. Each material will then have the ability to transform into any other, providing the raw material atoms are present. This process of raw material provision would be enabled by either growing materials in vats or ducting them in liquid form to the replicators. It is

possible to grow anything in a vat – a rocket engine perhaps!

These chemomechanical systems could herald the dawn of super-smart materials: 'Wetware'. Leaving aside the obvious potential of Nano-technology for rejuvenating the ill and indeed the dead, what does this mean for architecture? It could mean that designs for building will replicate. A building might have a mother, or owners or users could grow new book shelves, floors or walls. Obviously in a nano-building the air would always be fresh. Architecture would be responsive like never before; it might even disappear. Honeymoon couples could grow a new home whilst sunning themselves on a foreign shore, providing a neighbour made sure it did not dry up. Buildings would become conscious – alive. Descartes 'cogito ergo sum' translated by Spinoza as 'I am conscious, therefore I exist' becomes important in relation to the built fabric of our cities. It has recently been said that some apes have the intelligence of a two-year-old child and therefore should be given human rights. In time, buildings will become more intelligent than this: should buildings be given human rights? What of demolition without the building's permission. Is this murder? Or indeed with its permission, is this euthanasia? Perhaps what is needed is a series of laws akin to Assimov's Laws of Robotics which focus around protecting humans, obeying humans and protecting the self in that order of priority. This huge philosophical debate is one that is happening in the scientific community, particularly in reference to Artificial Intelligence, but not in architecture. Architects must research these avenues as architecture is where the philosophical issues of the 'aliveness' of smart materials will become paramount.

Living in a house is not the same as living with your home. When is a door not a door? When it is called Brenda and it is good enough to eat by its own light.

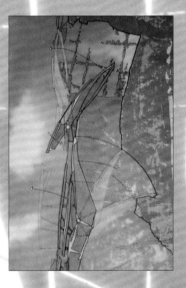

Images from Spiller Farmer research project 1993

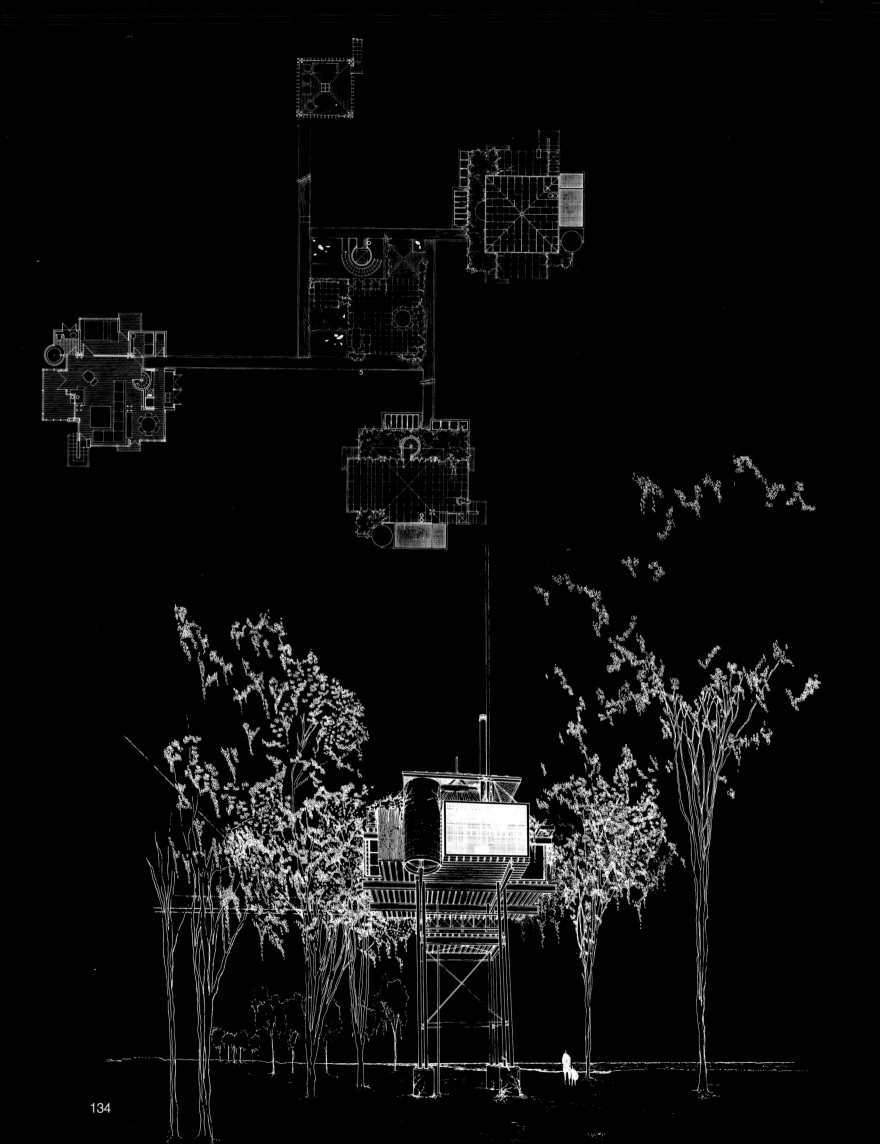

PUGH + SCARPA
TREE HOUSE PROJECT
Lakeland, Florida

The location was the principal inspiration for these four one-bedroom winter homes, each designed for the members of a single family. Adjacent to a lake in a Florida swamp with year-round standing water, the houses are surrounded by mature cypress trees and accessible only by foot on a raised, unpaved path.

Inspired by the Florida Cracker House, both in terms of imagery and energy efficiency, each structure respects the site's environmental fragility and is lifted 7.3 to 9.7 metres above ground level, into and sometimes above the treetops. The steel structures only imprint the site at four points, marking man's intrusion on the site, while the remaining ground plane is organic and unaltered.

Beams and columns are of steel, pile foundations of concrete, and walls and ceilings of timber frame. Other elements include exposed steel, cedar siding, exposed timber beams, and galvanised-metal siding and roof.

OPPOSITE: Plan; sketch; BELOW: Site plan

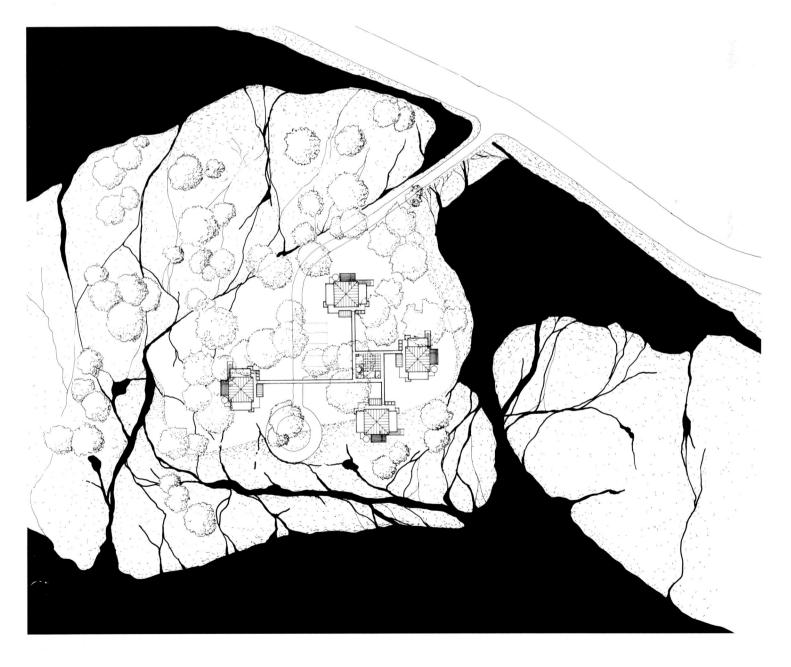

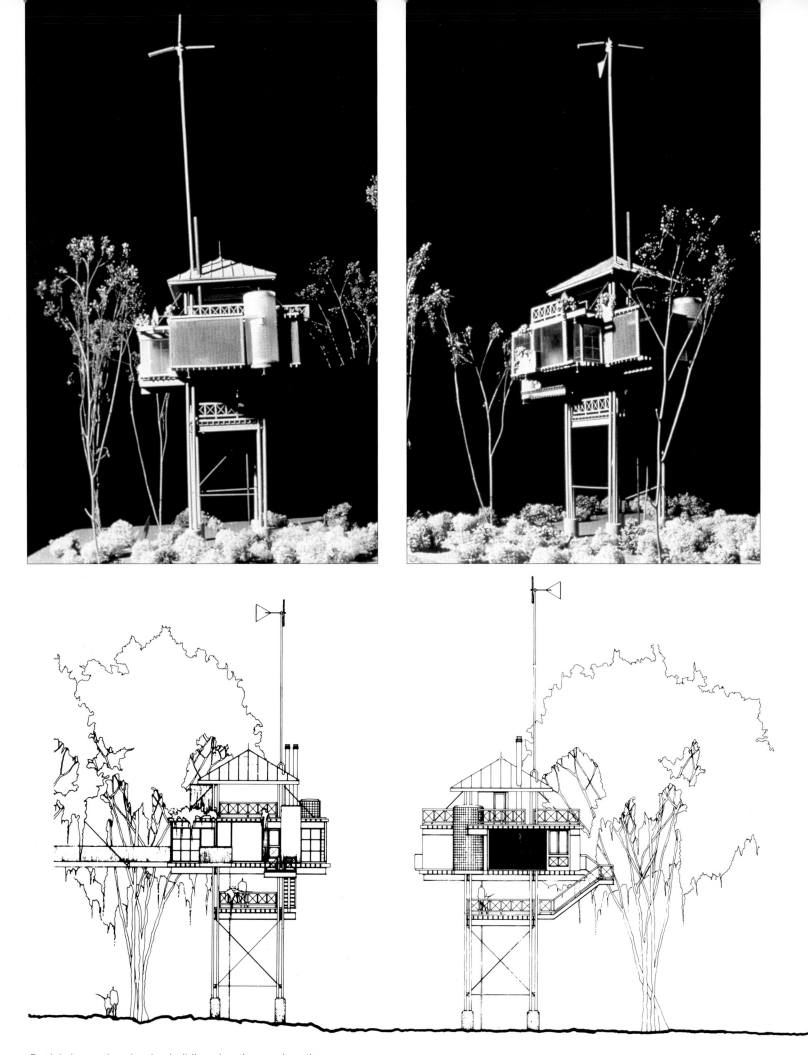

Partial site section showing building elevations and section

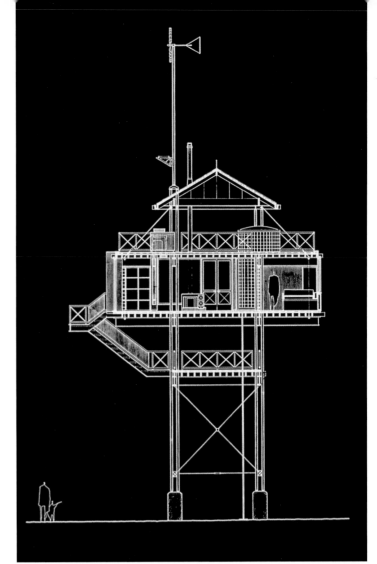

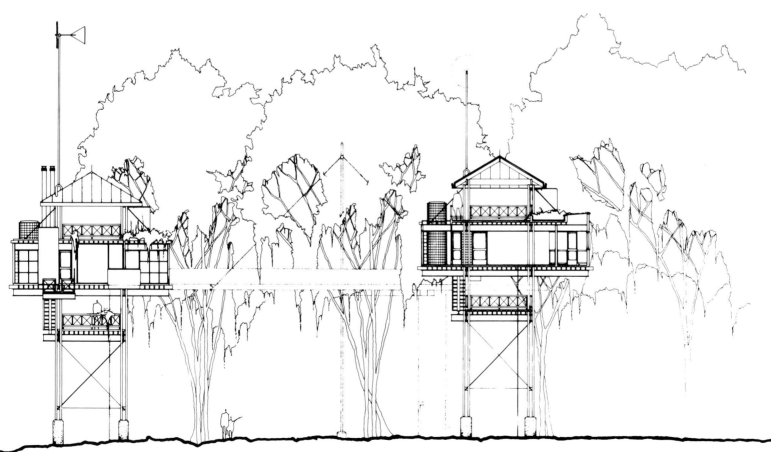

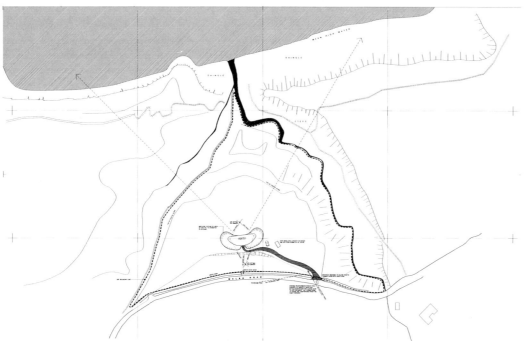

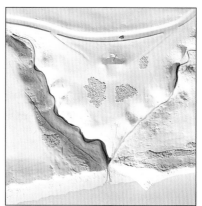

FROM ABOVE: Model view from the sea; site plan; aerial view, model

FUTURE SYSTEMS

PROJECT 222
Druidstone Haven, Wales

The beautiful and dramatic location of this house, set within the Pembrokeshire Coast National Park, was the driving force of the design. The objective of this project (1996) was both to maximise the stunning views of the Welsh coastline and to minimise the visual impact of the building by siting it in a way that makes it appear to be a natural part of the landscape.

The soft, organic form of the house is designed to melt into the rugged grass and gorse landscape, the roof and sides of the house being turfed with local vegetation. Views of the building are thus only of these grasses and the transparent glass walls outlined by a slim stainless-steel rim – an eye overlooking the sea. The surrounding landscape remains untouched, with no visible boundary lines or designated garden area, ensuring the building's organic appearance.

The simple plan is open and informal, reflecting the lifestyle of the clients, with the main seating area arranged around an open log fire. Two free-standing, brightly coloured, prefabricated pods house the bathroom and kitchen services without touching the roof, in order that the space is perceived as a totality. A continuous blockwork retaining wall and steel-ring beam support the roof, eliminating the need for internal columns.

The roof is an aerofoil construction covered with turf. Its curved plywood underbelly creates a soft interior, complementing the organic form of the structure. The house is entirely electrically powered, with under-floor heating elements arranged around the perimeter walls.

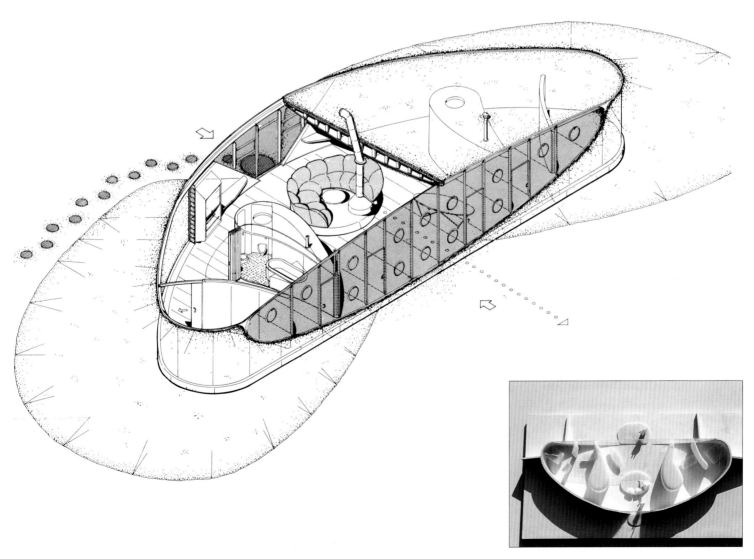

FROM ABOVE: Isometric; model

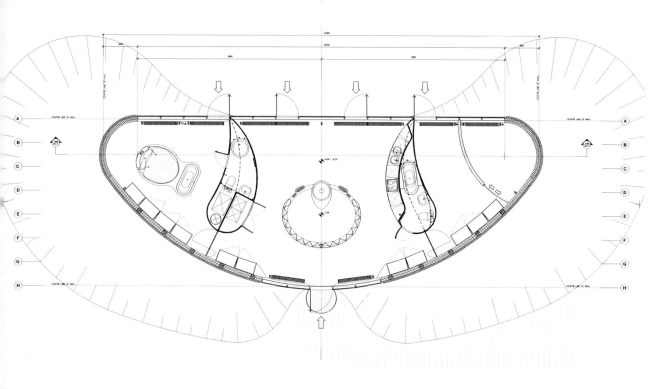

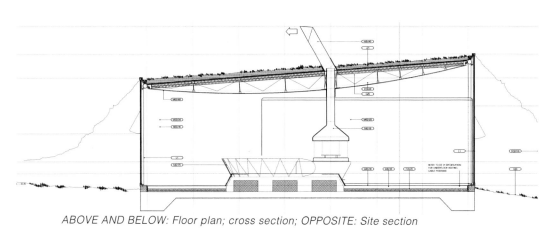

ABOVE AND BELOW: Floor plan; cross section; OPPOSITE: Site section

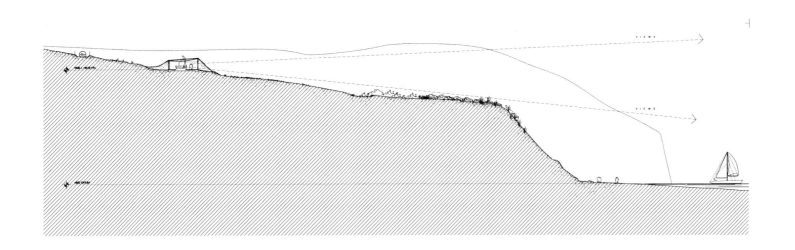

FRANÇOIS ROCHE

VILLA MALRAUX ARTISTS' RESIDENCES AND STUDIOS
Maïdo Road, Reunion Island

Introduction

Sites and territories nurture identities, preconditions and affects that architecture and urbanism have continuously restrained and eradicated. The architectural object, having claimed authority for four centuries,[1] has the power of unparalleled destruction of modernity to maturity. But in so doing it signals its own limits and end.

The numerous 'aesthetic orthodoxies' born in the antechamber of reason and the wastedumps of ideology have now not only become unworkable but are also criminal in their discrepancy with society.

Judging each operation on the validity of hypotheses within an enormous assortment of ever-increasing facts and artefacts is not an easy task. Signs and referents are not pre-given, like a symbolic reference, but have to be discovered in real time, on the 'real site'.

If architecture did not know or could not substitute for the modern culture of breaking-in a culture of place (more attentive to what it was bulldozing), it is because it was already contaminated – a genetic error, in short . . . The horizons of the world of perception, of corporeality and of place have only too rarely been the mediums of production.

Territorialising architecture does not mean cloaking it in the rags of a new fashion or style.[2] Rather, in order that the place gains a social, cultural and aesthetic link,[3] it means inserting it back into what it might have been on the verge of destroying, and extracting the substance of the construction from the landscape (urban or otherwise), whether a physical, corporeal substance within it, or climates, materials, perceptions and affects.

This is not historical regression, nor modern projection, but an attitude that affirms itself by what it doesn't belong to, outlined against a razor's edge, in permanent equilibrium. It is a process that is renewed at each new place, allowing for an *in situ* attitude rather than just another aesthetic code. From that a radical displacement of our function can be born.

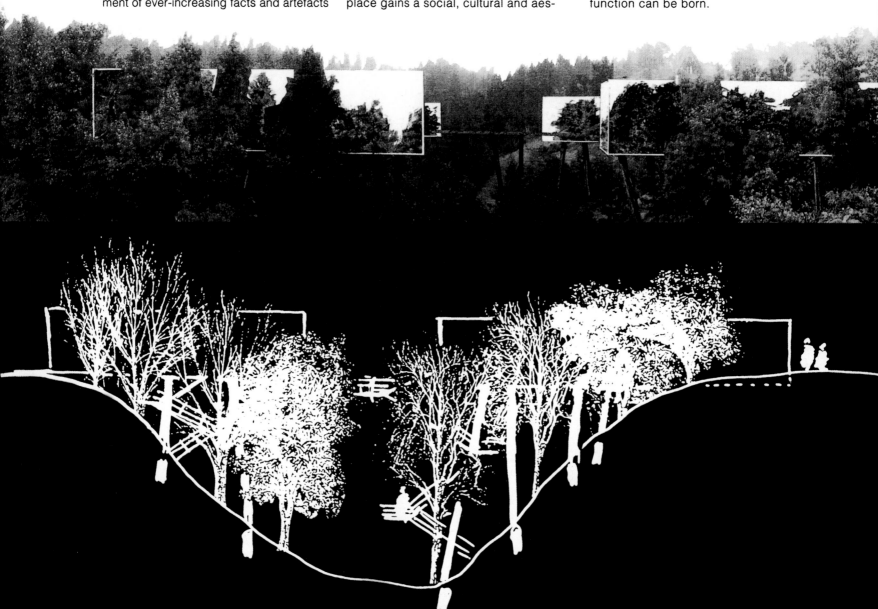

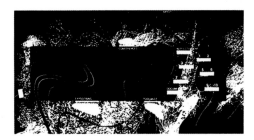

To identify that which characterises a place is already to interpret it and to put forward a way of operating on it. But linking a being to its ecosystem can only save linking the body to the body of architecture. This process of reactive mimesis is not a simulation of the 'exquisite corpse' game, a visual avatar, disappearing and camouflaging itself with an ecological alibi. Its ability to take hold of a territory without subjugating it depends on the unclear identity that develops within it, on the transformation it operates, on the gap of its implementation, on the ambiguity of the network of extraction/transformation that the materials have come from: from a gabion of loose stones to maple foliage, rusted metal to uncut plywood, quarried stone to false wood PVC, apple espaliers to walls of lichen.

This antidote to the separate,[4] autonomous body, this 'live' production process could not operate were it not nourished by these active materials: 'there are the images of materials . . . sight names them and the hand knows them'.[5] In order that these 'barren' propositions do not add, subtract but rather extract, and in order that the object of architecture can spur on the real, like a contorted alterity of the territory in abeyance, we should, perhaps, shift the origins of architectural referents into a precondition that states, 'there is'.

Villa Malraux Artists' Residences, Maïdo Road, Reunion Island

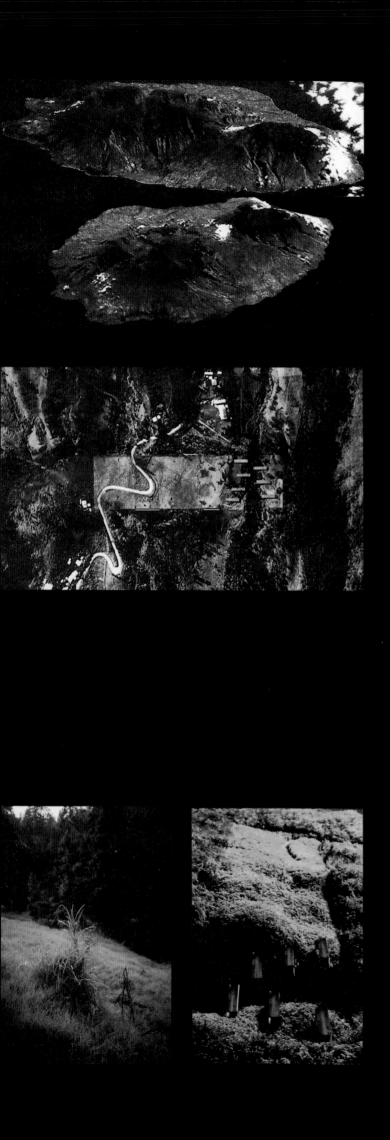

The Maïdo road, from the sea to the peak of the 2,200-metre high Mafate mountain passes an extraordinary sequence of terraces of tropical vegetation: from open dry grassland at 100 metres, sugar cane fields at 300 metres, bamboo ravines at 500 metres, forests of Eucalyptus, cryptomeria plantations, fallow fields of acacia mimosas at 1,000 metres, geraniums and reeds at 1,200 metres, tamarind woods at 1,500 metres, and broom at its peak.

The road offers a perspective of the land, yet at the same time is the agent of its destruction. Halfway up Mafate, at 1,200 metres, lies a clearing. The building is this empty space intensified: an enclosure open to the sky, bordered by cryptomerias, acacia mimosas, the edge of the clearing and a ravine.

The exhibition spaces and public places are developed randomly around the trees, with the clearing's edge bordering them at one side. A large, reflecting clear-plastic wall indicates the building. The cryptomeria trunks perforate the construction, so as not to interrupt the clearing's vegetation. The artists' residences and studios are constructed on stilts, embedded into the trees, their facades of plastic shutters reflecting the tops of the acacias.

The Ti-Jean Garden (landscaped by Gilles Clément) is located at an altitude of 1,500 metres. The entrance is accompanied by micro-facilities on a ravine (eg, cash dispenser services). The design is an extension of the layout of the Villa Malraux.

ROBERT KRONENBURG
EPHEMERAL ARCHITECTURE

The way in which you are and I am, the way in which we humans are on the earth, is dwelling . . .

Martin Heidegger[1]

An accurate definition of the ephemeral is that which lasts for just one day – more commonly we think of ephemeral experiences as transitory ones, though of indeterminate length. It is almost automatic to assume that such fleeting experiences are relatively inconsequential. However, though they may be temporary in duration, their impact can be lasting: the fleeting memory from childhood may become an individual's most potent recollection and its power be such that it helps focus, or destroy, an entire life. It is therefore the power of the experience rather than its duration that is more important in gauging its meaning and effect.

Heidegger believed that anywhere on the earth and under the sky became our dwelling once we became capable of dwelling – the whole of the world became part of our 'inside' space; dwelling did not need buildings to take place. Although the need for architecture springs from the pragmatic need for shelter, once this function has been fulfilled the role of architecture then serves other purposes such as identifying place, belonging and ownership. It is 'dwelling' in this sense to which Heidegger refers. These purposes are concerned with the spiritual part of life rather than the physical and are recognised by the mind and recalled in its memory.

In terms of architecture, even the most ephemeral structure has the power to form a sign that we identify as 'place', which in turn is linked intricately with other powerful concepts of occupation and definitions of territory. As temporary structures were the first forms of architecture to be erected, they have the potential to make a direct connection with every person's ability to make architecture in a way that more complex forms cannot. They also therefore have the power to encapsulate, in the most immediate way, the primal act of building.

The experience of making and remaking architecture is significant, both for those involved and for those watching the process. The erection of a building that takes place over a comfortable attention time-span has more power to be retained in the memory as an event. Temporary structures, built quickly and in connection with a specific occasion, have this intrinsic connection with the establishment of event phenomena, for they tap into essential 'of the day' ephemeral qualities. Such structures appear to have a latent energy encoded within their fabric – when dissembled there is the potential for erection into a usable form; when in use, there is the knowledge that one day soon they may be taken apart.

Portable architecture, made to be erected repetitively, uses forms of construction that are linked most intimately with its essence – in many cases its form is therefore expressive of its structural system, materiality and erection process. It can be argued convincingly that the form and character of these buildings are therefore easier to read for those involved in their operation and use.

The possibility of deconstruction (destruction!), which is inherent in all architecture, inevitably affects the notion of its creation, its use, and the knowledge that eventually it will, in time, fall into disuse. Buildings remain in use because of dedicated acts towards their maintenance and operation. If this system fails or is ignored the building fabric will suffer, eventually beyond effective repair. Unlike the normal course of events in nature, which is self-regenerating, architecture requires direct human action to ensure its continuity. Portable buildings can be perceived as relating more to the cyclic quality of life, for in their destruction lies their ultimate rebirth – the ebb and flow of construction/ destruction, the cycle of 'building/building-in-use/dismantling' reflects the growth/death cycle found in the living world.

The ephemeral qualities that are most easily observed in portable building also have value in buildings meant for continuous use on more permanent sites. These qualities may be utilised in static architecture in order to make it more immediate, more understandable, and more recognisable, and to help accentuate demarcations of place and space for building users. The notion of event in architecture is one which can also be appropriated by architects designing buildings for more permanent functions on a specific site, so that the individual will take note of time and event in their use of the building in ways that allude to the cycle of the day, the seasons, patterns of building use and life. The sensitivity to delicacy and economy of structure and form found in the best lightweight transportable architecture is a valuable tool in expressing the form of any building and the relationship between its space-making and space-generation qualities.

LEFT: Vincent Golding & Azlina Raja Azwa, *Fire Tower and Stair Platform*, 1998, detail; ABOVE: Tom Raymond, *Parliament Tent*, 1997; BELOW, L TO R: Henry Frankish, *Flat Pack Dreadnought*, 1992; Sang Il Hoon, *Rabbit Chariot*, 1997

MARK PRIZEMAN

INTENSITY
Portable Architecture as Parable

Looking down upon the face of the earth, it is only the remains of fixed buildings that survive to tell us of a society's aims. The only physical evidence of the transient and mobile societies are the paths, no different from the tracks of wild animals, that move from one hunting ground to another littered with scattered broken artifacts.

Today this transient architecture continues and the physical evidence is all too easily misunderstood. Like a bicycle pulled from a canal, merely a relic minus a few essential components, it is the act of moving that makes it understandable. The problem with describing portable architecture – be it a fireworks display, rock concert or the army of Genghis Khan – is that no part stays still at the same time as another. The whole edifice is never there long enough to be complete and it is the relationship of one space to another that has to be understood, after all.

It is in the transition from hunter gatherer to farmer that the origins of architecture are based. The remnants of the nomadic soul are the basic language of the historical forms of architecture. The bound reeds and vegetative decoration that are the coded ingredients of Ancient Egyptian, Mesopotamian, Mayan, Chinese, Greek, or whatever, telling us a cogent hierarchical story. Perhaps a clearer way of understanding the power of architecture is to start with the nomad placing portable structures in a variety of special places with due regard to the context and climate – the ability to adapt and lead one's life free from the requirement to leave physical evidence of it.

Nomads in their wanderings over the face of the earth consider the landscape as common territory and do not seek to leave their mark upon its face. The essentially all-pervading nature of the nomad's life (Berbers, gypsies, travellers, etc) that so annoys current governments is the same gadfly that so upset the ancient Greeks and their concept of citizenship. The restless urge to wander over the face of the Earth through an ever changing scenery, without altering it or possessing it, is anathema to the prescribed rules of civilisation. The punishment of landscape by architecture is as old as Ozymandias, but the nomad accommodates the natural features of mountains and streams in architecture, noting their relative placement and imbuing them with cosmic powers, much as the rooms in a temple. The ability to disappear and leave no trace is a common theme and one which volume house builders should be reminded of. But then real architecture nowadays is to do with having a fashionable sense of soul, or is it style?

The direct link from the nomad's yurt to Modernism is by way of Le Corbusier. His direct observations in his 'Journey to the East' are poignant: on seeing the Turkish houses stacked up the hills in Bosnia and Constantinople he conceived the tower block. The traditional Turkish house consists of a number of self-contained square rooms (*Odas*) which are derived generically and functionally from the open-plan yurt, organised around an open area (*Sofa*) which links the *Odas*. The arrangement of the

*FROM ABOVE: Alice Tang, Snail Stair, 1997;
Greg Sheng, Feng Shui non-aligning Tent, 1996;
Paris Sargolis, Wind powered Wheelbarrow*

houses up the hills allows a sense of privacy, while providing each house with a clear view over the neighbouring dwellings. If you imagine this stacked situation with the hill removed you are left with the Unité de Habitation.

The Tent Project, run by First Year Unit 3 at the Architectural Association in London for the past 11 years, has a variety of ancestors, living relations and disparate offspring. It was started in 1987 as a response to the then First Year Technical Study requirement for students to execute in the AA workshop a full-size detail of one of their designs for a building. The concept was to both introduce students to an understanding of the physical craft involved in architecture and illustrate that the detail of a building could contain the ethos of the whole.

The Tent Project takes the idea further by constructing a complete building: an individual's first building that has to perform within a group, the ethos of the whole then being truly reflected in the details. These details are all connected with the essential requirement of portability. Due to its longevity the project has started to display evidence of evolution and divergence. To spend a cold night in a futuristic structure made using essentially Medieval methods of construction is a test of the integrity of the design to reach a satisfactory resolution. Eleven years later the project has evolved within the changing academic context of the AA; the argument between whether a drawing is derived from the object or whether it is the drawing that should determine the result.

Conventionally, architects are taught that what they draw is what will happen. This is a very foolish handicap to be blighted with since it leads either to banality or loss of control once something is constructed. The success of a tent depends on the exploration of an idea in the workshop by wandering through the dream and not being restricted by the finite parameters of a drawn representation of the future object. So learning how to control the gestation of an idea by full involvement with its manufacture is achieved by using drawings as calculations. The resolution of the projects in drawn form happens only after the tents have been tested and includes descriptions of the events surrounding this occasion.

The request to spend a night in something that you have made appeals to the primal urge in us to make a house. Moreover, it is not a difficult task to make in a couple of hours something that will keep you warm and dry in inclement weather: tramps, soldiers and hunters all manage quite sufficiently. It is the idea that a combined collection of structures will form a settlement or miniature instant city that provides the inspiration to push the programme further. The tents have to be capable of being transported to a field and erected easily in the cold darkness of the English countryside in mid winter. The Unit is then thrown back on its own resources and demands the mutual cooperation of members to exist. Like explorers planning to venture into the unknown, an ability to imagine the consequences of what one takes and what one leaves behind is imperative.

A budget of £50 to £70 for materials for the Tent Project limits the indulgence of an idea and encourages a hungry eye for the opportune. Methods of construction are not prescribed and new ways are often chanced upon during the construction process, or are developed from the experiences of previous expeditions. Sponsorship, salvage and recycling all play their part. An agenda or manifesto is drawn-up to focus the investigations. New and untested possibilities often arise from the use of unfamiliar combinations of materials. Seminars are given by people working commercially at the forefront of manufacturing skills; for example, furniture makers, fashion designers and alternative research labs.

Making things in an almost Medieval manner and discovering techniques and methods in a hands-on improvisational way is a major design tool. If you do not know exactly how something is to be made intuition needs to be employed, and chance to force progress in realising the structure. A feel for materials and how they misbehave is only learnt by direct experience. The preconceptions of strength and weight become very abstract concepts and are replaced by an attitude of perfecting a method.

The workshop at the AA is equipped with wood and metal working equipment in a room measuring 6 x 20 metres. An enclosed yard suffices for trial erection and other techniques. The structures are then packed into a van and taken on a four-hour journey into the isolated countryside. Dark is usually setting in by the time the various components are unpacked, and the first structures to be assembled are those which have foreseen this occasion and can accommodate extra recumbents.

Each structure has its chosen social function and location within the unit's notional 'instant village'. These are first presented as 1:20 sketch models arranged in an imagined site around a central fire chalked out on the studio floor. In addition to the primal requirement of shelter, each tent had to provide a service for the community as a whole. Each year's selection contains the reworkings of some previous themes of Tower, Observation Platform, Shell Structure, Space Frame, Zoomorphic Shelter and good plain Service to the Community Tent. Eventually, shelter can be challenged. Pontus Brushwitz's 1992 Observation Tower started a cycle of proposals; subsequently also fertilised by the 1994 Machine Project.

In attempting to catalogue the projects we find similarities and affinities of, as yet, untold stories that will need to be with each other on that silent hill witnessing the fall of architecture in the valleys below.

Once on site, the weather and the landscape dominate and it is the responsibility of the group to pitch their structures in a manner that justifies the previous months' effort. By being in the field with the tents, one participates in a performance where everybody thinks that they know their lines and are disparately making others listen. It is the antithesis of suburbanisation, the industrial reconciliation with nature where the rules of civilisation

kill what is ugly. For it is in the field that one is literally 'left alone to one's own devices'. When all has passed and these devices are all but destroyed by the passing of time, they are left to inform the next generation with exaggerated tales of success and disaster. Erecting a structure on an isolated hillside and looking out at the twinkling evidence of the rapid descent of England into suburbanisation, one cannot help but think about how this inversion of territory and abuse of landscape has come about and how much one is participating in the situation.

The individual tent is seen only as a fragment, or component within a four-day event which has bound them together to make something else. They are no longer seen as isolated projects, set like advertisements within the beautiful setting. The community formed by the unit on the site is an unpredictable artifact that generates a common experience against which the structure is tested. The structures react and respond to the situation in a spontaneous manner. It is the more successful of these projects that later reflect on this chance collage of dreams on a landscape.

The photographs illustrate this particular moment in the project, that of the improvised setting of a structure against a landscape – as in all the best Westerns where the simple device of setting simple actions against monumental scenery evokes a heroism in even the most trivial domestic scene. It is perhaps part of the lesson that all bad architecture seeks to repress this montage of scales, for it is the simple everyday tasks of shelter and community that these edifices seek to provide. Like the 'benders' being inhabited at the same time 20 or so miles away by the protesters at the bypass, the relatively simple and crude methods of manufacturing could seek to test certain ideas of scale, presence and function in the English landscape.

It is an initial concept that is allowed to dream and grow that can accommodate the details for true portability. A selection of disparate unconnected objects from a museum feeds the initial reaction to the brief, for it is the manner in which something is made, the soul within that needs to be understood. Railway engines, boats and aeroplanes have evolved along similar lines yet their souls are as different as the elements through which they travel. The smoke-box door on a steam train is a facade of cast iron that speaks of the weight of all behind it; the hinges, solid expressive elements. The nose cone of Concorde is a casting of Araldite resin which droops to distinguish itself from other inferior modes of transport. The forming and steaming of green timbers make the hull of a ship of the line resplendent with its decorated stern.

Assembly details are a crucial element in the development of these structures as they should rely only on themselves for the best effect. The experimental 'Wooller' British motorcycle was an attempt to make a motorcycle that did not require any tools to maintain it. Using parts of the initial disassembly as tools for the next stages, speed of assembly, or the performance of assembly, are all considerations come to bear. A nomad uses what is to

ABOVE, L TO R: Takako, Polypropylene Slug, 1996; Lena Nalbach, Horse, 1996; David Lau, Maze, 1998; Yuka Suganami, Lycra Playroom, 1998; CENTRE, L TO R: Paul Mascaro, Gaudí Kitchen; Vincent Golding and Azlina Raja Azwa, Fire Tower and Stair Platform, 1998; Lena Nalbach, Horse, 1996; Vincent Golding and Azlina Raja Azwa, Fire Tower and Stair Platform, 1998; BELOW LEFT: Yoichiro Akiba, Thatched Ropeway, 1998; BACKGROUND: Yuka Suganami, Lycra Playroom, 1998, detail

FROM ABOVE, L TO R: Morten Bille Jorgensen, Steel Cathedral, 1998; Dimitrios Tsigos, Merry Go Round, 1998; Azlina Raja Azwa, Staircase/ Platform, 1998; Il Hoon Roh, Surveillance Centre, 1998; Asaf Mayer, Tensegrity Pod, 1998; Il Hoon Roh, Surveillance Centre, 1998

hand and able to be replaced or adapted, animal and vegetable sources that can be replenished with only the labour of processing (gleaning\refining) as the moderator. Neat, efficient joints that do not leave the maker groping for nuts in wet grass with a torch grace many of the more successful projects.

The loss of control of the destiny of one's work through a compression of time and situation gives all the more credence to how it is recorded. The unexpected failure, loss or damage of a part should encourage improvisation and invention (if only for a decent photograph!). Mapping of the event using symbols to describe change and the passage of time reveals aspects of the community that could have been foreseen; structural failures, convenient improvisations and the contributions of curious visitors staying for a night or two.

After this stage, the question is how to draw up the structures orthogonally and describe the event for the 'folio'. However, the drawings never quite acknowledge the simple poetic reality of things like gaffer tape wrapped wantonly about a sleeping cocoon as a makeshift repair, or the dusting of snow over a stained canvas hammock; but then it is the dream that is being drafted. Drawing what one knows, after the event, is often harder than drawing what one thinks one knows before. However, there are things that only drawings can capture: like the relationship between a group of first-year architectural students on a hillside and the possible futures that could have occurred.

The military establishment, comprising the most technically advanced nomads, is apocryphal in this role, re-inventing and driving forward technology behind a mask of implacable conservatism. Meticulously recording their history in image, symbol and word, the sergeants' and corporals' stripes in the army originate from the award given by the lord of the manor of a pair of cruck frames to build a cottage – the simplest form of shelter recorded on the sleeves of those given a role beyond simple serf.

The requirements of the project have much to do with developing an ability to explore the ramifications of making an idea physical, and potentially functional, in a previously unknown site that by inhabitation becomes extremely well known and tempered. The Object in The Landscape projects often seek to draw some inference from the site as a way of justifying their presence upon the site. This may be indicative of the modern dilemma concerned with context and the acknowledgement of a pre-existing set of architectural rules. It also harks back to the architect's mythical freedom to build and design in isolation, like a pioneer staking his claim in foreign lands. The nomad pitching up takes stock of the context and follows a portable set of rules or traditions. The difference occurs when one is merely the author of a fragment of the perceived whole and is not in such idealised control of the destiny of one's contribution, nor conversant with the improvised etiquette of the society that will use it. Like all real cities, this is perhaps where chance and time are the real planners.

This points to the real difference between architecture and sculpture. The molestation and layering that a work of architecture both performs and withstands is unacceptable to the mind of the sculptor. So the very nature of the tents' failings is their strength: the hidden stories of unfulfilled ambition resulting from lack of time or finance, and the unexpected uses to which the components can be redirected, create a genuine scene upon a site.

The nomad is bound by the seemingly fixed horizon of his tradition and uses invention as a way to survive starvation. Cro-Magnon man was over 6 feet tall and lived a hunter gatherer way of life, drawing from the resources at hand. It is only the limited diet of the agricultural-based societies that gave us shorter physiques. The change of diet in developing industrial cultures determines the hunter gatherer's stature, but the architecture still suffers the unyielding and fixed strictures of the settler, turning tradition into stone

The Industrial Revolution created a new role for architecture, which was perceived as being terrible and destructive. In the wake of the rapid and all-consuming power of production, the tenets of the Renaissance exploded; religion limping along behind. The factory/office became a temple to the God of Mammon and large chunks of the population were housed in vast cities laid out as scientific justifications for the above. These are all reasons that we now live in a post-industrial age in which architecture lacks the vigour to express a communal poetic relationship with the landscape and allow the individual to journey through it. Architecture can only now reflect the individual's soul and its reading of the world as subject matter. If that soul has no reading then so much the better, for then we can build banal mass-produced reproductions of copies that merely serve to decorate the function of comfort, but with no joy.

Guilt for the change wrought by society upon itself still has little effect in aesthetic policy beyond a concern for the remnants of the American tribes and the Aborigines' humiliation. Travellers and road protesters may still attempt to readdress the balance by reminding us of the importance of landscape and the differences between the routes people may choose to pass along, but essentially the concept of uncontrolled movement is anathema to subtopian society.

Another by-product of industrial mass production and release of labour from the drudgery of making life a matter of survival is the opportunity to make mistakes from experiments: the ability to combine an ever changing array of ingredients to realise any ambition that imagination can make understandable. The Trade Fair and Exposition are examples of occasions when the joy and excitement of structure and programme can be explored. The Crystal Palace and the Festival of Britain, respectively positioned at the blossoming and at the decline of this country's industrial history, sought to express the vigour of technology with a cultural re-examination, to produce situations in which architecture could return to its roots as a reflective mirror of society's beliefs. It is important that the savagery of imagination, too, is not tamed.

The experiments carried out by the students of Unit 3 attempt to bear this out in their application of an imagined future situation (camping in February in English open countryside), with a flexible range of skills and materials available. The imagination of expressing a structural concept is where the individual flavour of the structures shown begins to make the architecture. The possible combinations of the structures, with an urban arrangement in mind, give an uncertain aspect to the eventual placement. The imagination has to be as flexible as the structure is portable, and there is the crux of the dilemma. The intelligence to survive on the move is not judged by physical death, as in the past, but by the public reception of the image it beholds. In reality, the product is of a crude hand-crafted, thrown-together nature on close inspection; but it is one that, regardless, realises the full plethora of architectural potential.

ABOVE: Mobile Home for Kröller Müller, 1995; BELOW: La Bais-o-Drôme, *1995*

JOEP VAN LIESHOUT
In Conversation with Klaar van de Lippe

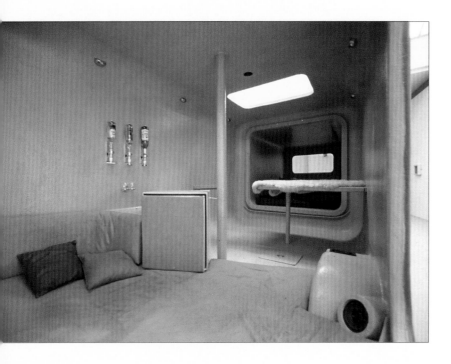

Rotterdam-based Atelier van Lieshout was established in 1995 by the artist Joep van Lieshout (born in Ravenstein, 1963), after he gained, in collaboration with the acclaimed architect Rem Koolhaas, international recognition for the design of several bars and sanitary units for the prestigious Grand Palais in Lille (1994). The artist is currently working on another project with Koolhaas to convert a former bank on 43rd street in downtown Manhattan into a theatre.

Perhaps Van Lieshout's most charismatic work is the creation of a series of provocative mobile homes – *La Bais-o-Drôme, Survival Unit Autocrat,* and *Modular House Mobile* – which have inhabited art galleries and roadsides in Cologne, Rotterdam, Reykjavik, Paris, New York, Los Angeles and Winnipeg. Although these trailers do contain pragmatic conveniences, such as toilets, sinks and kitchens, the interiors and exteriors also communicate exotic and romantic ideas about the possibilities for a portable dream home with fur-lined or slick and shiny spaces. The mobile homes are just a part of Van Lieshout's output, which ranges from furniture design to sculpture and environmental installations.

Klaar van de Lippe is an artist and collaborator in Atelier van Lieshout.

Klaar van de Lippe: In your earlier work with crates, and later the furniture, you operated a strict system of measurement. The work was founded on a rigid concept, although very physical in terms of the colours you used and the polyester material. The conceptual aspect now seems to be more a thing of the past. What you're currently making is more organic, more sensitive?

Joep van Lieshout: Yes.

KL: Was this conceptual aspect of your furniture perhaps more based on the production side than on aesthetic conviction?

JL: Hmm.

KL: You first worked under your own name, but some time ago changed it to Atelier van Lieshout. Is the creativity now collective?

JL: Sometimes.

KL: How does it work? Is it an *atelier* in the same sense as the old-fashioned artist's atelier?

JL: Yes.

KL: Thank you. Ah! So the house rules, turn up on time etc, they're the general rules, and then there are the job allocations. Everyone has their own assignment . . . I've got it. And you're the boss?

JL: Yes.

KL: Your own work, or the team's work, is bought by all and sundry and has a practical use as well as being exhibited as art. Do you rate one higher than the other?

JL: Hmm, hmm.

KL: So, is it more a question of people enjoying it?

JL: Yes.

KL: But to keep the business rolling, you must need to earn a lot of money. OK, so in principle you don't make a distinction between art and artifact – does that extend your potential market considerably . . . ?

JL: Yes.

KL: So this lack of distinction has a purely practical side?

JL: Yes.

KL: The things you make are getting bigger and bigger. First it was furniture, then baths and bathrooms, followed by diminutive houses and mobile homes. It will probably be proper houses and buildings next. If someone asked you to construct a building, a prison for instance, would the answer probably be . . . ?

JL: Yes.

KL: There used to be two clear sides: the strict side and the pricks. Let's say the rational and the irrational. I now see more of a mixture. The phalluses are still there, but even the strict things have become more organic. Take the skullrooms, for instance: intuition, desires, and even passions now seem more prominent – are these more important than severe concepts and intellectual reasoning?

JL: Yes.

KL: Yet your/the team's way of working is not woolly. The production methods are, in fact, extremely efficient. There is actually a dichotomy there – I would almost say a romantic capitalist or a practical utopian . . . are you laughing because you're pleased?

JL: Ha, ha, ha!

KL: There is an increasing drive towards autarky: to be self-sufficient, independent. That could be something purely pragmatic, but it could also be an idea that can be taken further; like, for instance, some of those religious sects – the Shakers, for example, whose ideology set them apart. Are you driven by any sort of political or religious conviction?

JL: No.

KL: So the fact that you make your own medicines, bottle your own vegetables, make your own machines – that's all driven by one idea: independence?

JL: Yes.

KL: There is no underlying, larger world-view? There is nothing that you absolutely accept or reject? In fact, you have no morals?

JL: Yes.

KL: That explains a lot of things, because I'm now eating a home-made sausage, from your own slaughtered free-range pigs, as well as some superb bottled vegetables. Very healthy. But you are also plying me with lots of your home-distilled pear brandy.

JL: Delicious isn't it?

KL: These drawings I'm looking at, of factories and machines and all sorts of people at work; sort of settlements, communes . . . only women seem to be working there. Oh no! I can spot a man over there. Are these drawings part of some kind of masterplan? A vision of the future?

JL: [?]

KL: I can't quite figure out whether you are planning one day to live in the kind of community shown in the drawings. I see it more as a romantic ideal than a concrete plan, although you also make guns: that really is for real. Hmm . . . it looks as though you would like to set up your own state; almost as though you're wanting to transform the proverbial artist's individuality from a *state of mind* into a literal *state of being*. Am I right in feeling that?

JL: Yes.

KL: I am suddenly reminded of your early work, when you were still at the academy. You copied Machiavelli's *The Prince* and took photos of yourself as a sad ruler. Has that drive to have your own domain always been there?

JL: [. . .]

KL: What about those huge beds you're making, and all that polygamy: is that serious? Is it also part of your masterplan?

JL: Yes.

KL: The sexual element is right at the centre; almost as a mainspring, a sort of creative power . . . ?

JL: Yes.

KL: But what dimension does that inhabit? Does love also play a part? Is there also a Guinevere, a woman you love and for whom you fight?

JL: [. . .]

KL: Or does it all revolve round lust? Lust with a capital L?

JL: [. . .]

KL: Can I take some elixir with me later?

JL: Yes.

KL: Give me the one for uneasiness and vague premonitions, the *sedative tincture*.

March 1998, Rotterdam.

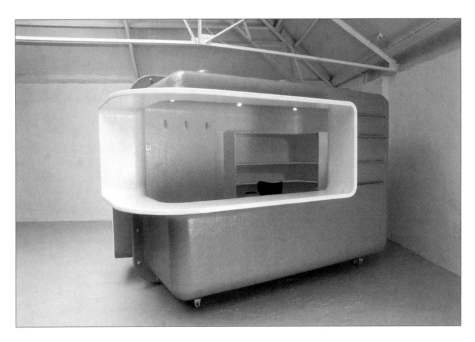

FROM ABOVE: Castmobile, Tilburg, 1996; Information Stand, Aalborg, 1996; Reception Unit, Zürich, 1996

GILLIAN HORN
EVERYDAY IN THE LIFE OF A CARAVAN

The image of row upon row of shiny boxes hugging the landscape is a familiar one across Britain. Rural, seaside or post-industrial, the pattern is the same: a glimmering plateau of roofs that hover ten feet above the ground. Hundreds of thousands of caravans[1] huddled together in holiday caravan parks form these landscape blankets which, through their proliferation, may well seem commonplace and ordinary.

The caravan park is perhaps exemplary of the *everyday*: its caravans mass-produced with cheap materials, low technology and largely unskilled labour; its owners and users predominately working- and lower-middle-class couples and families; and its facilities unpretentious and unexceptional in their planning and landscaping. From the gnomes and busy lizzies around their borders to their chintz and wipe-down, wood-look interiors, caravans, their parks and inhabitants, must surely be the epitome of the everyday in our constructed environment.

Unaspiring, unglamorous and unwelcome in our upwardly mobile communities, the caravan is treated with little more than disdain. Why is it that caravans are so consistently denigrated by the middle classes? Why do they have no status, allure, or cultural value to us? Why do we dismiss them as common and everyday? I would argue that, under closer scrutiny, the caravan reveals itself as a far from ordinary dwelling and the caravan park as an extraordinary place; a place where people escape from the everyday and reinvent it as a realised fantasy.

The status of the caravan holiday home is an ambiguous one: it is used like a home but not as home and although it feels like a home it doesn't look like one. Neither vehicle nor house, yet transportable and habitable, the caravan falls between the 'mobile' and 'home' of its namesake. Even its terminology is indeterminate: caravan, mobile home, static, holiday home and leisure home all describe the corrugated aluminium or plastic clad prefabricated unit that sits on a steel chassis two feet off the ground, revealing the incongruously small wheels which mark its identity and signify its ambiguity.

It is the flickering sense of 'home' captured in the caravan which lends it its particular qualities. The caravan is like a toy; a discrete box with openings through which you can see life-sized domestic interiors that have somehow been squeezed into its unyielding case. There is a thinness about caravans which is both literal and metaphorical; the interiors are the stage sets of home, with images of homeliness veneered onto every surface.[2]

There is a discernible formula behind the caravan interior founded on iconic images of home which are grafted together to form a ready-made house-set: a distillation of the domestic suburban interior. The living/dining area centres around the hearth with display mantel, TV stand and book/knick-knack shelf. To one side of this core is a glass-doored, perhaps even mirror-backed, drinks/ornament display cabinet and to the other is a framed or flute-edged mirror. The caravan interior is dominated by the presence of a large bay window at the end of the living

area, recalling the archetypal suburban home. Built-in, soft seating with warm patterned covers wraps around this bay which occupies the entire width of the caravan, exaggerating the sense of space. The aluminium windows are netted and framed by heavy curtains and pelmets, colour co-ordinated with the upholstery. The master bedroom boasts a vanity unit with fitted, decorative mirror, shelves and fitted cupboards. The kitchen comes with full-sized appliances with tile-effect vinyl covering the visible floor and wall surfaces. Elsewhere, fitted carpets and patterned wallpaper-effect walls complete the ensemble.

Emphasis is given to these homely constructs through their relative scale to the actual size of the interior – the footprint of a six-berth caravan can be as small as 27 square metres – with not a square inch of surface left unstyled or referentially ambiguous. These features become exaggerated in the compact space creating an appearance of home that seems both more ideal and more tangible than home itself, whose associations with the ideal have become lost in the everyday realities of home life.

There is a sense of the uncanny in the caravan that extends beyond its resonance with 'the unhomely' (the literal translation of *das Unheimliche*). The holiday caravan is more of a satellite addition to the home than a substitute for it, but it is enough like home to throw into question the very identity and value of what 'home' is. The caravan works like a Freudian double to the home.[3] The caravan's theatrical projection of homeliness creates a superficial reflection of its source, the home, and through this discordant familiarity throws suspicion on the security of the home ideal. This effect destabilises the myth of the home as a protected place of retreat that enables a return to a state of satiated need. It exposes the home itself as a substitute, rather than source, for a desired state of unity; in playing with the culturally ingrained symbols, ideals and dictates of behaviour associated with home, the caravan thus poses a threat to the validity of the myth of the home by exposing it as such.

Whilst the caravan interior is directly modelled on the generic, suburban home interior, the exterior makes no gesture towards the imagery or associated ideologies of the suburban house. Unlike the suburban house which can be read as an integrated facet of an articulated streetscape, the caravan is a dislocated object in the uninterrupted landscape of the caravan park. The dichotomy of the veneered, home-narrative construction of the interior to the pared down, no-frills vehicular narrative of the exterior is extreme. No attempt is made on the exterior to disguise the physical reality of the caravan. Nor is there any attempt to assume a house-like identity in its description; caravans are all sold and referred to by their exterior dimensions (in feet) which are inscribed on the cladding. Whereas the interior of the caravan exposes ideals and collective assumptions about the physical and ideological nature of home through its intentional, motivated similarities, the exterior reveals some of the inherent assumptions in our ideological constructions of 'house', 'home' and 'community' in its radical departure from them.

The signification of the house as the *real* home is made apparent in the exterior treatment of residential park homes in comparison to their second cousin, the caravan. Park homes, sold and sited for year-round living as primary residences, are essentially caravans that are dressed up to look like homes from the outside, rather than merely fitted out to feel like homes inside. Their pitched roofs, textured render walls and brick skirts all imply permanence on the site and an outward image of a secure home. For these everyday homes, mobility and temporality are disguised and denied, redolent as they are with associations of transience, instability, gypsies and social outcasts, in an attempt to display idealised virtues of stability, stasis and permanence that are deemed to be implicit within the typology of the suburban house. This identification with the grounding of the house signals a desire to belong in society and can be read as a gesture towards accepting its codes for belonging.

The interior layout of the caravan is arranged under the orthodox principle that separates private sleeping and washing areas from more open, cooking, dining and socialising areas. Although these boundaries are less rigid in the compact space of the caravan than in the conventional home, the established hierarchies of privacy are accepted. The siting of the caravan within the park, however, radically departs from these conventions and bears little relation to its suburban counterpart. Between the street and the suburban house, there is a sequence of thresholds leading from the public road, kerb and pavement to the semi-public fence, gate, path and drive to the semi-private planted border, garage, porch, doormat and solid front door. This serves to establish the physical and psychological detachment and privacy of the suburban home. In the caravan park, however, the physical boundaries tend to lie only at the site perimeter. There are rarely any material boundaries separating the caravans, or designating their proprietal limits, other than an access road, some occasional planting and the caravans themselves. Nor is there the elaborate sequence of barriers that, in a suburban house, serves to protect the domain of the home. In the caravan park these codes of ownership and separation are reduced to Tarmac strip, swathe of grass (*not* lawn), perimeter planting around the caravan and steps up to a plain glass door. Each caravan has its own territory for which it is responsible, but this area is not marked, with the effect that the control and codes of this territory become blurred and its boundaries become socially respected rather than physically enforced.

This dissolution of boundaries within the caravan park has the further effect of merging the positing, and protocols, of 'fronts' and 'backs' in and around the caravan. The distinction of 'front' and 'back' dominates the pattern of conventional housing in which the front garden, used for public display (of taste, order, wealth), is separated by the house from the back garden, used for private occupation. In turn, the front of the house, through its

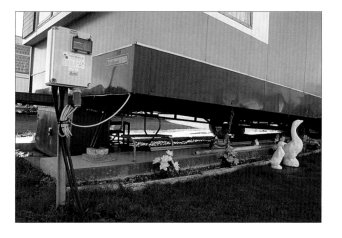

FROM ABOVE: Caravan park in Essex; caravans in a Kent caravan park; caravan undercroft

Living area of Atlas' Status Super caravan, 1997

Living area of ABI Leisure Homes' Montrose caravan, 1997

Living area of Cosalt Holiday Homes' Monaco Super caravan, 1997

weighted balance of wall to window, offers privacy for those within whilst maintaining the opportunity to observe those without, and the back of the house, protected by the buffer of the private garden, can afford to open and extend the home outside. In the caravan park, however, there are no front gardens for show and back gardens for (secret) pleasure; no front doors for visitors and back doors for family. Instead there are areas of occupation which are inhabited according to the orientation of each caravan on its pitch and the relative positions of neighbours, cars and sun. Deck chairs, plastic tables and cars all assume equivalence as accessories to the caravan park landscape.

It appears that the whole caravan park is a 'back', the boundary and formality of 'fronts' beginning at the park entrance, the threshold to the everyday, 'real' world. In the backyard of the site, the usual guards of the occupants waiver and their sense of propriety shifts. People live out what is commonly considered to be a nostalgic ideal of community: friendly, connected and informal. Weekend or holiday lives become what people would like their everyday lives to be, but it precisely because caravan life is not *every*day life that this fantasy is made possible.

In bringing the act of living out an imaginary everyday closer to its ideal, the caravan becomes more homely, in its lived experience, than the home itself. The caravan thereby transcends its role as a mere symbol of homeliness and takes on the function of a reality. In effect, through this shift in the status of the imaginary and reality, the 'real' home becomes secondary to the 'fantasy' home of the caravan. Indeed, its invisible presence becomes a critical support to the realigned set of relationships. By virtue of negotiating the balance between reality and illusion, the ordinary and extraordinary, such a fantasy of the everyday is able to be constructed and lived out in caravan parks.

Caravan parks are generally only open for nine months of the year, so it is assumed, and more often is the case, that the occupants all have 'real' homes elsewhere. The assumption that there is, out of view, a conventional property sited in a conventional community, following its conventional codes, is critical to the success of the reality of the caravan park community. The presence of an absent double to the caravan allows the necessary freedom, within the park, to detach from the stringent assessments which we use to form our 'real', but in effect mythical, communities outside.[4] These so-called communities are based on superficial identification rather than shared experience. There is a desire to belong (and a fear of exclusion), but 'belonging' is judged by criteria that are based on wealth, race, class and social status, evaluated through a set of associative codes attached to property. The affluent, acquisitive middle classes, to which our society aspires, display their mythical virtues of being proper, responsible and just, through their property which is symbolically loaded with their projected identities. Caravans bypass this identification process; they are not valued as property and are not considered as secure financial assets that have taken a lifetime's hard work to accrue. In this sense, they are not considered to represent a demonstration of commitment, faith and investment in a community.

The irony is that it is the caravan park which might come closest to being a community. That membership is voluntary, association is temporal and social pretences are removed offers the chance to relate, as needs be, through actual, lived, common ground, with some of the prejudices (which protect us from the risks of interaction), attached to our real, everyday lives put aside. Perhaps, then, in the caravan park's realised ideal of community, created through an imaginary construct of the everyday, there is an example and lesson for us all.

Notes

1 'Caravan' is used here as a generic term to describe semi-permanent, off-site manufactured holiday-homes-on-wheels.

2 Nothing is quite as it first appears, the seams between ceiling panels of the caravan are edged with timber to look as if they hold up the caravan as beams hold up a cottage.

3 Sigmund Freud, 'The Uncanny', *Art and Literature*, vol 14, The Penguin Freud Library, Penguin (Harmondsworth), 1990.

4 Richard Sennett discusses 'the myth of the purified community' in his book *The Uses of Disorder: Personal Identity and City Life*, Pelican Books (Los Angeles), 1973.

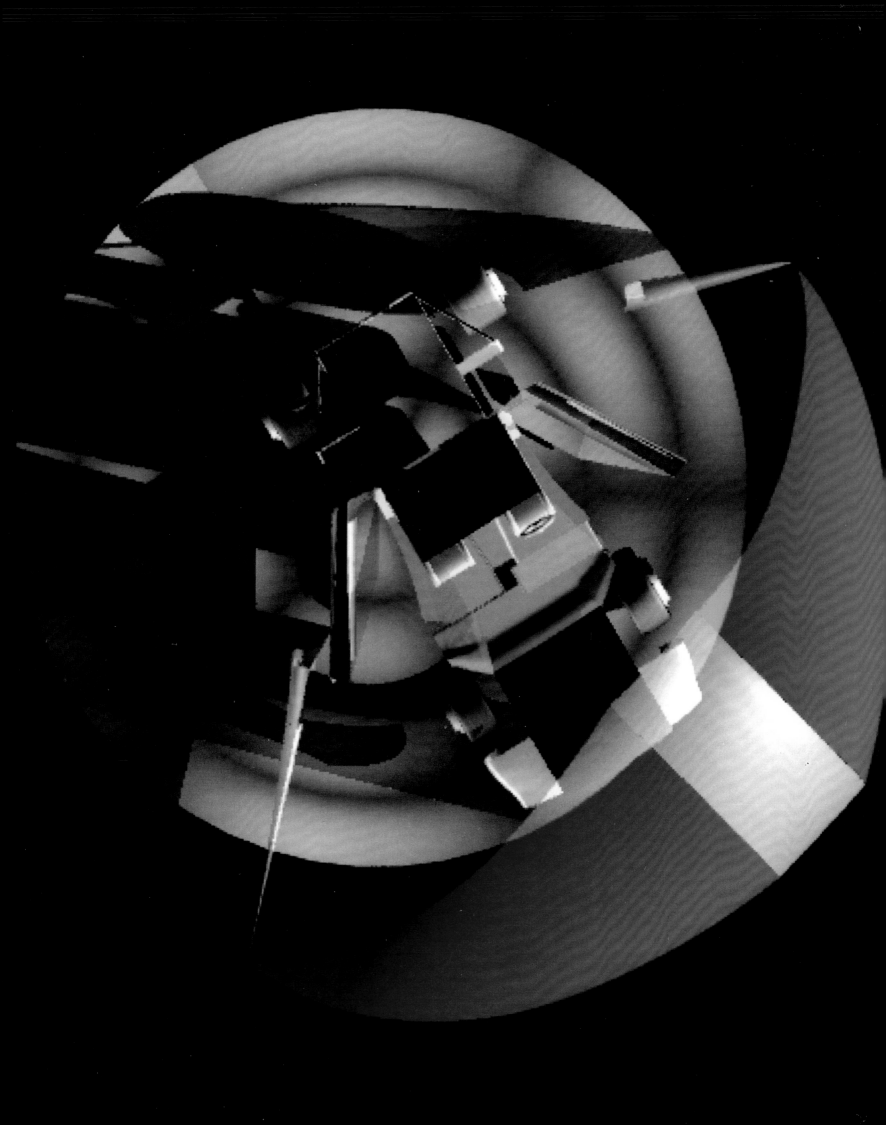

MICHAEL WEBB
DEPICTING THE DRIVE-IN HOUSE

Note from the author: when a word appearing in the text is followed by a bracketed numeral, eg, 'deiform (2)', the reader is encouraged to refer to the New Shorter Oxford English Dictionary *for the precise shade of meaning intended.*

The decorum of the 'crit' at Columbia University's new 'paperless studio'[1] is somewhat an inversion of its more traditional counterpart, ie, in the days when the visual medium – the *lingua franca* for discussion – was the steam[2] drawing. Consider the students' passion (1): two nights without sleep, and on the third day, to stand, flayed before the critters . . . that student now sits behind a monitor, hidden except for occasional glimpses of garishly illuminated temple, bringing forth wonders projected on a giant overhead screen. Power now rests with the student. The form of interaction is similar to that of being at JFK; you're pleading with a surly, indifferent booking agent, likewise hidden behind the deiform (2) monitor . . . you'll do anything, anything, if only the agent can get you on a flight to Heathrow!

Here are reasons given for failure to present work:

Paperless studio crit: 'my project is lost in the hard drive'.

Steam drawing crit: 'my pen broke'. For one whose work[3] has so much concerned motion and depiction, and who has figured, reluctantly, that the still (4) or series of stills may convey the mathematics of motion, but never its grace or its beauties, the opportunity of having computer animations made of the work was bemusing. Such was the case when MOCA, the Museum of Contemporary Art in Los Angeles, in preparation for its 'End of the Century' show asked the New York based architect Kent Larson to supervise the preparation of computer animations of certain twentieth-century projects, among them the 'Drive-in House'. Under his guidance, and my needling, and with the

help of MIT Professor Takehiko Nagakura and three MIT students (Chia Chang Hsu, Priti Paul and Marios Christodoulides), work was started on three separate manifestations of the project.

The Drive-in House (written 1976)
'My maiden aunts, now long gone to their reward, referred to the automobile as a 'horseless carriage', even as late as the 1940s. And well they might have, for, as old Buckminster Fuller loved to tell us, the car is still a coach and four . . . just with different styling and more horse(!) power: which didn't mess the village up too much when only the squire had one, but when everyone wanted one it led to the planning and ecological disaster that is America today.

So, if the basic programme of the car were to be extended to cover social issues, such as the journey from dining table to driver's seat, what happens to the car when left alone . . . were the architect's purview (2) to be extended beyond the limits of the site . . . ' (here the fragment ends).

Addendum (from 1966)
'The motivating force, behind the Drive-in House, was the observation that facilities existed such as movie theatres, restaurants or churches with drive-in options, where the management would provide the movie, food or the peace that passeth all-understanding, and you BYO mini auditorium, dining area or pew. What if a house were thought of in the same way? You might have as a fixed locus, the stuff that's too heavy to move: bathtub, stove, family heirloom, but the rest (that which is needed for the journey) could be folded down into the auto and driven away'.

Storyboards were prepared for three manifestations of the project: the '25 x 25' House of 1964, the Sky-rise Slab Block, and the Wankelhaus of 1988.

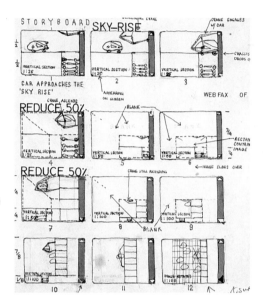

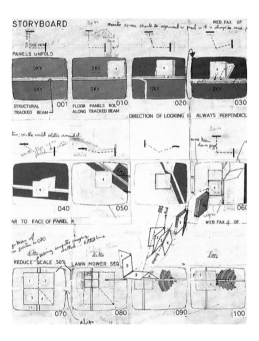

OPPOSITE: Drive-in House, detail; FROM ABOVE: Sky-rise 'storyboard'; '25 x 25' House 'storyboard'; PAGE 18: Wankelhaus, detail; PAGE 19, FROM ABOVE: Sky-rise, electric runabout cars; '25 x 25' House, lawn mower detail

163

The '25 x 25' House

Perspective projection 'privileges' (a popular locution among critters in the USA), a singular point, the location of the observer, and if there be no compelling reason within the scope of the overall projects for the existence of such a point, then the appropriateness of the choice of projection should be in doubt. Most students working with the computer, it seems to me, are blissfully free of such doubts. So, in my storyboard, the projection is orthographic, the direction of looking always perpendicular to the face of panel four. Stainless steel floor panels roll along a structural track system, each hinging open like a petal – a metal petal. Also shown is the lawn mower sequence.

The Sky-rise

Special electric runabout cars arrive at the base of the Sky-rise, at which point the body and chassis separate, the chassis to be stacked in subterranean racks and the body to be hoisted up via a travelling crane to the appropriate apartment in the sky, or perhaps more interestingly, to the inappropriate apartment. The devices developed by Macintosh to move text and/or images up and down (the scroll bar) or to change size (the dotted rectangles) were appropriated here to allow vertical scanning and scale changes.

The Wankelhaus

The Wankel rotary engine as exemplar of the miracle of the rotor (a quasi-triangular form) rotating within the cylinder (a quasi-circular form), yet maintaining constant contact at four sliding points. 'Epitrochoid' is the arcane word that describes this. In the Wankelhaus, the car as energiser and activator of the house (which is an empty shell when the car is gone), rotates the space – metal panels unfolding and sliding past each other so as to maintain a seal against external inclement weather. A nocturnal plan projection reveals slits in the metal panel skin, the shape of the car's lights and windows, illuminated as the car rotates.

Notes

1 Columbia University in New York has a computer-only studio
2 It was considered that the spread of television during the 1950s in England would mean the end of radio. At the same time, British Rail was eliminating its fleet of steam locomotives and replacing them with diesel power, so naturally, radio began to be referred to as 'steam radio'.
3 What pretensions are contained within this world. The US Internal Revenue Service classifies it as a 'hobby'!

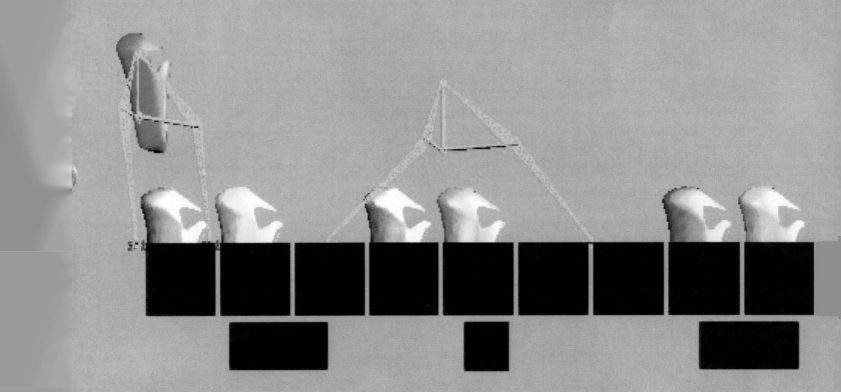

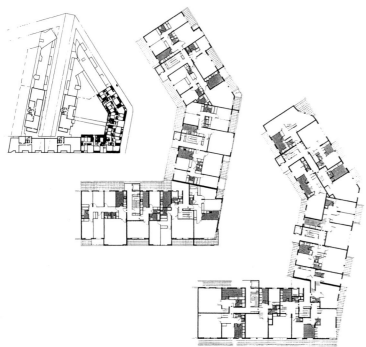

Bercy Corbineau, Paris, FROM ABOVE: Site plan; typical floor plans

FRANCIS NORDEMANN

FROM PRIORITY ZONES TO URBAN COMMUNITY

THE FUTURE OF 'LES 150 GRANDS ENSEMBLES'

During the post-war housing boom, millions of square feet of social housing, arranged in incomplete, isolated clumps, were tagged on to the outskirts of cities across Europe. Nowadays, these large residential districts, known as *grands ensembles* or 'big estates', are often run down. They have become problem-ridden zones, typically associated with the deterioration of urban life and social difficulty. Many countries continue to create such rational settlements, which cannot be thought of as truly urban. By exploring the past, we may be able to offer an urban future to these modern estates.

It is hard to believe – or to understand – what happened to social housing in the 20 years separating the construction of the low-cost housing estates of the Parisian belt, the Amsterdam southern extension, the garden cities of Britz in Berlin, or la Butte Rouge in Chatenay-Malabry, the Weissenhof in Stuttgart, and the Viennese Hofe, from the construction of standardised developments spread on the outskirts of large cities from Manchester to Barcelona, Amsterdam to Strasbourg, Lisbon to Frankfurt. It is tempting to see these projects in terms of a purely formal and stylistic analysis, which would ignore the structural causes of their problems, blaming them on the emergence of Modernism in architecture. It is also tempting to excuse them in the same rhetorical terms that were originally used to promote and justify them.

We might ask why, in the brief post-war boom, four million homes were mass-produced, stacked in towers and slabs on empty fields, far away from the existing urban fabric. Lying behind these projects are two myths – the myth of modern industry opposed to ancient, small-scale production, and the myth of hygiene opposed to the slum in the ancient city. The architecture of these estates was, in fact, a realistic, practical, even innovative, response to new complications that appeared after the war: the urgent need for the rapid construction of a large number of housing units, and the consequent demand for a greater number of low-cost dwellings (eventually produced *en masse* in imitation of industrial methods), plus the increasing desire to improve hygienic standards in housing. But in putting aside existing architectural, urban, historical and structural values, a new practice was also taking shape: normalisation.

Cultural values, which had long ruled the complex process of constructing urban settlements, were replaced by normalising and scientist values that impoverished urban form. Projects were reduced to schematic compositions, forcing design to respond to the new constraint of standardisation. The era imagined a rational, urban world, its rules gleaned from modern industry; but when the patterns of industrial production were applied to the urban world, the results were almost militaristic.

In response to this shift of values, builders, architects and engineers struggled to conform, sacrificing their *savoir-faire* in the process by giving up a cultural definition of their discipline. Rejecting the complexities of urban design in favour of schematic composition culminated in the destruction of urban form.

The new process was made up of three steps: analysis of needs; listing of programme specifications and project. The project was no longer the whole process, but a sort of customisation, tagged on to the end and forced into the background. It was a pattern that could produce new objects: towers, slabs, detached houses, but could not create urban forms, even if it claimed to use urban models.

The impact of this process on the landscape can be simply described: high-rise towers and horizontal slabs dropped on the *tabula rasa* of public open spaces, which could have been parks and gardens. Dead-end roads and driveways instead of alleys, streets or avenues. Residual spaces at the front of apartment buildings that create a minimal relationship between inside and outside, instead of a planned sequence of entry spaces. Insignificant institutional buildings instead of civic monuments. In other words, with these projects, urban logic gave way to the random dropping of objects on sites.

Given the context of their production, it is hardly surprising that, 25 years later, these giant housing districts are in crisis: physically degraded and socially unable to develop into real communities. Their conception created the conditions of exclusion, precluding any possibility of integration within the urban fabric. They want to be recognised as a 'piece of city', but the planning methods that created them succeeded in pushing the city out beyond its own limits. The experiment never took urban roots, yet it is still in operation today.

Every town bears in a more or less implicit way the traces of urban historical models. Urban form stems from the cultural, economic and technical conditions of its development and, most importantly, it provides a meaningful framework that accepts multiple uses and transformations. In spite of their weaknesses, these housing districts are subject to the same rule; but, unlike other urban areas, their meaning cannot be found in terms of any architectural or urban value system developed over time (a model that would have taken root). Their composition signifies only the particular terms of their creation.

The estates' masterplan is terrifyingly simple, an exercise in elementary zoning for the novice planner. By failing to offer a public-space network with various relationships from outside to inside, it becomes a homogenous, formulaic composition, heralding an era of traffic networks (rather than continuous cities). These schemes are highly profitable for architects, planners and developers, creating an opportunity for contractors to hire cheap, unskilled workers to put together rough, pre-cast components.

Several million people live in these big estates, which reveal the backstage of so-called urban fabrication. Now that their weaknesses can be clearly identified, it is time to re-examine their original design in the light of what they could become.

A primary design weakness lies in their isolation from the rest of the city, the result both of their self-sufficient layouts, which establish a discontinuity with neighbouring areas, and by their particular form. A second major weakness is the simplistic treatment of architectural volumes and the poor quality of the spaces between buildings (or total absence thereof). A repetitive succession of basic horizontal or vertical blocks, placed as objects on the ground, is connected only by geometric figures (laid out in plan). There are no public spaces, continuous constructions or urban sequences. The same weakness can be noticed in the landscape itself, where instead of malls, parks, gardens or city squares we find huge tracts of empty and undefined land. A third problem lies in the heterogeneity of public buildings, social facilities and housing. Sometimes public services are concentrated away from housing (according to a theory of segregation), sometimes they are mixed in with it (resulting in a reduced density and increased dispersion of housing). In both cases there is rarely a clear physical or structural liaison between public buildings and residential ones; they don't seem to relate to the same city. The historical city is made up of a dialogue between solid and void. It is driven by the continuity of facades along a succession of public spaces. Estates, by contrast, are made up of buildings dropped discontinuously on undifferentiated empty space.

Finally, the organisation of a *grand ensemble* denies centrality: a typical plan consists of a linear artery, along which the housing blocks are distributed arbitrarily. The notion of a community, based on links between people and expressed by the continuity of urban fabrics, is missing. The idea of a town, formed from housing organised around community buildings, with public areas structured hierarchically, and therefore easily recognisable, is also absent. If an acceptable urban environment is to evolve, then the negative effects of such built-in standardisation must be gradually effaced.

Social problems like unemployment and poverty accumulate in such big estates because of displacement of social and cultural facilities, concentration of diverse ethnic and cultural minorities, disaffection of captive tenants. Images of slabs and towers are often invoked as symbols of the miserable living conditions of disadvantaged populations, the poor quality of the spaces being put forward too readily as a cause of misery. The production of such estates deliberately precluded their integration into the larger urban context, and the social and economic crisis also results from such exclusion.

It might be tempting to consider only these social and economic 'facts', and to advocate the destruction of these projects in order to eradicate the poverty they shelter (as if one could erase a historical mistake). But calling for their destruction denies the environment and history of millions of people. It is a call for exclusion and 'urban purification'. Disused buildings, or those in a poor state of repair, might warrant demolition, but it is unthinkable to raze structures to the ground if this action serves no purpose, if it does not pave the way for an alternative urban project.

Another option is to retain the original 'solution', promoting restoration to reverse degradation and neglect. This approach, however, denies the theories of urban evolution, and replays the logic applied to their conception: it supposes that, as with a machine, the problem of the large estates is one of maintenance and replacement of parts.

The first cultural step to be made towards integration is to accept that lessons can be learnt from these estates. The field is open to complement, densify, diversify the urban framework in order to enrich it, in the same way the ancient quarters were built.

The making of cities is a sedimentary process, fed and renewed by addition and substitution on a limited piece of land. Instead of extending suburbia indefinitely, it is time to look at empty sites as portions of 'cities-to-be', to develop their qualities and extend their history, to enclose them within urban culture and integrate an urban process – that of the traditional city together with its extensions. It is a necessary function of cultural renewal to adopt a positive attitude to these estates. The first step towards a more urban future is to confront and eliminate the logic applied to their conception.

Similar cultural problems were raised some years ago by the rehabilitation of historic districts. These were considered to be slums calling for eradication until attention was suddenly paid to historic preservation, immediately followed by urban investment. The modern estates, with their specific qualities, can be thought of as sharing equal status with other parts of the city.

Densification will call for diverse new uses and will bring cultural and financial investment. It will confirm that housing districts can be given urban value, can adapt to social changes and therefore acquire greater status. As long as studies reveal the positive aspects of modern urban frameworks, such statements can give direction and sense to ambitious, long-term political strategies aligned in carefully programmed and properly targeted projects.

Another positive aspect of these developments is that they are arranged to maximise the utilisation of sites and avoid waste of land (an economy underlined when compared to more recent peri-urban development). They also provide housing for many inhabitants. Huge, empty, misused and undefined spaces may be present between constructions, but these are potential sites. A varied socio-cultural community surfaces as a result of the original functional programming of the 'community' (a community = a neighbourhood = housing + services).

When a series of interventions is programmed over the long term, based on specific site studies, the housing district can be transformed, ensuring the conservation of local characteristics (such as lines of communication, boundaries, landforms, original architecture). Restitution of the local context and the specific geographic, urban and socio-economic characteristics and neighbouring physical and cultural environments would be a major step towards the integration of each social housing district into the city (and proof that the impersonal logic applied in their conception has finally been abandoned). Each case must be examined separately if individual problems of local restructuring are to be defined in detail.

Investment in public space can act as a catalyst in the re-evaluation of a community. Building into the empty spaces of large estates is an urban-addition process that enriches a site. Projects will make non-public spaces out of empty fields, offering sites for densification, creating new links towards continuity and achieving an improved quality of urban life.

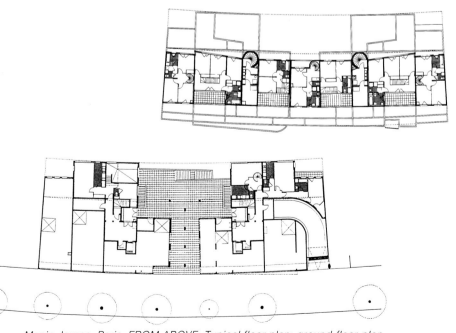

Manin Jaures, Paris, FROM ABOVE: Typical floor plan; ground-floor plan

TOWARDS COSMOPOLIS
UTOPIA AS CONSTRUCTION SITE
Leonie Sandercock

In the late 1990s the world of planning education and practice uneasily straddles an old planning paradigm, and one that is struggling to be born, in a way that is evocative of Matthew Arnold's great mid-19th-century image of wandering between two worlds, one lost, the other yet to be found. The old planning served modernist cities in a project that was, in part, dedicated to the eradication of difference. Metaphorically, this planning can be linked with the machine images of the great Fritz Lang film, *Metropolis*. The emerging planning is dedicated to a social project in which difference can flourish.

The metaphorical image of Cosmopolis is meant to suggest that diversity. To ensure planning's continued relevance into the next century as a significant social project, contributing to the creation of cosmopolis, it is important to give more flesh to these bones. I do this by developing three notions: the importance of an expanded language for planning (involving a re-linking with the design professions); of an epistemology of multiplicity; and of a transformative politics of difference. This extract can deal only with the first of these. My personal vision is for a profession embracing concerns for social and environmental justice, for human community, for cultural diversity and for the spirit. In post-war planning's rush to join the (positivist) social sciences, some of its capacity to address these concerns was lost because it turned its back on questions of values, of meaning, and of the arts (rather than science) of city-building. The language, and the mental and emotional universe of planning were thus constricted. We can expand this universe by talking about the city of memory, the city of desire and the city of spirit.

City of memory

Why do we visit graves? Why do we erect sculptures to dead leaders or war heroes or revolutionaries? Why do we save love letters for thirty or forty years or more? Why do we make photo albums, home movies, write diaries and journals? Why do we visit the sites of cave paintings at Lascaux, at Kakadu? Because memory, both individual and collective, is deeply important to us. It locates us as part of something bigger than our individual existences, perhaps makes us seem less insignificant, some-times gives us at least partial answers to questions like, 'Who am I?' and 'Why am I like I am?'. Memory locates us, as part of a family history, as part of a tribe or community, as a part of city-building and nation-making. Loss of memory is, basically, loss of identity. People suffering from amnesia or Alzheimer's are adrift in a sea of confusion. To take away a person's memories is to steal a large part of their identity. The past dwells in us and gives us our sense of continuity, anchoring us even as we move on.

Cities are the repositories of memories, and they are one of memory's texts. We revisit the house(s) we grew up in, we show our new lover the park where, as a kid, we had our first kiss, or where students were killed by police in an anti-war demonstration ... Our lives and struggles, and those of our ancestors, are written into places, houses, neighbourhoods, cities, investing them with meaning and significance.

Modernist planners became thieves of memory. Faustian in their eagerness to erase all traces of the past in the interest of forward momentum, of growth in the name of progress, their 'drive-by' windscreen surveys of neighbourhoods that they had already decided (on the basis of objective census and survey data, of course) to condemn to the bulldozer, have been, in their own way, as deadly as the more recent drive-by gang shootings in Los Angeles. Modernist planners, embracing the ideology of development as progress, have killed whole communities, by evicting them, demolishing their houses, and dispersing them to edge suburbs or leaving them homeless. They have killed communities and destroyed individual lives by not understanding the loss and grieving that go along with losing one's home and neighbourhood and friends and memories. Since nobody knows how to put a dollar value on memory, or on a sense of connection and belonging, it always gets left out of the model.

This is not an argument against change. (Decaying and growing, cities can't choose to stay the same. They have to choose all the time between alternative changes – blight or renewal, replacements or additions, extensions outwards or upwards, new congestions or new expenditures.) It is rather an argument for the importance of memory, for the need to pay attention to it, to understand that communities can and do go through grieving processes, to acknowledge these in some sort of ritual way. We need to remind ourselves of the importance of memory, and of ritual in dealing with loss. If we need to destroy, as part of our city-building, we also need to heal.

Recent work by planner-historians like Gail Dubrow, Dolores Hayden and John Kuo Wei Tchen, among others, indicates that there is a new multicultural sensibility at work in planning in the 1990s. Hayden's *The Power of Place* dwells on the ways in which public space can help to nurture a sense of cultural belonging and at the same time acknowledge and respect diversity.[1] She writes of the power of ordinary urban landscapes to nurture citizens' public memory, and notes that this power remains untapped for most working people's neighbourhoods in most American cities, and for most ethnic history and women's history. Urban landscapes are storehouses for individual and collective social memories. Both individuals and communities need to find ways to connect to the larger urban narrative. Some urban planners are now working with artists, anthropologists, land-scape architects, archaeologists and communities to do just that in public history and public art, community mapping and urban landscape projects that seek a more socially and culturally inclusive approach to our urban memories.

City of desire

Why do we enjoy sitting alone in a coffee shop, or outdoor cafe, or on a park bench, apparently day-dreaming? If city dwelling is in part about the importance of memory and belonging, it is also about the pleasures of anonymity and of not having to belong. These are closely related to desire, to sexual desires and fantasies. We sit on a bus, empty seat beside us, watching new passengers come on board, wondering whether anyone will sit next to us, and if so, who? This is the thrill and the fear of the chance encounter.[2] We sit on the beach or stroll through a park, watching others and being watched, and in that watching are hidden fantasies and desires, sometimes unacknowledged, other times a conscious searching. This is the eroticism of city life, in the broad sense of our attraction to others, the pleasure and excitement of being drawn out of one's secure routine to encounter the novel, the strange, the surprising. We may not want to partake. But we enjoy the parade. If city life is a coming together, a 'being together of strangers', as Iris Young suggests in *Justice and the Politics of Difference*, we need to create public spaces that encourage this parade, that acknowledge our need for spectacle – not the authorised spectacle of the annual parade or the weekly football game, but the spontaneous spectacle of strangers and chance encounters.[3] Yet the opposite is happening. Planners are systematically demolishing such spaces in the name of the flip side of desire – fear.

The city of desire – and its place in city planning – is one of the aspects of city life that has only just begun to (re)surface in writings about the city. (It was certainly there in Walter Benjamin's writings in the 20s and 30s.) There are many themes to be unravelled and stories yet to be told relating to desire and the city, to sexuality and space. Elizabeth Wilson's *The Sphinx in the City* argues that the anonymity of big cities has been liberating for women (at the same time as it increases our jeopardy from sexual assault);[4] and George Chauncey makes the same point with respect to gay men, in his history of gay New York, noting how many gays have moved from the oppressive, homophobic atmosphere of small towns to the anonymity of New York.[5]

In Barbara Hooper's account of the origins of modern planning in 19th-century Paris, 'The Poem of Male Desires', the role of desire on the one hand, and fear of it on the other, produces the desire to control desire, which Hooper argues has been a central organising theme of planning practice.[6] Hers is a story of 'bodies, cities, and social order, and more particularly of female bodies and their production as a threat to male/social order'.[7] Hooper investigates planning's texts and uncovers the theme of 'disorderly bodies'. 'Significantly, this list of disorderly bodies includes not only prostitutes, but lesbians, excessive masturbators, nymphomaniacs, and hysterics – also suffragettes, female socialists, feminists, independent wage-earners.'[8] She argues that planning developed in the late 19th century as a participant in new forms of social control directed at women.

In making the hitherto invisible visible – that is, the significance of desire, of eros, in urban life – we also make it discussable. In breaking the taboo, the silence, we move slowly

ABOVE AND OVERLEAF: Computer-generated montages by Peter Lysiottos

towards a richer understanding of urban life and of what has been left out of planners' models and histories. Billboards are an ongoing issue for planners, especially those advertising bill-boards that explicitly link sex/desire/the body with the sale of merchandise. As the ads get more explicit and provocative, there are pressures on city councils and planners to ban such displays. The pressures come from left and right, from feminists objecting to the objectification of the female body, to fundamentalist religions objecting to any public acknowledgement of eros. This conflict over billboards is, then, more than an aesthetic issue. It is about the (unresolved and unresolvable) 'problem' of desire in the city.

But there is much more to the city of desire than eros, as philosopher Iris Young has suggested:

> The city's eroticism also derives from the aesthetics of its material being: the bright and coloured lights, the grandeur of its buildings, the juxtaposition of architecture of different times, styles and purposes. City space offers delights and surprises. Walk around the corner, or over a few blocks, and you encounter a different spatial mood, a new play of sight and sound, and new interactive movement. The erotic meaning of the city arises from its social and spatial inexhaustibility. A place of many places, the city folds over on itself in so many layers and relationships that it is incomprehensible. One cannot 'take it in', one never feels as though there is nothing new and interesting to explore, no new and interesting people to meet.[9]

The city of desire is also an imagined city of excitement, opportunity, fortune. It is what brings millions of people from the countryside to the big city – Nordestinos to São Paolo, Turks to Frankfurt, Anatolians to Istanbul, Michoacans to San Diego, the Hmong to Chicago, the people of the Maghreb to Paris. It fuels dreams. By not understanding the power of such dreams, or by dismissing them as irrational, planners' own dreams of rational control of migration processes, of orderly human settlements, will remain just that – dreams. The daily stories of border-crossings from Mexico into the United States, crossings in which people all too often risk, and sometimes lose, their lives, illustrates the point. Such is the power of the city of desire, a power strikingly rendered in Gregory Nava's movie, El Norte, and John Sayles' Lone Star, both of which also show how easily the city of desire may become the inferno. One symptom of the narrowness of modernist planners' horizons is the fact that they find it very hard to focus on desires rather than needs. A need is supposedly an objectifiable entity, identified in 'needs surveys': 'I need a more frequent bus service'; 'I need more police patrols in my neighbourhood'. A desire, by contrast, involves the subconscious, a personal engagement, dreams and feelings, an ability to intuit the atmosphere and feeling of a place. How does the city of desire translate into planning? Perhaps by giving more attention to places of encounter, specifically those which are not commercialised – the street, the square – and which are not placed under the gaze of surveillance technologies. Perhaps also by recognising that some places of encounter must necessarily be appropriated, and not trying to regulate the uses of all public spaces.

City of spirit

What draws many of us to visit places like Machu Picchu, Stonehenge, the Dome of the Rock or the Wailing Wall in Jerusalem, the Kaaba stone at Mecca, Chartres, or Uluru, in the apparently empty centre of Australia? Why do certain mountains, springs, trees, rocks, and other features of landscape assume symbolic and sacred values to certain peoples and cultures? Historically we have invested our surroundings, urban as well as non-urban, with sacred or spiritual values, and we have built shrines of one sort or another as an acknowledgement of the importance of the sacred, the spiritual, in human life. The completely profane world, the wholly desacralised cosmos, is a recent deviation in the history of the human spirit. Beginning perhaps in the 19th century we have created landscapes, cityscapes, devoid of the sacred, devoid of spirit. The tall chimneys that arose in the nineteenth-century factory landscape (Mumford's 'Coketown') and the skyscrapers of the late 20th-century city, perhaps symbolise the excessive dominance of the masculine yang force and its values. From East Germany and Russia to California or the Mississippi Delta, parts of the devastated countryside are left sterile and dead, a monument to the consequences of human rapacity unchecked by considerations of spirit. We are so deadened by our Western industrial landscapes that we now go in search of comfort to Aboriginal songlines or Native American sacred places.

The environmental message is clear. It is time to re-introduce into our thinking about cities and their regions the importance of the sacred, of spirit. In his superb book about black and white Australians' relationship to the Australian landscape, Edge of the Sacred, David Tacey calls for such a 'resacralisation' as a social and political necessity.[10] 'White Man Got No Dreaming' was the partial title of a book by anthropologist WEH Stanner.[11] The Aboriginal Dreaming and Western rationality stand to each other as thesis to antithesis. What the one affirms, the other denies. In Aboriginal cosmology, landscape is a living field of spirits and metaphysical forces.[12] Our English word landscape, as the poet Judith Wright has pointed out, is wholly inadequate to describe the 'earth-sky-water-tree-spirit-human continuum which is the existential ground of the Aboriginal Dreaming. Obviously white Australians cannot appropriate Aboriginal cosmology, tacking it on to their own overly-rational consciousness, and nor can alienated North Americans adopt the cosmology of Native Americans (although much of so-called new age spirituality, the world over, seems to be attempting something very much like that). But there are Western traditions of re-enchantment to which we might connect. The point is that perhaps our modernist/progressive longing for freedom from the non-rational is inherently flawed; out of date and out of touch with the real needs of our time.

How can cities/human settlements nurture our unrequited thirst for the spirit, for the sacred? In the European Middle Ages, it was in the building of cities around cathedrals. But that was long ago. In the more secular cities of today, at least in the West, life does not revolve around the cathedral, although in many communities the church, synagogue or mosque continues to play a vital role in social organisation. But if we look at cities as centres of spontaneous creativity and festival, then we get a different sense of the presence of spirit around us. Our deepest feelings about city and community are expressed on special occasions such as carnivals and festivals. Our highest levels of creativity are seen in art galleries or heard in symphony halls. But the nourishing of the spirit, or soul, also needs daily space and has everyday expressions: two women on a park bench 'gossiping'; a group of students in a coffee shop discussing plans for a protest; an old Chinese man practising his tai chi on the beach or in a park; amateur musicians busking in front of cafés and museums; an old woman tending her garden; kids skateboarding among the asphalt landscaping of sterile bank plazas . . . Rational planners have been obsessed with controlling how and when and which people use public as well as private space. Meanwhile, ordinary people continue to find creative ways of appropriating spaces and creating places, in spite of planning, to fulfil their desires as well as their needs, to tend the spirit as well as take care of the rent.

There is another dimension to the city of spirit which has begun to actively engage some planners, in collaboration with artists and communities. That is the process of identifying what we might call sacred places in the urban landscape. The works of Hayden,[13] Dubrow,[14] and Kenney,[15] are suggestive. Kenney's work in mapping gay and lesbian activism in Los Angeles reveals the connections between place and collective identity which are at the heart of gay and lesbian experience of the city. Kenney evokes Stonewall – the scene of three days of rioting in Greenwich Village in 1969 in protest at police entrapment and harassment in a bar frequented by African American and Puerto Rican drag queens – as essentially a sacred site for the gay and lesbian movement. The labour movement, the women's movement, African Americans and Native Americans could each name such 'sacred urban places', and have begun to do so, and to commemorate such sites.

What the above discussion suggests is the need for a diversity of spaces and places in the city: places loaded with visual stimulation, but also places of quiet contemplation, uncontaminated by commerce, where the deafening noise of the city can be kept out so that we can listen to the 'noise of stars' or the wind or water, and the voice(s) within ourselves. An essential ingredient of planning beyond the modernist paradigm – planning for cosmopolis – is a reinstatement of inquiry about and recognition of the importance of memory, desire, and the spirit (or the sacred) as vital dimensions of healthy human settlements and a sensitivity to cultural differences in the expressions of each.

Adapted from Towards Cosmopolis: Planning for Multicultural Cities, *by Leonie Sandercock, John Wiley & Sons (Chichester), January 1998*

Notes

1 Dolores Hayden, *The Power of Place. Urban Landscape as Public History*, MIT Press (Cambridge, Mass), 1995.

2 Dora Epstein, 'Afraid/NOT: Psychoanalytic Directions for Planning Historiography', in Leonie Sandercock (ed), *Making the Invisible Visible: A Multicultural History of Planning*, University of California Press (Berkeley), 1998.

3 Iris Marion Young, *Justice and the Politics of Difference*, Princeton University Press (Princeton, NJ), 1990.

4 Elizabeth Wilson, *The Sphinx in the City: Urban Life, the Control of Disorder and Women*, University of California Press (Berkeley), 1991.

5 George Chauncey, *Gay New York: Gender, Urban Culture, and the Making of the Gay Male World 1890-1940*, Basic Books (New York), 1994, p135.

6 Barbara Hooper, 'The Poem of male desires: female bodies, modernity, and "Paris: Capital of the Nineteenth Century"', *Planning Theory* 13, 1995.

7 Ibid, p105.

8 Ibid, p120.

9 Iris Marion Young, op cit, p240.

10 David Tacey, *Edge of the Sacred*, Harper Collins (Melbourne), 1995.

11 WEH Stanner, *White Man Got No Dreaming: Essays, 1938-1973*, ANU Press (Canberra), 1979.

12 David Tacey, op cit, p148.

13 Dolores Hayden, op cit.

14 Gail Dubrow, 'Redefining the Place of Historic Preservation in Planning Education', *Planning Theory* 13, 1995, pp89-104.

15 Moira Kenney, 'Remember, Stonewall was a Riot: Understanding Gay and Lesbian Experience in the City', *Planning Theory* 13, 1995, pp73-88.

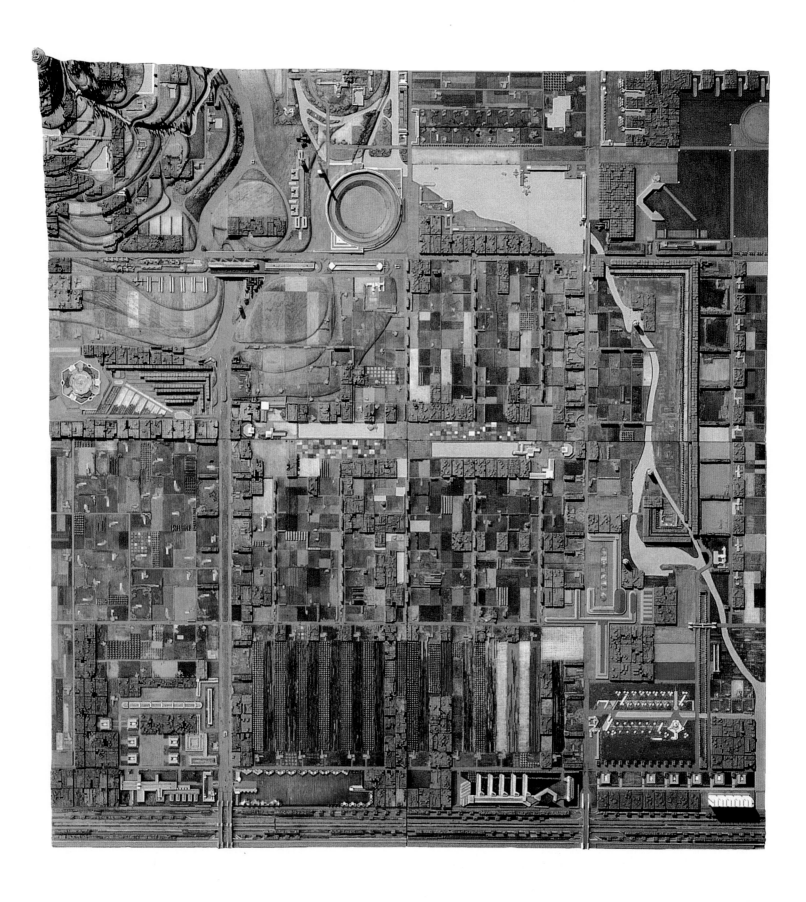

ROBERT FISHMAN
SPACE, TIME AND SPRAWL

The overwhelming fact of 20th-century world urbanism has been the creation of a new kind of decentralised city; but we do not see this city clearly because, unlike all cities of the past, the new city has no defined centre or periphery, no core, no manufacturing or commercial districts, and no hinterland. Instead, urban functions spread out along highway growth corridors in low-density settlements that combine urban, suburban and rural elements in a seemingly random and endless collage. This new city exists in its most advanced form in the United States but the economic, social and technological forces which have created it can be seen worldwide.

The developers of a massive retail and office centre outside Atlanta, Georgia have called their development Perimeter Center. This seeming self-contradiction points to a revolution in urban form and a radical new sense of space. Since the first cities of the ancient Near East, cities have existed to define a centre. The Egyptian hieroglyph for city was a cross inscribed in a circle – the idea of a crossroads or centre combined with that of a defined border. In Hellenistic and Roman times the very form of the classical city expressed the idea of a centre around which the hinterland was organised; later, the Renaissance used the techniques of linear perspective along great boulevards to reinforce the meaning and dominance of the core. Piranesi's classic engraving of Bernini's colonnade and piazza for St Peter's Basilica with the obelisk at its centre makes especially vivid the idea of urban space and world power organised around a great centre.

The coming of the global trading city and the 19th-century industrial city did not contradict but reinforced the desire to create classical urban space at least at the city's core. This is perhaps best demonstrated by Haussmann's rebuilding of Paris and by Daniel Burnham's monumental Plan of Chicago (1909). Burnham's plan is especially interesting in this context, for he started from the functional integration of the region around a unified transportation network which converged in the core, the Chicago downtown or Loop. This functional integration was then combined with and expressed by the creation of a consciously classical urban space organised around a monumental government plaza. This, for Burnham, was the modern city.

Yet precisely in the years 1905-15 when Burnham was laying out his plans for a monumental and classical modern city, new technologies and a new concept of urban time and space were being created which would fundamentally challenge not only Burnham's city but every other concept of the city since classical times. I have borrowed the title of this piece from Sigfried Giedion's Space, *Time and Architecture* (originally published 1941) because I follow his basic thesis that cubism brought to consciousness a new space time continuum that stands in sharp distinction to classical space. Combined with new technologies – especially the automobile which was in the course of rapid development during this very decade – a new city was born.

Giedion defined cubism as 'the new space conception: space-time', and this in turn meant the essence of space as it is conceived today is its many-sidedness, the infinite potential for relations within it. Exhaustive description of an area from one point of reference is, accordingly, impossible; its character changes with the point from which it is viewed. In order to grasp the true nature of space the observer must project himself through it.[1] Giedion was referring to Picasso and Braque's paintings in the years 1909-14; yet I believe he has given us an excellent description of post urban space in the late 20th century.

But, as Space, *Time and Architecture* reveals, Giedion himself never grasped the radical implications of his ideas for city planning. As secretary of CIAM, Giedion was closely allied to the great generation of European modernists, especially Le Corbusier. And, however radical his architecture and town-planning were in many other respects, Le Corbusier was a severe classicist in his basic conception of the city. In his Contemporary City for Three Million People (1922), Le Corbusier conceives his city from one point of reference, the perfect zero-zero point formed by the intersection of the east-west and north-south axes. Like Burnham, Le Corbusier centralises the city's transportation network around the single centre. Indeed, in the relentless symmetry of his artificial city, Le Corbusier out-Burnhams Burnham,

I believe there was a great architect-planner of the early 20th century whose city-concepts exactly embody 'the new space-conception' that Giedion announced. This was the American architect Frank Lloyd Wright with his Broadacre City design, which dates from the 1920s. More than any other urban design concept, it speaks directly to the most radical elements in the late 20th-century city. Giedion knew Wright's work well, including Broadacre city, which is referred to specifically in *Space, Time and Architecture*. Indeed, the book contains a description of the author's visit with Wright in 1940 at Wright's home and masterpiece, Taliesin in Wisconsin. But Giedion was also committed to an interpretation of modern architecture that relegated Wright to the status of an honoured precursor. Moreover, the Broadacre City design as Wright presented it was deeply enmeshed in a very American utopianism that owed far more to Thomas Jefferson and Henry George than to Karl Marx, making it difficult for a sophisticated European modernist to see its radical implications.

As early as the 1890s, Wright was in opposition to Daniel Burnham and Burnham's movement to bring classical form to the American city. Where Burnham had attempted to re-orient the city around a single dominant centre – the Chicago downtown or Loop – Wright envisioned a city that would have no downtown or centre at all. He attacked what he called the undemocratic and pseudo monarchical centralisation of cities around a dominant set of intersecting axes. This opposition was political, economic and aesthetic; Wright saw the large city and especially its downtown core as the locus of royalist power that threatened democracy. Decentralisation meant the return of the United States to a society of universal landowners whose economic independence would result in cultural individualism and whose direct contact with the land would mean a resurgence of democratic culture.

Wright asserted that his new city was not only a return to the basic Jeffersonian values of the country; it also embodied advanced technology and a new way of experiencing time and space. It is significant (he writes):

> That not only have space values entirely changed to time values, now ready to form new standards of movement measurement, but a new sense of spacing based upon speed is here . . . And, too, the impact of this sense of space has already engendered fresh spiritual as well as physical values.[2]

Where Burnham and Le Corbusier had built their ideal cities around a single transportation hub (a virtual necessity for rail based cities), Wright organised Broadacre City on a grid system of automobile highways. Derived ultimately from Jefferson's 1787 gridplan for mapping the Northwest Territory, this highway grid, like Broadacre City itself, extends indefinitely in all directions. The city had no centre, or rather, as Wright put it, 'The only centre (the only centralisation allowable) in Broadacre City is the individual family home.'

By this he meant that in Broadacre City each household would now be free to create its own city. That city would consist of all the destinations they chose to reach, moving along the grid system of highways at speeds of 60 miles per hour. Scattered within the open landscape would be industries, offices, schools, shops, churches and all the other facilities for an advanced industrial society. Each household, living on a generous plot of an acre or more, would create a diverse city out of its multitude of destinations.

Broadacre City thus had no downtown, no industrial or worker's quarter, no slum areas or upper class suburbs. It could not be comprehended from a single point of view, only from the multiple centres or points of view of each household in its cars moving at great speeds over the landscape. As I hope to show, this utopian city based on what Giedion called the new space conception: space time describes better the way the majority of Americans now live than any other design model. But this new American city did not arise from a mystical appreciation of cubist space concepts, nor from an adherence to Frank Lloyd Wright and his particular combination of modernism and Jeffersonian individualism. It arose as the unplanned and unanticipated convergence of many uncoordinated initiatives which converged spontaneously on a new urban form.

I can only sketch out the many forces which gave rise to the new American city. Firstly, there were the many new technological networks that all had in common the displacement of the hub and spoke network that had sustained the great city at its core and replaced it with a grid network that gave the same advantage to those at the periphery as to those at the core. I have already mentioned how Wright seized on the most important of these new networks: the highway system as opposed to the rail system. But there were other systems of decentralisation: the telephone, the electrical grid, and the peripheral factory that left the crowded urban factory districts for open space at the edge. At the same time new networks of retail distribution made it possible to bypass the urban core and go directly to the neighbourhoods, and these retailing outlets were supported by parallel networks of cultural distribution that went directly to the home: radio and television.

As important as the technology that all advanced industrial countries shared were the particular social and economic factors unique to the United States. America shared with Britain a strong cultural attachment to the single-family suburban home and to the residential suburb: middle class, low-density neighbourhoods, at the periphery of the great city from which both industry and the working class had been excluded. But only the United States made suburbanisation a goal of government policy.

After the house building industry collapsed in

the Great Depression of the 1930s, the federal government intervened strongly with several New Deal measures which, taken together, amounted to a virtual industrial policy to promote the suburbs. Savings banks for small savers, bankrupted by the Depression, were refinanced by the federal government to provide mortgage money for suburban houses; further government guarantees made possible long term, low-interest mortgages for new home buyers; and other loan guarantees encouraged builders to undertake more efficient, large-scale operations that came close to industrialising suburban home building.

This home building industrial policy was strongly seconded by two others which also date from the 1930s and 40s. These were the automobile policy that supported road building to the exclusion of rail and other forms of mass transit, and the defence policy that encouraged defence contractors to build new plants on the suburban periphery.

Finally, the massive migration of poor blacks from the rural American South to large Northern cities during and after World War II made those cities the sites of intense racial conflict. At the same time, government policies designed to aid suburban house building created an ample supply of new suburban houses to which the white urban population could flee. In the years 1950 to 1975 land and building costs were so low that not only the middle class but much of the white working class could also become suburbanites. Because most American suburbs are independent cities supported by local property taxes, these suburbs could set up their own well financed public school systems and other services limited to their own residents. Meanwhile the central cities were forced to provide increasingly expensive services to an increasingly impoverished population but with an ever shrinking tax base to support those services.

The result was a massive shift in the American population, which was less than 25 per cent suburban in 1950 and is now more than 50 per cent suburban, ie living in a metropolitan area outside the central city. This new city has not, as Wright predicted, completely replaced the old urban cores, but these post-urban, post-suburban regions have become the real centres of American society.

Ironically, the very success of the new decentralised city has revealed the limitations and contradictions at the heart of Frank Lloyd Wright's utopia. A city based on the infinite multiplication of single family houses on larger lots necessarily destroys the very landscape it was designed to enhance. A city whose survival requires a multitude of individual automobile journeys necessarily creates 'low density congestion'. Where the congestion of older cities reflected the intensity of downtown life, the congestion of the new Edge Cities reflects a single mode transportation system too simple for the needs of a real city. As Le Corbusier observed, 'The city that achieves speed achieves success', and the new decentralised city is failing as congestion slows it down.

Finally, a city that exalts the individual and the isolated household cannot create these forms of community every true city requires. Wright struggled with this problem both in his architecture and in his personal life throughout his career, and now the new city that represents his principles has inherited his struggle. The challenge is to impose effective boundaries and limits to growth on a city whose very nature, Wright recognised, is to be everywhere or nowhere; to create or to redevelop genuine cores for a decentralised city that has grown by ignoring centres; to build new transportation systems that provide alternatives to the automobile and feed pedestrian; policies that connect that the people in Edge Cities and the people in inner cities indeed belong to the same society.

As this special issue of *Architectural Design* shows, our most creative architects and planners are already responding to this challenge. The real question for American society is whether the habits and expectations formed during the era of unlimited suburban growth are still too strong to permit meaningful change.

Notes

1   Sigfried Giedion, *Space, Time and Architecture: The Growth of a New Tradition*, fifth edition, Cambridge, Mass: Harvard University Press, 1967, pp435-436

2   F L Wright, *The Living City*, Horizon Press, 1958, p86

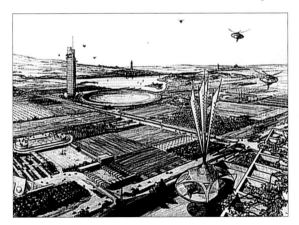 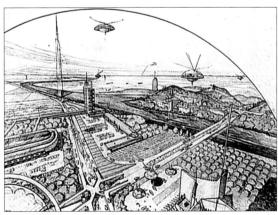

Perspectives of the Broadacre City project

ALEJANDRO ZAERA POLO

ORDER OUT OF CHAOS
The Material Organisation of Advanced Capitalism

At the end of the 60s, due to the rise of the late-capitalist mode of production, emerging patterns of urban organisation began to consolidate as new forms of urbanity and material organisation. These changes in the urban topographies coincided in time with the emergence of a new scientific paradigm which has come to replace the long-lasting validity of conservative systems – those based in models where systems are considered isolated and maintaining matter and energy constant – by an emerging epistemology that understands systems as vaguely delimited locations crossed by flows of matter and energy.

As a result of the realignment of scientific paradigms according to the new demands of production and culture, we undergo since then an epistemological change.[1] To study the analogies between the emerging urban processes and the epistemologies appearing within the productive-economic-cultural models of the so-called *advanced capitalism*, could help us to approach the chaotic behaviour of the contemporary city as part of a process of reformulation of orders, rather than as a sign of their disappearance.

This text attempts to connect a series of urban topographies which have appeared within the last 25 years, with the body of knowledge emerging simultaneously within different fields – generically labelled as 'chaos theory' or 'science of complexity'. And to propose them as a key to reformulate the disciplines concerning material practices.[2]

Flexible Accumulation: Spatial Organisation as Economic Strategy

The models of advanced capitalism originate at the crisis that affected the economies of developed countries at the end of the 60s, as the forms of economic integration able to incorporate the problems of over-accumulation inherent to the capitalist development. Urban topographies entered a period of radical restructuring which characterises the production of space to the present day.

If urbanisation has historically developed as a process of accumulation and location of surpluses, within late-capitalism the city is determined by its capacity to incorporate a circulation of surpluses. David Harvey has named as a regime of 'flexible accumulation' that form of economic integration characteristic of advanced

capitalism where over-accumulation problems are solved through 'mechanisms of spatial and temporal displacement'.[3] Within the 'regimes of flexible accumulation', the crisis inherent to capitalist development tends to be absorbed through periodical reorganisations of space. The areas required for the system's growth are produced not through territorial expansion, but through an increasing mobility of resources and capital, and the implosion of transport and communications.

This periodical restructuring of the capitalist space unfolds a 'liquefaction' of rigid spatial structures. Urban structures are required to maintain the flexibility so as to absorb a continuous spatial reformulation without losing their specificness and centrality. The production and organisation of urban space acquire within late-capitalism an extraordinary importance, despite the decreasing value of spatial boundaries.

The growth of the 'organic composition of capital',[4] which once characterised the capitalist development in its 'fordist' regime, reverses its direction within late-capitalism: the quotient variable-to-fix tends to increase as a strategy to enhance the flexibility of production.[5] The evolution from an economy of *scale* to an economy of *scope* – from *industrial* to *informational* – shows that production is no longer competitive through a good cost/price relationship, but through its diversification and capacity to adjust to a constantly evolving demand.[6] Consequently through this growing disorganisation of the composition of capital, the contemporary city tends to constitute itself as a *non-organic* and *complex* structure without a hierarchical structure nor a linear organisation.

The Processes of Globalisation as Origin of Differences

If in the traditional city, the stability of the economic and productive structure, the homogeneity of the constructive techniques and the uniformity of the social composition was translated into stable, homogeneous, continuous and hierarchic spatial and material organisations, where exchange and flow processes had only a relative importance, the contemporary city is characterised by the incoherent coexistence of social groups, economies and technologies, and the growing importance of flows and exchange with

OPPOSITE: Hybrid public/ private space, Trump Tower, New York

179

external milieus. The globalisation of the financial system within advanced capitalism is one of the most determining factors of contemporary urban topographies: capital can operate instantaneously on a global scale resulting in the devaluation of spatial delimitations. Simultaneously, cities evolve into poles of attraction whose success depends on their offer of specific facilities to attract certain activities.

Contrary to the homogenisation of urban topographies that could be expected from the process of globalisation, the mobility of capital and resources develop a sharp consciousness for the specificity of each enclave, establishing a regime of strong competition: those locations which offer more developed mechanisms of spatial-temporal displacement (improved transport and communications, developed research and educational facilities, more trustworthy credit systems and fiscal advantages) will become poles of attraction for labour and surplus. The process of territorial competition is evidence of the supremacy of spatial variables over historical processes within advanced capitalism: the battle becomes territorial instead of class-oriented.

The processes of economic globalisation do not lead to a spatial homogenisation, but on the contrary to the enhancement of diversification and heterogeneity by increasing our awareness of differences, the particularities of a location and its specificities. We witness an artificial regionalisation, an artificially enhanced nature, where the local flavour becomes synthetic. The success of the contemporary city as a topography, relies in the ability to articulate the 'space of flows' with the consolidation of topographies of centrality with enough 'critical mass' to ensure its structural stability.[7]

Constellations of Attractors – Polycentric City

Traditional urban structures had developed an organic growth scheme that informed the classical planning techniques, constructed on models of centrality, homogeneity, continuity and hierarchy. The contemporary city, exposed to the instability of late-capitalist production, can not maintain the rigidities of an organic structure that articulates urban events within a global structure. Urban topographies grow today in a milieu which is no longer structured on the city/territory opposition, but rather on the transport infrastructure as a vector of mobility. The territorial organisation derived from a 'liquid economy', disintegrates the urban body and spreads it over the territory in a multiplication of centrality. The non-organic, polycentric structures which characterise emerging urban topographies are more efficient at dealing with the erratic demands of late-capitalist production.

The 'liquefaction' of the urban structure unleashes a discontinuous, unarticulated urban

growth. The polycentrality of the Parisian Ville-Nouvelles, the cities of the American Sunbelt, and the centro-European conurbations, such as the Ruhrgebiet and the Randstat are examples of the discontinuity of the emerging urban fabrics. They are cities constituted as constellations of attractors which defy both the gravitational criteria of traditional urban models and the isotropic, decentralised modern organisations.[8] Within the emerging urban models, the centre/periphery, full/void and exterior/interior oppositions tend to disappear, evolving towards polycentric, a-hierarchical systems, 'networks' or 'rhizomes', more operative within unstable conditions.[9] The city is built around lines of displacement and connection, operating in a topological rather than geometrical mode. The urban structure turns into a de-regulated, superconductive topography, capable of continuous reorientation to follow erratic flows.

Paris' Ville Nouvelles originate from a political decision which sought to solve the sclerosis of the overcrowded metropolitan area of Paris without decreasing its centrality within the network of European cities. Paul Delouvrier's, *Prefect of the Parisian Region*, set in motion an ambitious programme for the Île de France, which would connect five Ville Nouvelles and an airport zone.[10] Unlike the English New Towns, the political nature of the Île de France operation did not just try to solve the growth of the urban structure, but also to keep Paris as the 'capital of Europe'. Delouvrier designed a system where the distance between the primitive nucleus and the new centres would keep the interdependence between them, and therefore the unity of the structure.

The cities of the American Sunbelt are those placed in the band that crosses the continent between parallel 42 and the Mexican border: Los Angeles, Phoenix, Dallas Fort-Worth, Houston, Atlanta, Washington and Miami. The Sunbelt area had a strong development during the 60s and 70s, in the period in which the great cities of the American East Coast were starting a process of decay. The Sunbelt Cities were created on the territory generated in the second colonisation of America: the construction of the Interstate Freeways in the 50s. If the first colonisation established the cities of the East and West coasts, and on the Great Lakes, the Interstate Freeways made accessible the interior territory. A new accessibility, a good climate and cheap labour, were the reasons for the flow of investment that produced one of the quantitatively most important urban developments of recent history. Contrary to what was happening simultaneously in Paris, the development of the Sunbelt Cities occurred with a remarkable lack of state control, driven mostly by economic demands.[11] The Sunbelt Cities have

Views of a complex urban environment, Times Square, New York

developed a polycentric structure of dense cores, approximately ten miles away from each other. Amongst the 'attractors', motorways and open spaces serve as a buffer which allows the system to evolve in an a priori undetermined direction. In the Sunbelt Cities, the urban territory is determined by the topological continuity of the infrastructures, rather than through the geometric pattern of the fabric.

The conurbations of the Ruhrgebiet and the Randstat do not originate directly from a political decision nor as a spontaneous speculative process. They grow as a mutation of a pre-existing urban structure by means of a new accessibility. What, in both cases, was a medieval network of small cities evolves, by way of the development of transport infrastructure during the 50s, into a series of urban enclaves which operates as a sole urban structure. Each one of the existing centres undergoes simultaneously an important growth and a functional specialisation. (In the Ruhrgebiet, Düsseldorf becomes the service centre, Bochum the industrial one and Essen the commercial area. In the Dutch Randstat, Rotterdam assumes the industrial role, Amsterdam specialises in services and culture, and The Hague develops the administrative centre.) Both conurbations are good examples of the enhancement of differences as a weapon for competition within a territory where spatial boundaries and metrics are becoming increasingly irrelevant.

The Hybrid as Device for Local Accumulation

Late-capitalist production mode and its quest for a greater flexibility of the urban structure derives in the weakening of hierarchies and organic unity within the contemporary city. Urban events become less understandable through typological definitions: when the integrating ability of urban structure has disappeared, urban events develop into devices of local accumulation. Hybrids are programmatic structures able to capture surpluses and fix them in specific topographies once the traditional urban organism becomes too rigid to operate efficiently within the unstable territory of flexible accumulation. Hybrid programmes articulate between erratic economic flows and their consolidation as urban topographies, without the mediation of a unitary urban structure. Where urbanity is constituted as a *discontinuous* and *non-organic essence*, the 'hybrid' becomes the 'quantum' of urbanity.

Hybrids, or complex programmatic structures, approach the programme as a relational essence. Their proliferation underlines the complex nature of the contemporary city, which can no longer be analysed through linear models (ie metric distance, centre-periphery gradients, public-private structure and inside-outside boundaries). Each point on the territory is determined by a superposition of laws whose effects cannot be analysed as linear functions. Hybrids are to complex processes what types are to linear processes.

The spatial juxtaposition of functions and programmatic adjacencies in hybrid buildings revalues the three-dimensional organisation of the city versus its planimetric determination. The complex formed by the AT&T, Trump and IBM headquarters in Manhattan not only integrates a multiple programmatic structure, but also incorporates systematically the public space within the buildings: a subversion of the established urban boundaries between public and private. Similar deformations of a pre-existing urban structure are very frequent in American Downtowns, where the gridded geometry of urban fabric is being systematically undermined in the most dense areas by a series of underground and above ground-level connections which links adjacent buildings, developing topologies of the public space that defy the existing urban structure.[12] (Although perhaps the very concept of the *grid* as an a-hierarchical structure, may imply already an accumulation 'on the spot'.) In their invisible form, they shape a clear diagram of the asymmetries of urban growth.[13]

In the so-called 'fashion buildings' of central Tokyo, we can find a similar phenomenon, this time adapted to the structure of property of a pre-existing urban topography, and to the smaller quantification of the investments implicated in the urban development.[14] Fashion buildings are hybrids where a multiplicity of programmes shares an unusually compressed space: small service companies, small hotels or groups of apartments, shops and showrooms. They are constructions where the iconographic, topological and scalar operations are more evident than metric or geo-metric determinations: to attract people with a surprising image, to promote vertical movement to the basement and to the top of the building, and to create urban density in a certain area of the city.

Unlike the New York hybrids, the fashion buildings are not supported on the economic power of large corporations – trans-urban, transnational structures – but rather on the sum of small local investors: the buildings would not be named IBM or AT&T, but Tepia, Scala, Santeloco, Nani-Nani and a variety of fantasy names which singles them out as autonomous and different enclaves within the city. If the American case exemplifies the localisation of multinational surpluses, in the Japanese case we witness a process of local accumulation that bypasses the urban structure to act as a capturing device of more global and indeterminate flows (franchises are, for example, preferential clients of the fashion buildings). They are a step forward in the

FROM ABOVE: Complex post-capitalist spaces of: the Bonaventure Hotel of John Portman, Los Angeles; atrium, Marriot's Hotel, Atlanta

formulation of a complex urban structure. Their extravagant individuality is a result of the articulation of multiple interests. If we analyse Maki's Spiral, (curiously enough Maki was one of the prophets of the mega-structures of the 70s) or Suzuki's Joule-A, as two typical examples of fashion buildings, we witness the mixture of public and private spaces, and the exploitation of the vertical dimension as a public realm, which we had already found in the Manhattan hybrids. The possibilities of programmatic adjacencies become one of the most interesting events within these structures.

Japanese hybrids operate within the urban fabric, by densifying specific areas or streets: this form of developments is often coordinated between several investors, to launch the economy of a certain location within the city. This type of strategy seems to be more efficient within the contemporary city than the metric and geometric operations characteristic of urban planning techniques. Fashion buildings genuinely operate as 'attractors', establishing fields of influence within the urban fabric by raising the property value around them, unleashing processes with much more capacity of transformation than geometrical determinations.

Fashion buildings operate within the urban fabric in a similar way to the previously analysed developments in the Sunbelt, Paris and the European conurbations. What defined the urban structure in those cases was not a coherent geometry, or the conservation of scale and geometrical pattern throughout the territory, but rather the generation of an urban topography structured as a multiplicity of centres of urban density.

Geometries of Complex Dynamics: Morphogenesis, Topology and Self-Similarity

The dynamics of contemporary urban phenomena are the manifestation of emerging complex orders, rather than a result of a random process. Within the non-conservative urban paradigms that we are trying to approximate, urban development is a morphogenetic process. The city as a field of permanent formal genesis rather than as a completion and conservation of a pre-existing state. It is increasingly difficult to project the city as an extrapolation of a predetermined linear process or to operate by limiting possible variation to consolidate a certain geometrical structure. It is precisely the instability of the regimes of flexible accumulation that brings the variable conditions of the urban structure to the forefront, putting into crisis conservative attitudes, both from an historical and contextual viewpoint, as well as from an Utopian perspective.

The consideration of the temporal variable within the morphogenetic process approximates the pre-existing urban structure as a base for

evolution subject to potentially radical modifications. To incorporate time within the planning of the contemporary city does not mean that urban entities are strictly determined by their past, but rather the acceptance of the bifurcations in the evolution, the asymmetry of the process of growth, and the irreversibility of the development process.[15] Therefore, both types and urban models, in what they insist on the constants of form and structure, lose their primacy as tools for planning.

In light of this, it seems more adequate to plan urban systems as entities in permanent change rather than to force processes of formal determination, legislation, delimitation and assignment of competence; to operate within a process of continuous appraisal which allows the incorporation of the complexities of contemporary production methods.

The loss of an organic and hierarchical structure from both city and territory provokes the fragmentation of the urban system into nuclei that compress the complexities of the urban organism. Instead of the organic unity and continuity of the classical city and its opposition city/territory, the new urban forms spread over the territory as a discontinuous essence. The interaction with the territory becomes a complex problem of 'multiple attractors', rather than a linear, 'gravitational' function determined by a central point. This discontinuous organisation of urban structures develops a self-similar condition, independent from the scale in which the system is analysed.[16] From the increasing influence on the cities of the competition on an international scale, through to their polycentric structure, up to the resulting hybrid building, we always find an analogous composition of force-fields. Within contemporary urban structures, relationships of scale, measurement and proportion become far less significant than those of density, size and topological structure, in parallel with the replacement of the *scale* economics of modernity by late-capitalist *scope* economics. Scale relates always to a fixed reference point, man, state, place, and is consequently an operative method of little efficiency within the unstable geographies of late-capitalism.

Hidden faces of geometry arise from the necessity to operate within the emerging material culture of late-capitalism. If we look at the maps that describe the nature of contemporary urban structures (ie La Défense in Paris, the transportation network of Tokyo and the development of the Minneapolis Downtown) we will find that the correspondence between the formal structure of the city and the urban systems (the communication systems and public space) is not regulated, as in traditional urban systems, by a common metric and geometric structure. Irregular geometries versus ideal forms, compositions of

FROM ABOVE: Hybrid public/private space, IBM Headquarters, New York; time/space compression, Headquarters of CNN, Atlanta

traces rather than of closed forms and boundaries, these seem to be the manifestation of the complex formal logics which late-capitalist modes of production are bringing to light. Emerging urban systems are topologies defined by relations of contiguity, discontinuity, deformation, unification and density rather than metric systems. The predominance of flows, deformations and dimensional and dynamic heterogeneity within the urban structure of advanced capitalism, puts into question the static spatiality, homogeneity of magnitudes and constance of the form in time, that once characterised traditional urban structures and planning methods.

Knowledge is essentially an operative tool: its bases do not necessarily correspond to the essences of reality, but rather with the ability of an emerging organisation to enter into an intelligible and therefore *operable* domain.[17] Knowledge irradiates from the needs of a mode of production, rather than approximate an eternal reality. Maybe what finished the Enlightenment-Modernist project and its ambitions of universal rationality was a question of spatial organisation, a matter of geometry: the emergence of a global space that enhances local differences. To operate within the contemporary city we have to evolve the disciplines related to material practices: it may be by looking at the sciences of complexity that we understand a reality that our disciplines are no longer able to operate.[18]

Notes

1 Thomas Kuhn, *The Structure of Scientific Revolutions*, The University of Chicago Press, Chicago, 1962.

2 See the synthesis of these theories elaborated by James Gleick, *Chaos: Making a New Science*, Penguin Books, New York, 1987.

3 'Mechanisms of temporal displacement' are those which permit the instant conversion of fixed to moving capital. These mechanisms require the existence of financial institutions capable of guaranteeing the validity of these conversions. 'Mechanisms of spatial displacement' are those which allow for the opening of new areas of growth to absorb surpluses in production, capital and labour. Technological and educational research, and construction of transport and communications infrastructures are exemplary processes. David Harvey, *The Urbanisation of Capital*, John Hopkins University Press, Baltimore, 1985.

4 The '**organic composition of capital**' is the ratio between the fixed capital and the variable capital within a productive structure. In Marxist theory, that quotient is supposed to increase over time, following the development of a productive structure in order to improve its productivity.

5 Henri Lefebvre, *La Production de L'Espace*, Anthropos, Paris, 1974.

6 In the sense used by Manuel Castells of the term 'informational' in *The Informational City*, Basil Blackwell, Oxford, 1989.

7 *ibid* Castells, M.

8 Term 'attractors', taken from contemporary physics, is used to determine certain areas of structural stability within an evolving system. René Thom, *Structural Stability and Morphogenesis*, The Benjamin/Cummings Publishing Company, Reading, Mass, 1975.

9 This term characterises material or conceptual structures which articulate multipliers. Deleuze & Guattari, *A Thousand Plateaus. Capitalism and Schizophrenia*, The University of Minnesota Press, Minneapolis, 1987.

10 Île de France in HV Savitch, *Post-Industrial Cities: Politics and Planning in New York, Paris and London*, NJ, Princeton University Press, Princeton, 1988.

11 Joel Garreau, *Edge City. Life on the New Frontier*, Doubleday, New York, 1992.

12 LG Redstone, *The New Downtowns*, McGraw Hill, New York, 1976.

13 Henri Lefebvre compares the urban network to a mechanism which already suggests the loss of the organising capacity of urban structures by the elimination of hierarchical structures, and by granting each point within the territory an 'area of free enterprise', *La Production de l'Espace*, Anthropos, Paris, 1974.

14 Deyan Sudjic, *The 100-Mile City*, André Deutsh, London, 1992.

15 In this respect the interest lies in the models of evolution of a formal urban model, symmetrical and homogeneous towards a distorted model proposed by Ilya Prygogine as an example of the evolution of a complex system. Prigogine, I, & Stengers, I, *Order out of Chaos*, Bantam New Age Books, New York, 1984.

16 In fractal mathematics, in which automorphic structures are defined in each of their scales. Benoit B Mandelbrot, *The Fractal Geometry of Nature*, Freeman & Co, New York, 1977.

17 Instead of logically establishing Geometry, one must establish logic within Geometry, to obtain a general view of a world made up of emergences and pregnancies: the emergences are objects which are respectively impenetrable; the pregnancies are hidden qualities, effective virtues which emanating from source will impregnate themselves to other emerging forms and produce visible effects (figurative effects). René Thom, *Esquisse d'une Semiophysique*, InterEditions, Paris, 1988.

18 Michel Serres proposes geometry as the origin of knowledge. Michel Serres, *Les Origines de la Geometrie*, Flammarion, Paris, 1993.

FROM ABOVE: The experience of post-capitalist urban environment, JFK Airport, New York; superposition of urban structures, Atlanta, underground parking OMNI Center

GUY BATTLE AND CHRISTOPHER McCARTHY
MULTI-SOURCE SYNTHESIS
The Design of Sustainable New Towns

By the 21st century 70 to 80 per cent of the world's population will live in concentrated urban centres. Nowhere is the demand for new towns going to be greater than in the developing world. As technology renders the field worker redundant and as population increases, more and more people will migrate away from their rural settlements to the urban centres, demanding housing, feeding, higher standards of living and thereby increasing pollution and placing greater demands on the world's already depleted natural resources.

To find the solution, we must first ask the right questions, for example, 'What are cities, how do they work?' Cities and towns are a complex mesh of people, lifestyles, machines, buildings, politics, power. However, from a purely engineering basis, they can be more simply defined as systems that import raw materials (input) to fuel a 'metabolism', that exports goods (output) and refuse material (waste).

This 'metabolism' can be fairly accurately defined in terms of input, useful output and waste, using a simple accounting and balance sheet. Typically a metabolic balance sheet would indicate that the actual useful product is small compared with the input (ie often less than 1%). Such studies also show the vast amount of waste that is typically put directly back into the biosphere (approximately 70%). In many cases, this goes back as raw pollution, leaving the biosphere to 'absorb' and process it for us. Following this philosophy, the earth can be viewed as a series of reservoirs (for resource) and sinks (for waste), both the reservoirs and sinks having finite capacity. At present rates the reservoir will quickly become empty and the sink full. It is therefore necessary to identify the various processes that go on to make up this metabolism so that their efficiencies can be improved, not only as individual cycles but also in the manner in which they can beneficially interact. There are two basic ways to view a city's metabolism. Either as a linear process, (input gives output plus waste) or as a cyclical process that produces feed back loops and recycles wastes. The key difference between these two viewpoints is that the linear system will eventually reach full capacity, whereas the circular system is sustainable.

The system can be identified by the following characteristics – *Linear*: water use high and is polluted; sewage is discarded; toxic fumes pollute; building materials and 'wastes'; trees felled without replacement. *Circular*: low water consumption, treated and recycled; wastes reused for fertiliser, heating and energy; fossil fuel used efficiently; building materials recycled and used discarded; trees replanted.

Any city can be designed (or evolve) from two starting points. That is the smallest module outward (ie building – streets – urban clusters – city, eg London) or from a strategic level inwards (macro planning, street scape, city blocks, buildings eg Manhattan). In most historic cases, this has been a process of evolution. London grew from a series of small clusters to become a massive urban conurbation, with the transportation and water systems being added as a result of growth (micro – macro). In contrast, Manhattan, grew from an initial orthogonal planning grid (macro – micro). But essentially both are the results of evolution rather than any real strategy, and thus the metabolism is generally linear rather than cyclical (eg refuse is rarely used to provide energy, it is merely transported out to sea and dumped as in the case of Manhattan). Indeed, both London and New York in comparison to many other 'mega' cities are extremely wasteful, producing 950 tonnes of rubbish per year per person compared to Mexico City which produces only 350 tonnes per person per year (a reflection on an affluent and effluent rich society!). However, within the developing world, with the ever increasing demand for new housing and new towns, neither approach has proved to produce an ideal result. The only real way to design sustainable cities is by being able to effect (ie design) both the macro and micro levels of the town simultaneously. For instance, it is no good designing an efficient energy production system if all buildings are going to be air conditioned and profligate energy users. Thus, it is absolutely essential that the designer (urban planner) has some means of regulating the amount of energy any building plot may use by legislation or guidelines. This does not mean that there would be a heavier handed planning approach, merely that there would be a more rigorous set of guidelines and targets for the designers to work to, encouraging them to

ABOVE: Stockpile of cattle bones; Early inhabitants of the Galapagos Islands introduced horses as a means of transport, with little regard for the environmental consequences

FROM ABOVE L TO R: Beehive; New York City;
Travelling Buddhist priest

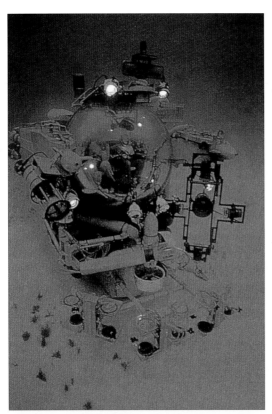

FROM ABOVE L TO R: Johnson Sea-link Submersible can descend to 1000m (3000 ft) from a surface support ship; Nutrient laden water supports plankton that feeds millions of fish; Snake hatching

maximise energy efficiency in return for floor area. Within existing cities, this is notoriously difficult to achieve. However, in the developing world, where new towns on green field sites are more common place, then such an approach is viable and essential for the well-being and balance of the earth.

A formula for sustainable development

A town's metabolism is comprised of six cycles which each have their own individual patterns but in some way all affect one another: transportation; energy; water; waste; micro climate, landscape and ecology; materials, construction and buildings. Naturally, many of the decisions to be made with respect to the above, are site specific and would necessarily take into account fundamental factors, such as: the climate (solar, temperature, humidity, precipitation, wind); geology (site conditions, materials resources, topology); location; economics of country, etc. However, in many cases the general objectives remain the same.

Sustainable transportation

This can be defined as transport which aids the mobility of one generation without compromising the mobility of future generations. Clearly many of today's transportation modes are not in keeping with this definition: the private car – the first choice of many in the developed world – is one of the major causes of the current high levels of pollution in our urban areas and in many places automobile accidents are the major cause of death in the under 50 age group.

Whilst the developed world is only now beginning to realise the irredeemable damage the car has done to society in terms of land-take, inner city deterioration, accident levels, air quality and noise, for the rapidly modernising and expanding economies of the developing world the problems are only just beginning. Rapidly increasing car ownership levels coupled with climatic humidity may soon mean that in many industrialising countries, environmental pollution indicators may soon exceed those currently being experienced in the industrialised nations. The challenge therefore is to prevent this foreseeable disaster from actually occurring without denying citizens of the developing world the indisputable benefits which increased personal mobility, facilitated by the car, can bring.

The key to a sustainable transportation system is the implementation of a transport hierarchy which gives priority to the pedestrian and public systems above the car. This does not necessarily imply positive discrimination against the private car: successful implementation of such a hierarchy can be achieved by merely creating an environment which does not cater for the car. This can be accomplished by limited parking spaces, traffic calming, cheap mass transit and by establishing a network of roads unsuitable for vehicular traffic: pedestrian; cycle based; mass transit (public); car. The hierarchy chosen will dictate which modes have 'design' priority over others. Successful implementation of such a structure will depend upon a segregated environment and will fundamentally effect design decisions. The dominance of the car is based on its convenience. In order to encourage people to use public network and then walk (or cycle) it is important that the system must be of a high quality and provide similar or better service.

An acceptable walking distance within any town is about 150–300m or 5–10 mins maximum. Thus any mass transit system and urban plan should be based around this module. If walking is essential then pedestrian (and cycle) routes must be carefully planned to be scenic with good views; shaded from sun and passively cooled; streets narrow enough to provide shade; protection from rain; interaction with wild life and effect on the fauna.

There are two options for mass transit: high speed with large stop spacing (monorail) needing secondary modes such as taxis to cover intermediate distances; or slower speed (LRT, trolley bus) providing a comprehensive coverage to negate the need for other modes (except walking). Costs depend largely on the ground conditions and topography, however a broad cost comparison is as follows: Monorail $132m-$360m; LRT $48m-$162m; Trolley bus $19m-$25m.

Phasing is an essential element of any choice for it will effect timing and the magnitude of costs. One of the major perceived advantages of rail based (LRT) systems is this huge up front capital investment required, with no opportunity to accrue revenue until they are fully operational, despite the fact that environmentally and urbanistically they have great advantages. It is therefore essential to examine the possible phasing of such a system to achieve the same end goal: roads constructed for a bus system (Bio diesel); bus upgraded to 'trolley bus' (electricity produced from waste or CHP); profits used to fund rail infrastructure; light rail system (LRT) installed (clear electricity control over country roads can be pedestrianised).

Energy

Energy in the form of electricity, gas, oil is used within three broad categories: buildings 50%; transport 25%; industry 25%. The underlying principle of any energy strategy must be to firstly reduce the demand and secondly to provide the energy required from a renewable source thus creating a self sustaining (and in this case, even self sufficient) system. It is clear however that to achieve this, both the demand

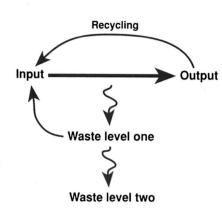

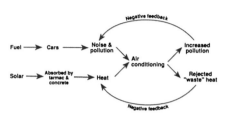

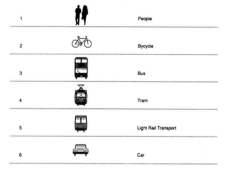

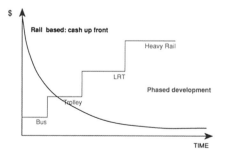

FROM ABOVE: Circular metabolism; Self-propagating use of air conditioning; Two methods of analysing the transportation hierarchy

187

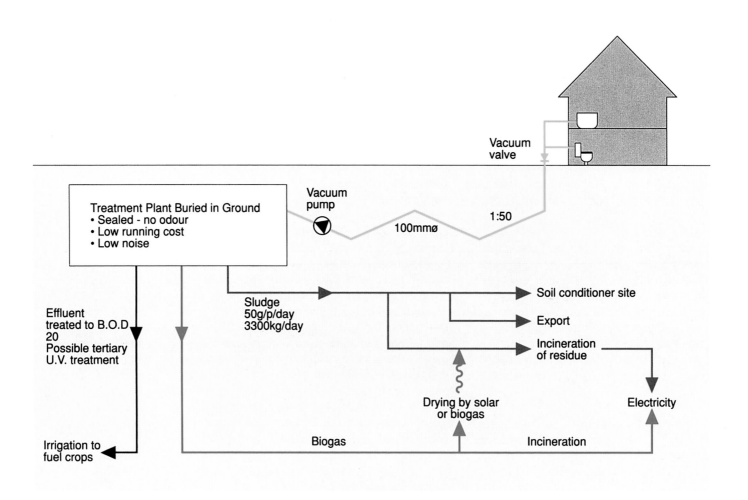

Vacuum valve

Treatment Plant Buried in Ground
• Sealed - no odour
• Low running cost
• Low noise

Vacuum pump

100mmø

1:50

Effluent treated to B.O.D 20 Possible tertiary U.V. treatment

Sludge 50g/p/day 3300kg/day

Soil conditioner site

Export

Incineration of residue

Drying by solar or biogas

Electricity

Irrigation to fuel crops

Biogas

Incineration

Waste management

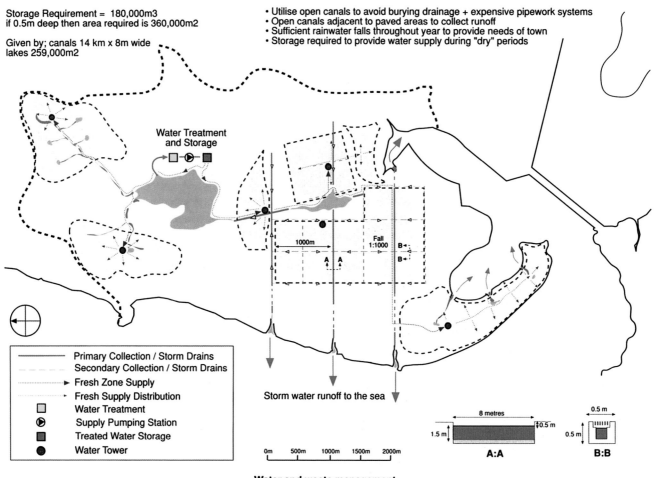

Storage Requirement = 180,000m3 if 0.5m deep then area required is 360,000m2

Given by; canals 14 km x 8m wide lakes 259,000m2

• Utilise open canals to avoid burying drainage + expensive pipework systems
• Open canals adjacent to paved areas to collect runoff
• Sufficient rainwater falls throughout year to provide needs of town
• Storage required to provide water supply during "dry" periods

Water Treatment and Storage

1000m

Fall 1:1000

B
B

A A

Storm water runoff to the sea

——————— Primary Collection / Storm Drains
– – – – – Secondary Collection / Storm Drains
·····► Fresh Zone Supply
·····► Fresh Supply Distribution
▢ Water Treatment
◉ Supply Pumping Station
◼ Treated Water Storage
● Water Tower

0m   500m   1000m   1500m   2000m

8 metres
0.5 m
1.5 m
A:A

0.5 m
0.5 m
B:B

Water and waste management

and supply must be tackled simultaneously and by the same strategic design body.

Building demand can be limited by producing design guidelines and energy targets for given plots of land. Typically, this will influence decision making with respect to both the building systems and architectural response. Importantly, it will place greater emphasis on the architect to develop a building type that is environmentally responsive (or selective) rather than being environment rejecting. Thus buildings will need to be: naturally ventilated wherever feasible; daylit; limit use of air conditioning; utilise solar energy for heating, cooling and ventilation efficient systems; careful orientation and planning; appropriate materials choice. By adopting these principles, it may be possible to reduce the actual energy demand by up to 70%.

Energy is traditionally supplied in three forms, oil, gas and electricity. Both oil and gas used for heating, cooling, etc can only result in reduction in natural resources, and thus are *not* sustainable. Electricity, although traditionally produced by the combustion of oil, gas or coal, can be produced by the combustion or collection of renewable sources such as: incineration of waste or energy crop (Biomass); solar collection (photovoltaic or solar thermal); wind turbines. However, in all of these processes, the efficiency of the actual electricity production is less than 30%, the remainder being lost as heat (usually up a cooling tower). Essential to the achievement of a sustainable energy policy is the use of this 'waste' heat by the utilisation of combined heat and power plants (CHP). The heat can be used not only to provide winter heating and hot water but also (more importantly) as a source for driving absorption cooling machines. In this manner, the energy production process can achieve up to 85% efficiency.

Renewable sources include – *Biomass*: This includes plant materials that may be specifically grown for energy production (fuel crop) as well as organic wastes that will be generated on site. There has been significant progress with respect to the utilisation of energy crops for energy production. Such an approach has significant advantages in developing countries as they utilise local agricultural skills, low first cost implementation – quick to implement (1-2 years for first crop). *Solar energy*: Photovoltaic – utilises solar cells to convert direct sunlight into electricity (dc). They are fairly inefficient, (10– 20%) and at the moment costly. *Solar thermal*: Uses solar energy to heat water to produce steam to drive a turbine etc. Used extensively in California – High capital costs, although they have great potential in sunny climates. *Winds*: Tried and tested systems. Their performance can be enhanced by integration into architectural building form. Following this philosophy, all

the new town would be all electric, with all heating, cooling, lighting, cooking, transportation and industrial systems (tram and/or electric cars) being based on electricity supply.

Water: In most countries, water is a valuable and scarce resource. It is thus important that a specific strategy is adapted that sets, as its prime objective, the achievement of a self-sufficient system; reduce demand; collect and store water over days or months to ensure that it is available all year round; treat and distribute water to areas of need efficiently; recycle waste water where possible for use in WCs or landscape. In any site specific area, it is necessary to carefully examine the precipitation and evaporation data. In many areas of the world, although there are long dry periods of little rainfall, there is often enough rainfall over the wet periods of the year to satisfy the yearly demand. However, essential to this strategy is an efficient collection and storage system. A typical balance for a new town development in a tropical climate indicates that enough rain falls through the 'wet' season to satisfy requirements during the dry season. In the example shown the town has been designed around the need to collect and store water in underground areas, tanks and lakes. The tanks form central squares and act as a significant thermal heat sink creating a cool micro climate within their immediate vicinity, whilst the above ground lakes and canals not only provide visual amenity but also a degree of evaporative cooling. In addition the canals from primary routes along which the landscape can be integrated to form pedestrian walkways and wildlife corridors.

Waste: Waste from a typical city can be broadly categorised into four forms: human effluent; bio-degradable/combustible waste (paper, vegetable materials); non-combustible waste (metals, glass etc); toxic waste. It is essential that the waste strategy is set to carefully deal with these four categories and that the 'waste' is not necessarily seen as something to be disposed of but as a resource to be recycled and re-used. Human effluent produces gas for heating/cooling/power, sludge for composting and water for landscaping. Biodegradable/combustible waste can be cleanly combusted to provide power and heat, can provide compost and ash, can be used for road constuction/ aggregate. Non-combustible metals (metals, concrete, glass, etc) – can be recycled or sold on to other areas. Toxic waste must be reprocessed by specialist offsite plant. The simplest means of dealing with this is to ensure that all industrial processes are environmentally friendly and their waste can be easily dealt with.

Microclimate

The creation of a 'comfortable' urban micro-

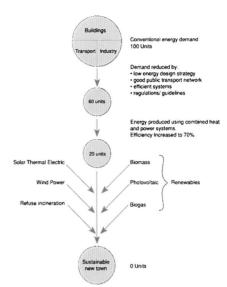

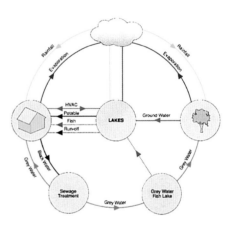

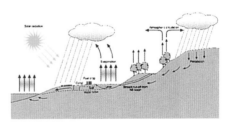

FROM ABOVE: New town energy strategy; Two methods of illustrating the natural water cycle; OPPOSITE FROM ABOVE: Waste management; Water and waste management

climate is essential to the successful operation of the urban transportation strategy of the new town. This will fundamentally affect the planning and layout of the urban environment. The response however will be site specific, primarily responding to the prevailing climate. The climatic elements within the urban area that can be modified by a sensitive urban design include: air temperature and humidities; radiant temperatures (surface) to which occupants are exposed; wind speeds in streets and around buildings; concentration of air pollution within traffic arteries; potential for natural ventilation; shading and potential for daylight; solar exposure and potential for solar energy utilisation. The urban factors that the urban designers have control over and that will effect these aspects are: topographical features of town; density (land cover) of buildings; distances between buildings; orientation and width of streets; urban parks, landscape; colour of buildings and streets; material choice (heavyweight versus lightweight). The aim of adopting such an approach is not to create an even level of comfort throughout the town, which would place too many restrictions on the design, but to create a changing thermal, air quality, acoustic and light 'topography' that recognises the need for varying landscapes. Thus streets may have a combination of fixed and variable shading systems. Bus stops and public squares may have a concentration of evaporative cooling systems (in hot/dry climates such as Seville) or permit good solar penetration (typical northern climate).Landscaping and green areas will play a vital role in the creation of the urbanscape and have a marked influence on the urban environment: provide outdoor shading, protection from cold winds; provide evaporative cooling; absorption of solar radiation; reduction in natural dust and air pollution particles; rainwater absorption; can impede or redirect wind to improve natural ventilation to buildings or surrounding areas. The landscape will also play a vital role in allowing fauna, flora and wildlife a natural path into and through the city. So that the town rather than merely destroying existing habitats can in some cases improve them or introduce new habitats and create opportunities for human and of wildlife interaction.

Materials
The choice of construction materials will play an important part in the sustainability of a new town. The primary objectives being that the materials should be: appropriate to the climate and the climatic response required; of local origin; low embodied energy; utilise local skills for construction; can be recycled; appropriate for the chosen structural regime.

In many cases, new towns comprise two to four storey developments. Although the use of steel or concrete is traditional for these buildings, there are many other alternatives, that in many cases can be sourced locally using local labour. *Stabilised soil blocks*: rammed earth; local soils, made locally; low cost and low embodied energy; can be used up to five or six storeys; recyclable. *Locally fired earth*: clay bricks; local skills; low cost; can be used up to five storeys. *Timber*: low cost, easy to use; sourced locally; replenishable source; low embodied energy; recyclable; *Fibre Concrete*: tiling (roofing); uses local materials (coconut and mud or cement). *Risk Hush Ash* (RHA); used to manufacture cement; burnt to provide energy and ash (100 tonnes rice = 5 tonnes ash).

Design Strategy
The very nature of this approach means that at first, each of these cycles should be analysed independently of each other and the urban plan in order to idealise their operation. It is then possible to create a multilayered design which is made up of all the individual components including the urban objectives. They can then be moulded together to create a working metabolism. This design process will involve highlighting the areas of both positive and negative interaction, leading to an emphasis of certain areas, that will inform the urban and architectural design. Thus, the plan for water may highlight a need for open lakes or canals, which can then be utilised as part of the landscape plan, and form an important element of the urban streetscape. Or the transport requirements for drop off points every 300m could form a module upon which the urban centres are clustered, which in turn may tie in with the requirement for water storage, etc.

In this manner, the urban planner, the architect and the engineers can work together with the various specialists to create an integrated plan and strategy based upon informed decision making. This approach to urban design is, however, more involved and more complex than the traditional methodologies for it involves examining the problem in not merely two or three dimensions, but in seven or eight dimensions. All towns and cities have metabolisms, that ultimately form part of the global eco-system. These metabolic cycles must respond to the demands for increased efficiency interaction so that they become sustainable Urban Environmental Design separates, idealises and then recombines these component cycles of the metabolism creating an environment and ecological topography that better satisfies todays demands for cleaner and better cities – *Towards a sustainable future*.

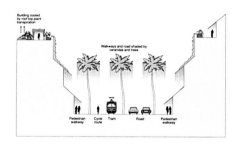

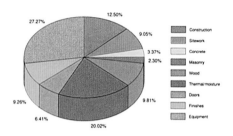

FROM ABOVE: Microclimate; Typical embodied energy in housing; OPPOSITE FROM ABOVE: Autonomous Living Capsule; Kayangez Atoll, Palau Pacific Ocean.
Thanks to: The Ngiom Partnership; Energy for Sustainable Development; University of London, Centre for Sustainable Development, The Martin Centre, Cambridge

THE FRACTAL CITY

MICHAEL BATTY AND PAUL LONGLEY

Abstract

A new science of form based on fractal geometry has emerged during the last 10 years. Fractals, or fractal objects as they are called, are irregular in shape but their irregularity is similar across many scales, thus enabling them to be described mathematically, and to be generated computationally. Fractals cannot be described using the geometry of regular figures based on points, lines, planes – the geometry of Euclid – for they exist between dimensions and therefore must be measured by means of their fractional or fractal dimension. Good examples are natural features and systems such as coastlines, mountainous terrain, and trees, but man-made artefacts such as silicon chips, stock market behaviour and even social organisations are fractals. Here we show that the morphology of cities is fractal. Their study using fractal geometry enables rich, predictive models of their structure to be developed, yielding new insights into how cities develop and how ideal cities can be formed.

The new science of cities

In the mid-20th century, those thinking about cities believed that they were clearly organised, simply ordered, and thus predictable, capable of being designed and planned in such a way that the quality of life of their residents could be directly improved by manipulating their physical form. This was a view that was widely held throughout architecture, indeed throughout the social sciences. It was founded on the belief that the social world, and its representation in physical artefacts such as cities was coherent and understandable in the same way that the physical world had been understood since the Enlightenment. The evident success of physics in providing an intellectual foundation for material technologies and the triumph of rationality through the application of the scientific method could be transferred wholesale and emulated in the social world, it was argued. Conscious and deliberate attempts at social engineering, as in the kind of architecture and urban planning which has dominated Western societies for the last 50 years and now the developing world, was the result.

As we approach the millennium, all this seems naive. The rational scientific programme has been split asunder in the last 20 years. Our understanding of systems in the small does not add up in any measure to our understanding in the large. Our theories and methods do not scale. The whole is more than the sum of the parts and physics as a basis for everything has been widely discredited. The limits imposed by theories of incompleteness, uncertainty, and complexity have destroyed any hope of a complete understanding and although there are some who still believe that physics will yet produce deeper theory, there is little hope that this will provide anything other than a mathematical tidying up of ever more tortuous logic. Dreams of a final theory are a chimera. Systems everywhere are simply too complex to be reduced to the tenets of conventional science. In the social world, prediction is logically impossible – although magic in the form of unpredictable new technologies is not! – while attempts at social engineering in the blunt manner of the mid-century have made the human condition worse rather than better.

Cities, the way we understand them, and the way we plan them demonstrate all the features of this crisis of rationality. Attempts at building mathematical models of their structure which began more than a generation ago were unable to yield realistic predictions even in the narrowest terms. They proved incapable of dealing with any kind of future which embodied creative development, surprise or novelty, now largely regarded as the seeds of social change. The massive explosions of population and their subsequent taming, and the emergence of world or global cities were not anticipated. Likewise, the impact of information and communication technologies and the rise of the network city could not be predicted, while at more local scales the development of edge cities, the refocusing of the city on suburbia, and the collapse of public transport systems inside Western cities have only been explicable in hindsight. In short, conventional science was unable to predict or even sense the emergence of new kinds of cities, new urban forms. In parallel, the repercussions of the disastrous experiments in social housing, of detailed planning controls on stifling economic development, and of transport systems which generated ever greater pollution and congestion, were nowhere anticipated. It is little surprise that the public and the polity, even the planners themselves, turned against the ideologies which produced such abhorrent results in our cities in the name of efficiency and equity.

The general response to these dilemmas has been the retreat into post-modernism. New urban theory is based on understanding cities in terms of their superficial structure through the kaleidoscope of social and physical complexity that clearly marks the intractability and ambiguity of the late 20th-century city. The search for order in cities in traditional scientific terms which associates cause to effect has all but been abandoned by the avant-garde. But amidst the ruins of this old science, a new science is emerging. Over the last 20 years, the view has been gaining ground that *insight* not *prediction* must be the goal of science. This has been spurred on by discoveries in mathematics in the late 1960s that superficially simple, deterministic systems from which equally simple and incontestable predictions have always been assumed, were not predictable in the traditional sense. The fact that simple systems were manifested with a level of complexity that was completely unknown, went some way to explain why more complex systems, which were often built from such simpler elements, were entirely unpredictable, in fact even chaotic. Cities, the weather, stock markets, are all examples which demonstrate chaotic behaviour under certain regimes, whose traditional models were unable to yield predictions with scale and form known in advance. In mathematical terms, this is largely due to the fact that the mathematical space within which such models operate is so convoluted and infinitely divisible that it is impossible to guess the accurate starting position of the systems within this space. In fact, it is impossible to know the position of the system and therefore impossible to make any form of prediction in the kind of precise terms that Newtonian science demands and assumes.

Such systems (and it can be shown that many, in fact most real systems can be so characterised) are thus largely unknowable. Even if their initial conditions and positions could be known, slight perturbations – random effects – would push their evolution into uncharted territory. Predicting weather is the classic example of such chaos. Edward Lorenz, who originally discovered chaos, presented a famous paper in 1972 entitled: 'Does the Flap of a Butterfly's Wings in Brazil Set Off a Tornado in Texas?'. In short, simple and small effects are magnified quickly into large-scale effects due to the action of positive feedback whose effects build spontaneously and cumulatively on each other. Chaotic systems are thus very different from those that science has worked with for the last 200 years. We traditionally assumed that most systems were linear. When they change, they change gradually, in proportion to what is there already, and thus their future behaviour is predictable, knowable. In fact, many systems are not like this for they show discontinuities in their behaviour, marked by catastrophes and bifurcations; weather, the stock market, prison riots and in our own case, the emergence of edge cities and out-of-town centres, are all examples of systems which cannot be understood and predicted by the traditional methods of science. Systems which shoot off into new domains and realms, which bifurcate, characterise those where surprise, novelty, and creative effort are central, where qualitatively different kinds of outcomes occur which cannot be predicted by methods which assume that the future is a simple linear function of the past. In fact, when science is scaled up to the real world, when we work with real systems like the weather, the physics of the small scale and the laboratory no longer applies and everything we deal with shows signs of chaos. Chaotic systems are the rule, not the exception which is what has been discovered slowly and painfully in science during the last 20 years.

There are many aspects of this new science which can be used to generate insights into the growth and structure of cities but here we will focus on how this helps us to understand their physical form, their morphology. One of the reasons why chaos lay undiscovered for so long in science and mathematics was that the mathematical space in which chaotic systems exist is irregular in a way that defied conventional geometries. The same kinds of irregularity are widespread in the non-mathematical, in the material world, in the morphology of cities, in geomorphology, in ecology, in biology, and in social organisation. Features such as boundaries, the way forms are packed into each other and

into space, the way terrain is structured and the way objects vary across scale, can all be seen in terms of a new geometry of form which has intrinsic connections with the new science of complexity. We will explain this geometry herein.

Fractals: the new architecture of urban form

Mid-century, our understanding of cities was largely based on responses to their physical form. Urban problems and their solutions were predicated in physical terms but as the quest for a deeper understanding began, the link between physical form and socio-economic functioning was broken. Although urban patterns were suggestive of such functioning leading to analogies, for example, between the city and the human body, the city and the machine, a convincing theory of urban form in the manner proposed for biology by D'Arcy Thompson, was never forthcoming just as it never materialised in biology either. Consequently, physical form became abstracted to the point where socio-economic functioning was loaded on to highly simplistic spatial structures, with little direct relevance to the ways in which architects and planners continued to manipulate, transform, design, and plan the city. But a generation passed, the world changed, and slowly but surely, interest in physical form revived: a new approach emerged.

Let us begin by explaining this new approach to studying urban form which is rapidly becoming an essential cornerstone in the post-modern science of cities. Imagine an ideal city of Renaissance times with an elaborate fortified wall built in the shape of the snowflake shown in the sequence in Figure 1 overleaf. The reason for the shape of such fortifications was to maximise the length of the wall so that as many soldiers as possible could be packed into the town's defence. Let us make the assumption that to design a good wall, we can repeat the basic motif which elongates the wall at different scales, thus maximising its length from the basic triangle in Figure 1(a) to the snowflake in Figure 1(d). In this sequence of figures, we might think of the way the same shape or detail is added at each level as the way we see the outline of the town at different scales, 1(a) being the coarsest scale where we can only see the triangular outline, to the finest level, 1(d), where we have three levels of similarly-shaped detail superimposed on one another. In these figures, we have taken the wall on the north side of the town and reproduced its line between each shape, clearly showing how the town wall gets longer as the scale gets finer. The rule for Renaissance town design is: to get the longest wall possible, add the same kind of crenellation at each finer and finer scale until no more soldiers can be packed around the wall.

At the first scale, we can consider the basic length of wall as being 1 unit but divided into 3 subunits, each of 1/3 length – Figure 1(a). At the next scale down, we add another subunit of 1/3 length by taking the central subunit and forming a triangular displacement with two sides of 1/3, thus making the length of the

LEFT: *Figure 1*. Generating the Koch Snowflake: a model of a fortified Renaissance town; RIGHT: *Figure 2*. The Manhattan skyline; *Figure 3*. The Manhattan skyline at two different scales

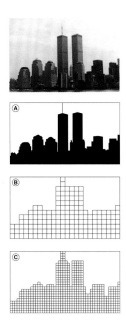

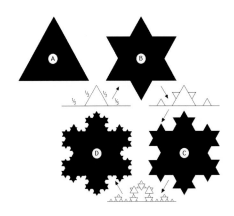

new line 4/3. This is equivalent to taking the old line and introducing a kink in it to make it longer as we show between Figure 1(a) and 1(b). We can of course keep on doing this at each scale. At the next scale down, we take each subunit of 1/3 and introduce a triangular displacement of length 1/9, thus leading to each subunit increasing in length from 1/3 to 4/9, and the overall length of the line increasing from 4/3 to (4/3)*(4/3) = 16/9 as in Figure 1(c). At the next scale, doing the same leads to the length of the overall line increasing to (4/3)*(4/3)*(4/3) = 64/27, as in Figure 1(d). We could speculate that if we continue this process indefinitely, the length of the line increases without bound: its length is unlimited – infinite – with the length being $(4/3)^k$ where k is the index of the scale. Of course, the scale from which we see this snowflake is fixed at the scale of the page, but you might imagine this going on for ever, picking up more and more detail as the scale gets finer and finer, from earthscale to subatomic levels.

This poses a paradox: how can a line continue to increase in length when it is clear from the sequence in Figure 1 that the area which the line encloses is finite? In fact, the area of the snowflake will converge to a fixed value as more and more detail at smaller and smaller scales is added. This conundrum was first stated for a coastline in a famous paper called 'How Long is the Coast of Britain?' by Benoit Mandelbrot (1967), who launched the field of fractal geometry 30 years ago. When you view a coastline on a map, it is at a certain scale. As the scale gets finer, then more detail around the coast is picked up and its length increases. If you go down on to the beach, then you would have to make a decision as to whether you were to measure around every pebble, and definitional problems would loom. But in general as you descend to the microscopic level, the length of the line increases without bound and it is easy to show mathematically (as we have shown pictorially in Figure 1) that the answer to the Mandelbrot question is that the length of the coastline is infinite; or rather, not infinite, but undefined. In short, for objects like coastlines, length depends on scale and absolute geometric

measures are no longer relevant. These are the kind of objects which are fractals, and it is clear that every boundary in nature must be fractal.

This geometric paradox was known in the 19th century in mathematics and in geography. There is some evidence that Leonardo da Vinci reflected upon it and if Leonardo knew about it, there is a good chance that the Greeks knew about it too. The paradox is as old as the hills. What is new is that for the first time, we now understand it and we have a new geometry to deal with it. But there is much more to fractals than the problem of length. To progress, consider the snowflake in Figure 1 which is the clearest kind of example. We constructed this fractal and were able to calculate its length routinely by taking a simple motif – the triangle – which we reduced in scale, transforming its position so that the snowflake might be constructed at any scale. It is quite clear that the design is similar from scale to scale and that at finer scales, the fractal is constructed from scaled down versions of the larger scale. We say that the fractal is self-similar in that the whole is formed from scaled versions of its parts. Fractals, like this snowflake curve (sometimes called the Koch curve after its originator, Von Koch) are exactly self-similar but if a little bit of randomness is introduced, as in a coastline, the object might be statistically self-similar or self-affine. The point is that seemingly random and transformed shapes can repeat themselves across scale and are thus fractals in the formal sense.

Besides scale invariance shown through self-similarity, fractals have precise mathematical properties. Using the traditional geometry of Euclid, a point has dimension 0, a line dimension 1, a plane dimension 2, a volume dimension 3, and so on. Fractal lines lie between dimension 1 and 2. Look at the line in Figure 1. It is more than the straight line of dimension 1 but it fills less than the plane with dimension 2. It twists to fill some of the plane and intuitively we might think its dimension lies between 1 and 2. For the Koch curve, we can compute the dimension as 1.26 (or in exact terms (log 4)/(log 3)) but if we think of lines which are more irregular such as fjord coastlines or if we make the kink in the

snowflake more exaggerated, the fractal dimension rises. Lines that twist and turn all across the space have a fractal dimension nearer 2. In fact, if you were to colour a square with a pencil and impose the rule that you are not to take the pencil off the paper but colour the square with one continuous line, you generate something resembling a fractal with Euclidean dimension 1 – it is a line – but fractal dimension 2 – it is a space-filling curve.

Fractals can of course exist in any dimension. Groups of points that follow a line are fractal dusts which have a dimension between 0 and 1, terrain has a dimension greater than 2 but less than 3, and cross-sections through terrain generate fractal lines with dimension between 1 and 2. City skylines look like obvious candidates. In Figure 2, we show the Manhattan skyline and in Figure 3, we show how the simplified outline of the skyline – Figure 3(a) – can be represented at two scales, Figure 3(c) being half the scale of Figure 3(b). By counting the number of cells at these two scales and then normalising by scale, we use a method (called box-counting) to work out the fractal dimension of the Manhattan skyline which gives a value of 1.56. If we looked at the suburbs, which are all composed of one- and two-storey buildings and open space, the dimension is more likely to be around 1.1 or 1.2. Once you start looking for fractals, you will find them everywhere (which is the title of one of the basic mathematical books on the subject by Barnsley, *Fractals Everywhere* (1988). In fact, most natural and man-made objects are not composed of simple points, lines and planes but of irregularly scaled versions of these. Fractal geometry is clearly the geometry of nature which is in the title of Mandelbrot's classic work defining the field, *The Fractal Geometry of Nature* (1983), but is also the geometry of cities as we reflect in our book *Fractal Cities* (1994). It is time to look at how we can describe and model cities in these terms.

Fractals in nature and fractals in cities

Any form which is self-similar is likely to be fractal. If there is a regular motif or design which repeats itself as the structure grows or scales – through time or across space, then that structure can be envisaged as a hierarchy, and thus fractal organisation is hierarchical organisation. The very best example is a tree. A tree is clearly self-similar in that its branches usually split regularly as they contract (scale) with distance from the root or main trunk. Any part of the tree mirrors the whole tree from the roots to the twigs and even into the structure of its leaves. In fact a tree is the literal embodiment of a hierarchy in that if you turn it upside down, the resulting structure shows the order in which the branches and twigs are formed as the tree grows from its roots. Indeed, if you look at the roots, then these, too, have the same shape as the tree, with the same fractal growth reaching into the earth as well as the sky. A wonderful demonstration of a fractal is to break some twigs from a tree, and view these twigs by blurring one's eyes, imagining that the twigs are the whole tree: the effect can be startling, just as the same can be seen in rock scree that has been formed by erosion on a mountain slope – the entire mountain form is contained within the scree, the scree being a smaller version of the same: this is what fractals in nature are all about.

Trees can be measured in two dimensions as elevations, or as plans, as cross-sections in the plane, or as objects that fill the plane, all giving rise to different fractal dimensions in the same way that cities can be envisaged as maps, as building structures that fill the third dimension, or as boundaries, or cross-sections such as the Manhattan skyline. We show the self-similarity of a number of trees in Figure 4 where the idea of hierarchy is quite clear and where suitable rendering provides very realistic looking trees. Note also that in the Koch curve of Figure 1, if the displacement is made into a spike, the resultant shape resembles a tree-like form, the so called Koch forest. Wherever self-similarity is generated across scales by repetition of a simple branching, then tree-like structures emerge as we will see for cities in terms of road networks, in geomorphology in terms of river and other water channels, and in the human body in terms of nerves and blood flow. In Figure 5 we show what is perhaps the best example of a fractal model of nature developed to date. This is Barnsley's fern (1988), which has been generated using a special mathematical technique which takes a real fern, computes how its branches transform into one another at different scales and then literally throws random dots at the page in such a way that only those dots that reflect the mathematical structure stick. In this way you can generate ever more levels of detail in a fractal object from whatever scale, with ever more realistic rendering.

So far, we have illustrated idealised fractals and real fractals, and fractals which are generated using models which reflect reality. The snowflake is idealised, the Manhattan skyline real, Barnsley's fern a model of reality. These distinctions run throughout science, and certainly throughout our use of fractal geometry to design, measure, and model cities. All our examples here reflect these distinctions and in the rest of this essay, we will show how different characterisations of urban form develop these different aspects of fractal geometry. Part of the challenge of this new science is to use this geometry creatively to measure, model and design; our book *Fractal Cities* contains many examples of this approach and we will now develop some of these here to illustrate their wide applicability.

Let us look at the way we might generate hypothetical fractal cities, starting with the assumption that cities of the past largely grew around their historic core. We plant a seed and then apply some local rule which embodies our shape motif, to the development already created. In Figure 6, we show four variations on this theme. The first, where we get rings of development, is the situation where everything is developed in the vicinity of each seed. No motif is applied and everything is developed with the shading showing the order in which the city grows around its core. The city fills its entire space and its fractal dimension is 2, the same as its Euclidean. As we make the motif more structured, sparser cities are grown which form the other three examples in this figure. In the top right-hand corner, the structure assumes that a cell is developed if there is one, and only one, already developed cell in the local neighbourhood. The bottom left-hand figure is the same with one or two developed cells in the neighbourhood. The bottom right-hand shape is created when the neighbourhood is restricted to cells north, south, east, and west of the cell in question with the rule that a cell is newly developed if only one cell in the neighbourhood is already developed. We can of course generate landscapes of these cities by planting many seeds and we show the kind of fractal carpet produced by applying the single cell rule in Figure 7. There are many other variants. In Figure 8 we show how we can grow a sparser structure – one which is called a Sierpinski gasket after the mathematician who discovered it – which spans the space and wraps around it. This is the kind of structure that we might envisage would be required when we colonise outer space – the kind envisaged by Arthur C Clarke in his recent book *3001: The Final Odyssey* where space cities require sparse, light structures which span space in more economical ways than the way we have built high density cities like London and New York.

There are three important points that need to be made about these hypothetical patterns. First, fractals do not only exist in space but also in time. The fractal carpets in Figures 6 to 8 illustrate how the motifs appear both spatially and temporally as the colour coding shows. Finding fractal patterns in time is harder than in space because the way we represent cities is usually in terms of space and we must disentangle space in terms of time to discover these. The second point relates to the

way we generate fractals. Clearly the procedures we use must be repetitive, iterative, or recursive as mathematicians call them. The way we constructed the snowflake in Figure 1 shows the basic idea of repeating and scaling the basic motif and placing it appropriately on the object as smaller and smaller versions of the overall pattern. Barnsley's (1988) iteration function system (IFS) is one such method but in Figures 6 to 8 we have defined the motifs in terms of cells or pixels on the computer screen and used a technique called cellular automata to generate these pictures. This way of modelling is basic to the new science of complexity which is being used widely to simulate space-time patterns, and it forms the essence of the creation of artificial life which represents the current synthesis of biology and computer science.

Thirdly, fractal geometry would be of no more than cursory interest if it were not for the profound idea that complex entities can only be understood in terms of very simple entities that comprise them. Cities display enormous variety but there is order to this variety and this order is clearly made up of very simple elements. Much of economic urban theory is premised on such order: for example, the distribution of places of different sizes and the way they grow is consistent with fractal theory, and although these theories have been under development for over one hundred years, they have been hard to tie to real city forms. Fractal geometry not only explains how order emerges from simple, local components but how complexity emerges. There is now real hope that appropriate ways of anticipating urban change, of generating new insights into how cities are formed and how new structures emerge, can be used to inform better urban design and urban planning which will be robust and relevant in a way that the plans of the past were not. To take the argument further, we must now turn to real places and see how the new geometry is consistent with urban patterns both within and between cities.

Growing cities

The skeletal structure of the industrial city is tree-like with radial street systems converging on the historic core. As cities grew around this core, they expanded into their hinterland in radial fashion, a little like the hypothetical square city in Figure 6. The street system is itself hierarchical with a few main radials, a larger number of district streets, and many neighbourhood roads. This hierarchy is easily seen in any modern city. In Figure 9 overleaf, we show the street system of the British industrial town of Wolverhampton in the vicinity of its centre. We have colour-coded the system according to the distance from the centre of its retail core. It is fairly clear that this mirrors the way in which Wolverhampton grew, except that in the last 30 years, a ring road has been used to divert traffic from the core. If you look at the radial road structure of the Greater London region, which is at the next scale up from Wolverhampton, the routes converge on the City, and layers of ring road – the North Circular Road, the M25 Orbital Road and so on – have thence been added during this century. The route structure has clear, hierarchical organisation as can be seen in Figure 10, while this picture also shows the fractal nature of the coastline and river estuary east of the metropolis. If we were to zoom in on this structure, we would see radial routes focusing on lesser order centres appearing at every level down, even to the level of the neighbourhood. Interestingly, as traffic focusing on centres has increased, the need to bypass such centres, has grown and a new hierarchy of circumferential

LEFT: Figure 6. Fractal carpets: land use patterns in hypothetical cities; CENTRE: Figure 7. An urban landscape; RIGHT: Figure 8. Sierpinski cities: colonising space with sparse structures

roads – orbitals and beltways – is emerging. The basic pattern of radial routes and the new pattern of orbitals repeats itself through the scales as fractal geometry dictates.

Different types of fractal structure exist in planned street systems particularly at the housing and residential scale. From the 1920s, innovative forms of pedestrian-vehicular segregation where cars and people were separated, were introduced in the Garden Suburbs and the New Towns schemes. At Radburn, New Jersey, in the late 1920s, Henry Wright and Clarence Stein developed such systems where there was a clear hierarchy in terms of local and distributor roads for vehicles, and paths for pedestrians. A schematic of the original plan for Radburn is shown in Figure 11. It is easy to see hierarchical organisation here. This has been replicated in many such housing layouts which are closer to the kinds of hypothetical fractals discussed earlier than are the organic and slowly growing forms that characterise the way most areas in cities develop. In fact, fractal geometry makes no distinction between planned and organically growing forms other than the fact that organically growing forms are often deterministic fractals with some noise or randomness added.

When these tree-like structures are embedded into urban development, we begin to see typical patterns emerge which are clearly fractal. If we also consider population densities, we see how cities begin to fill their space. Figure 12 shows the population density of Greater London where higher to lower densities are illustrated through the yellow to red colour spectrum. The pattern looks tree-like to a certain extent, yet its complexity suggests that it must have been built up not from one seed but from many. Many scales are represented in this pattern, and it can only be represented effectively using processes that build up from the small to the large – in short, processes which scale. The fractal dimension of London in these terms is nearer 2 than 1, while its boundaries which represent another way at looking at space-filling, are nearer 1 than 2. If we were to consider the third dimension, then life gets more difficult. Most of London with the exception of the City, the West End, and parts of the inner area, is largely two-storey residential and overall, it is likely that measuring fractal dimension into this third dimension would yield a dimension close to 2 than 3. Given the number of holes in the two-dimensional map, dimension measured in this way may even

be below 2. However, were we to look at the City, then we might find dimensions greater than 2. In fact we computed the dimension of the Manhattan skyline as 1.56 and a good rule of thumb in fractal geometry is that if the same processes occur in the next dimension up, the fractal dimension would simply be the first one plus 1, in this case 1.56 + 1 = 2.56. No one to our knowledge has really looked at cities in this way, although readers of AD might have expected our fractals to be those in 3D rather than 2D. However, this represents a frontier still to be explored and hopefully, some readers of this article will be encouraged to do this.

There are several ways of building fractal models which generate structures which fill space around some seed which acts a starting point. The most ambitious attempts to date are based on processes of local diffusion such as those found to generate structures such as crystals, electric breakdown, viscous fingers and such-like growth phenomena in physics. Let us refer to one specific technique which we have used extensively to simulate different kinds of fractal city called Diffusion-Limited Aggregation or DLA. This works as follows. Consider a seed which is planted at the centre of a space criss-crossed by a fine lattice and imagine that a series of particles is launched randomly one at a time from a long distance away from the seed. When a seed is launched, it wanders one lattice step at a time in any random direction. If it strays too far (outside the limits of the space), it dissolves or is destroyed and a new particle is launched. If the particle stays within the space, then eventually it will reach the seed and when it does it sticks; a new particle is launched. When this reaches the cluster it, too, sticks, and thus the cluster begins to grow in this manner. What do you think the cluster will look like eventually? Well, it turns out that this simple process generates a growing tree or dendrite around the seed. The reason is that as a particle sticks to a seed, it forms a branch which makes it ever more likely that when particles reach the growing cluster they will stick to already forming branches and avoid the fissures in-between. In fact, they are likely to encounter the branches first, just as if you drop a stone through a tree from above, although there may be many more spaces between branches than space occupied by the branches, the chance of the stone hitting a branch is very high because of the convoluted nature of the branches.

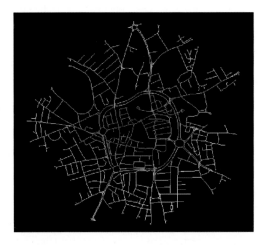

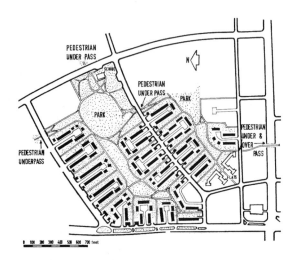

*ABOVE: **Figure 9**. Tree-like Wolverhampton; CENTRE: **Figure 10**. Fractal road networks, Greater London; BELOW: **Figure 11**. Hierarchical route segregation, Radburn, New Jersey; OPPOSITE: **Figure 12**. The fractal metropolis: London's population density*

We do not have to simulate the structure in this fashion although this is easy enough to do so. A more general version of the model exists in which we can weight the probability that the particle sticks to a growing branch. When this weight is very high, this means that when a branch begins to form, every particle will stick to the tip of the branch and a linear structure will emerge. If the weight is zero, then the particle can stick anywhere and an amorphous mass will form. As we vary the weight from zero to a large number, the structure changes from a 2-dimensional solid mass to a 1-dimensional line. All interesting cases lie between these limits. As the value of the weight falls, the structure becomes more and more dense with its fractal dimension falling from 1 towards 2. Classic dendrites associated with DLA have a dimension of 1.71. In our book *Fractal Cities*, we argue that this is the likely *a priori* dimension for industrial cities, near many of the dimension values we have measured for actual cities. We have generated typical cities using DLA and its generalisation and we show some of these in Figure 13. Our model does in fact have real meaning. To generate a linear city naturally (with a fractal dimension of 1), we have to constrain development so much that we only allow development on the end of what has been developed so far. Thus for any structure that fills space sparsely, we need very tight restrictions such as those used to generate the fractal carpets in Figure 6. As we relax these controls, we generate cities which fill ever more of their space, and when there is no control, everything gets filled, which is what would happen if you had no planning controls whatsoever. Or would it? We doubt it because human behaviour itself provides structure, and thus the ultimate quest of our new science is to find the rules that generate real cities.

Our last examples take urban form to the higher scales, to the region and to the nation. In Figures 14 and 15, we show the fractal structure of the megalopolis centred on south-east England, alongside the urban structure of Great Britain. When we examine the system of cities that form at these scales, it is clear that their number and their frequency as well as their form follow fractal laws which in physics and biology are called scaling laws. These reflect the scale invariance of fractal phenomena; if we were to take away the visual cues from Figures 14 and 15 which are the coastlines and the sea and which lead us to recognise the forms as being part of Britain, then the patterns could be at the same or at any scale down to the most local. London could be a small town while the nation could be the metropolis. At the global level, the distribution of the world population is, of course, also fractal, revealing that for the first time, we have a framework which enables us to link form to function, geometry to geography, space to time, and the present to the past. On this last point, there are now many examples which show how urban structure evolves through space and time and it is becoming clear how fractal structure evolves and changes.

Throughout our discussion, we have emphasised spatial structure, notwithstanding the fact that we have generated these structures through a kind of mathematical time. In Figure 16, we show the growth of the Washington DC-Baltimore metropolis from the late 18th century to the modern day. From this it is clear how fractal structure evolves. Two seeds start the growth which accelerates, eventually fusing the two urban areas as the sprawl gains speed. What the future form of urban society might be is uncertain. Some argue that all places will be urbanised but that fractal laws will still operate at every scale. Within this, there may be transitions to new forms of city which match radically new

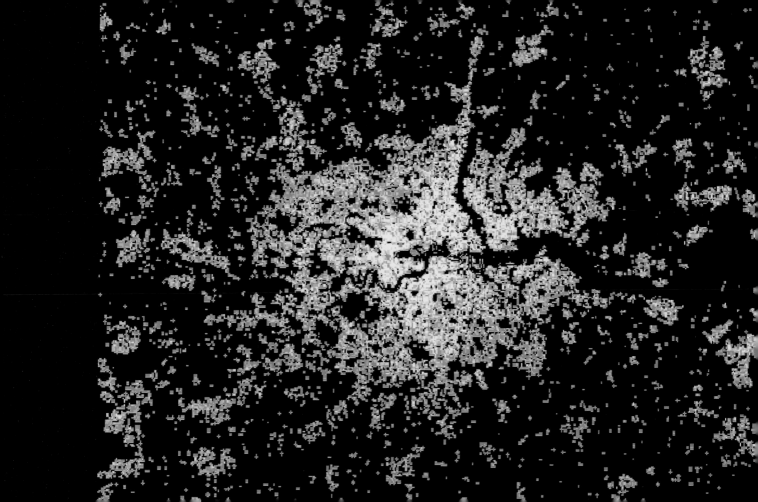

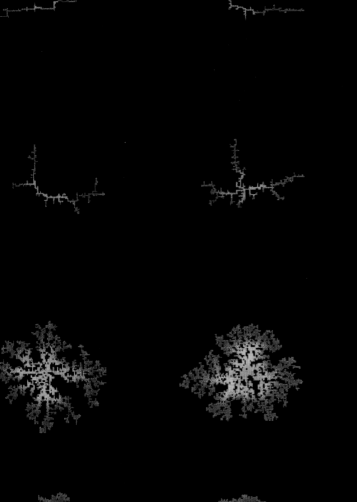

technologies. But whatever the future, in developing relevant insights about urban form, fractals and its place in the new science will be essential.

Towards a postmodern science of cities

The continuing challenge which has at last begun through these developments in fractal geometry is to link social process to spatial and physical form. This was David Harvey's challenge to urbanists almost a generation ago which dominated his book *Social Justice and the City* published in 1972 (by Edward Arnold, London). In fact Harvey's challenge was issued at the beginning of the long retreat from physicalism into social theory but the new science and the rise of post-modernism marks the beginning of the return. However, it is easier to see fractal form at more aggregate scales, in 2-dimensions rather than 3 and for cities in their entirety rather than in their elements. The real challenge is to build the continuing link through the scales, from the metropolis through the neighbourhood, to the street and the building plot and even beyond into the building itself.

We have no doubt that fractal geometry has much to say at more micro scales but so far, formally structured data has been lacking in this domain and architects have not been exposed sufficiently to the new geometry to be able to see its potential. It would be nice to think that within a decade, work will have begun in developing a fractal geometry for architecture linking form to

process, just as there have been developments of shape grammars and cellular automata at these scales already.

The quest to move into higher dimensions is also important. The core of the city could be seen as a sculpted fractal, as a volume that is successively unpacked as well as packed by smaller volumes of different sizes. There is much in the geometry that is suggestive here. Look back at Figure 1 and consider how we might extend all this into the third dimension. With an increasing number of high density city centres being available in digital, solid geometry – CAD – form, the quest to interpret such development through fractals is now feasible. Finally, none of this would be significant were it not for the possibility that we are on the threshold of developing ideas of how fractals are generated, how they evolve. If fractal geometry is the way of linking form to function, the next decade should see new theory emerge which shows how forms and functions co-evolve spontaneously and through design.

Michael Batty is Professor of Spatial Analysis and Planning, Centre for Advanced Spatial Analysis, University College London, 1-19 Torrington Place, London WC1E 6BT, UK (email: m.batty@ucl.ac.uk)

Paul Longley is Professor of Geography, University of Bristol, University Road, Bristol BS8 1SS, UK

Further reading

There are many more examples in our book *Fractal Cities* (Michael Batty and Paul Longley, Academic Press, San Diego, CA, 1994) which provides a systematic introduction to the measurement and simulation of urban structure using fractal geometry but the bible is by Bennoit Mandelbrot, *The Fractal Geometry of Nature* (W H Freeman, San Francisco, CA, 1983), which is a marvellous, esoteric, mindboggling book, well worth delving into time and time again.

A source of great inspiration. Michael Barnsley's *Fractals Everywhere* (Academic Press, San Diego, CA, 1988) is equally arcane, almost inaccessible to non-mathematicians but a wonderful illustration of the power of modern mathematics and a *tour de force* when it comes to methods.

A very readable and cogent introduction to the entire field is Hans Lauwerier's *Fractals: Endlessly Repeated Geometrical Figures* (Princeton University Press, Princeton, NJ, 1991, and Penguin Books, Harmondsworth, Middlesex, UK, 1992).

Applications abound. Physics is full of fractals, as is computer graphics. The various books by Heinz-Otto Peitgen, Harmut Jurgens and Dieter Saupe are worth

consulting especially *Fractals for the Classroom: Part 1 and Part 2* (Springer, Berlin, 1992) for these contain many applications to diverse fields and provide a useful overview.

Links between fractals and chaos can be mystical but a good medium is James Gleick's *Chaos: Making a New Science* (Viking, New York, 1987). However, if you want to delve into the essence of chaos, pursue the eminently readable book by the father of chaos, Edward Lorenz's *The Essence of Chaos* (University of Washington Press, Seattle, WA, 1993).

Another readable exposition which links the field to other branches of complexity theory is by Peter Coveney and Roger Highfield, *Frontiers of Complexity* (Faber and Faber, London, 1995).

Finally, let us note some papers. Mandelbrot's 'How Long is the Coast of Britain ?', *Science*, Volume 155, pp 636-8, 1967, marks the beginning of the field, while other related applications to cities can be found in Michael Batty, 'Cellular Automata and Urban Form: A Primer', *Journal of the American Planning Association*, 63 (2), pp266-74, 1997, and in journals such as *Environment and Planning B*.

WILLIAM MITCHELL
SOFT CITIES

Each window on my computer screen is an electronic forest *avantureuse*, a digital Broceliande. When I choose to enter this microworld, I have to play strictly by its rules.

Any piece of software creates a space in which certain rules rigorously apply, but with video games, the rules are the whole point. Without them there would be no game, and hence no fun. *Vide*!

Lemmings! Minimunchkin-mannikins tramp across the pixel patterns, timed to the tinny beat of the endless electromuzak; cast as an old softy of a God, I must intervene to save these tiny numskulls from otherwise-certain self-destruction.

'Eat fire, bug-eyed scum!' Suddenly I'm lost in the testosterone-fuelled fascist funhouse of Strike Squad; I must blow away successively more fearsome insectoid gladiators or face gory extinction myself. Kill or be killed.

SimCity! I get to play earnest urban policy wonk, but don't have to face an angry community when (as wonks are apt to do) I screw up. Its creator wrote, 'Access to a "toy" city gave me a guinea pig on which I could try out my city planning experiments'.[1] Good, clean fun until you notice the implicit political agenda. Its underlying structure is that of Jay Forester's mechanistic, conservative planning models from the 1950s and 60s. It presents you with a microworld magically free from racial divisions, labour unions, developers, or preservationists – one in which planners always win by building infrastructure (even when it carves up communities), lowering taxes, attracting industry, and creating jobs.

Realms of Arkania! 'Game features: more than 70 towns, villages, dungeons and ruins; twelve character archetypes; seven positive and seven negative character attributes; over 50 skills; twelve magic realms with over 80 spells; auto-combat option; and parties of up to six characters may be split and regrouped'.

F-15 Strike Eagle III! 'Surround yourself in a revolutionary new three-dimensional graphics system that provides you with a digitised map of downtown Baghdad complete with every bridge, the TV famous Air Ministry building and the "Baby Milk" factory! Cheat death in three explosive scenarios including Desert Storm, Korea and Central America!'

Metal & Lace: The Battle of the Robo Babes! 'Give your joystick a thrill . . . With the intense heat and action, you'll both end up with less than full body dress'.

Doom! The geography of this hack-and-slash masterpiece – the shareware sensation of 1994's gloomy winter – is three-dimensional, realistic, and extensive; you have a whole virtual city to get to know. The architecture is complex, the surfaces are textured, and the lighting and sound effects are eerily convincing. But the really big hook is that it's a fast-paced, cooperative, network game; physically separated game freaks can get 'together' in virtual spaces to explore them 'side-by-side'. You can see the computer-animated 'bodies' of your companions and they can see yours. You can communicate with each other as you blast thorny brown hominids with plasma rifles, or chainsaw flaming skulls that come flying at you out of nowhere. You get to gloat guiltily as your comrades-in-arms are mugged by the monsters that they meet and come to grisly, twitching ends. And in the 'death-match scenario', the instructions are to 'Kill everything that moves, including your buddies'.

Read the ads (bizarre as Borges, quirkier than Calvino) in *Computer Gaming World* or *Electronic Gaming Monthly*. Imagine yourself a mips-driven Marco Polo, a cybersurfing Gulliver; visit a few video game microworlds and engage in the action. The petty-Faustian bargain that all software offers will soon become vividly apparent; enter a digitally constructed world, accept its constitution and its rules, and you buy into its ideology. Love it or leave it.

Real estate/cyberspace

I was there at the almost-unnoticed Big Bang – the silent blast of bits that begat the universe of these microworlds. UCLA, the fall of 1969, and I was a very young assistant professor writing primitive CAD software and trying to imagine the role that designers might play in the emerging digital future; in a back room just down the hallways from the monster mainframe on which I worked, some Bolt Beranek and Newman engineers installed a considerably smaller machine that booted up to become the very first node of ARPANET – the computer network that was destined to evolve into the worldwide Internet.[2]

From this inconspicuous origin point, network

tentacles grew like kudzu to blanket the globe. Soon, cyberspace was busting out all over, and the whole loosely organised system became known as the Internet. During the late 80s and early 90s more and more networks connected to the Internet, and by 1993 it included nearly two million host computers in more than 130 countries. Then, in the first six months of 1994, more than a million additional machines were hooked up.

While the Internet community was evolving into something analogous to a ramshackle Roman Empire of the entire computer world, numerous smaller, independent colonies and confederations were also developing. Dial-in bulletin board systems such as the Sausalito-based Well – much like independent city-states – appeared in many locations to link home computers.[3] Before very long, though, most of these erstwhile rivals found it necessary to join forces with the Internet as well. There would not have been a great deal to connect if computers had remained the large and expensive devices that they were when ARPANET began in 1969.

But as networks developed, so did inexpensive personal computers and mass-marketed software to run on them. The very first, the Altair, showed up in 1974, and it was followed in the early 80s by the first IBM PCs and Apple Macintoshes. Each one that rolled off the assembly line had its complement of RAM and a disk drive, and it expanded the potential domain of cyberspace by a few more megabytes of memory.

Somewhere along the line, our conception of what a computer really was began to change fundamentally. It turned out that these electronic boxes were not really big, fast, centralised calculating and data-sorting machines as ENIAC, UNIVAC, and their mainframe successors had led us to believe. No; they were primarily communication devices – not dumb ones like telephone handsets, that merely encoded and decoded electronic information, but smart ones that could organise, interpret, filter, and present vast amounts of information for us. Their real role was to construct cyberspace.

Wild West/electronic frontier

It was like the opening of the Western Frontier. Parallel, breakneck development of the Internet and of consumer computing devices and software quickly created an astonishing new condition; a vast, hitherto-unimagined territory began to open up for exploration. Early computers had been like isolated mountain valleys ruled by programmer-kings; the archaic digital world was a far-flung range in which narrow, unreliable trails provided only tenuous connections among the multitudinous tiny realms. An occasional floppy disk or tape would migrate from one to the other, bringing the makings of

colonies and perhaps a few unnoticed viruses. But networking fundamentally changed things – as clipper ships and railroads changed the pre-industrial world – by linking these increasingly numerous individual fragments of cyberturf into one huge, expanding system.

By the 1990s, the digital electronics and telecommunications industries had configured themselves into an immense machine for the ongoing production of cyberspace. We are rapidly approaching a condition in which every last bit of computer memory in the world is electronically linked to every other. This vast grid is the new land beyond the horizon, the place that beckons the colonists, cowboys, con-artists, and would-be conquerors of the 21st century. And there are those who would be King.

It will be there forever. Because its electronic underpinnings are so modular, geographically dispersed, and redundant, cyberspace is essentially indestructible. You can't demolish it by cutting links with backhoes or sending commandos to blow up electronic installations, and you can't even nuke it. If big chunks of the network were to be wiped out, messages would automatically reroute themselves around the damaged parts. If some memory or processing power were to be lost it could quickly be replaced. Since copies of digital data are absolutely exact replicas of the originals, it doesn't matter if the originals get lost or destroyed. And since multiple copies of files and programs can be stored at widely scattered locations, eliminating them all with certainty is as hard as lopping Hydra heads.

Cyberspace is still tough territory to travel, though, and we are just beginning to glimpse what it may hold. 'In its present condition', Mitch Kapor and John Perry Barlow noted in 1990, 'Cyberspace is a frontier region, populated by the few hardy technologists who can tolerate the austerity of its savage computer interfaces, incompatible communications protocol, proprietary barricades, cultural and legal ambiguities, and general lack of useful maps or metaphors'. And they warned: 'Certainly, the old concepts of property, expression, identity, movement, and context, based as they are on physical manifestation, do not apply succinctly in a world where there can be none'.[4]

Human laws/coded conditionals

Out there on the electronic frontier, code is the Law. The rules governing any computer-constructed microworld – of a video game, of your personal computer desktop, of a word processor window, of an automated teller machine, or of a chat room on the network – are precisely and rigorously defined in the text of the program that constructs it on your screen. Just as Aristotle, in *The Politics*, contemplated alternative constitutions for city-states (those proposed by the theorists Plato, Phaleas, and Hippodamos, and the actual Lacedaemonian, Cretan, and Carthaginian ones) so denizens of the digital world should pay the closest of critical attention to programmed polity. Is it just and humane? Does it protect our privacy, our property, and our freedom? Does it constrain us unnecessarily, or does it allow us to act as we may wish?

At a technical level, it's all a matter of the software's conditionals – those coded rules that specify if some condition holds then some action follows. Consider, for example, the familiar ritual of withdrawing some cash from an ATM. The software running the machine has some gatekeeper conditionals; if you have an account, and if you enter the correct PIN number (the one that matches up, in a database somewhere, with the information magnetically encoded on your ATM card), then you can enter the virtual bank. (Otherwise you are stopped at the door. You may have your card confiscated as well.) Next the program presents you with a menu of possible actions – just as a more traditional bank building might present you with an array of appropriately labelled teller windows or (on a larger scale) a directory pointing you to different rooms: if you indicate that you want to make a withdrawal, then it asks you to specify the amount; if you want to check your balance, then it prints out a slip with the amount; if you want to make a deposit, then yet another sequence of actions is initiated. Finally, the program applies a banker's rule; if the balance of your account is sufficient (determined by checking a database), then it physically dispenses the cash and appropriately debits the account.

To enter the space constructed by the ATM system's software you have to submit to a potentially humiliating public examination – worse than being given the once-over by some snotty and immovable receptionist. You are either embraced by the system (if you have the right credentials) or excluded and marginalised by it right there in the street. You cannot argue with the it. You cannot ask it to exercise discretion. You cannot plead with it, cajole it or bribe it. The field of possible interactions is totally delimited by the formally stated rules.

So control of code is power. For citizens of cyberspace, computer code – arcane text in highly formalised language, typically accessible only to a few privileged high-priests – is the medium in which intentions are enacted and designs are realised, and it is becoming a crucial focus of political contest. Who shall write the software that increasingly structures our daily lives? What shall that software allow and proscribe? Who shall be privileged by it and who

marginalised? How shall the writers of the rules be answerable?

Physical transactions/electronic exchanges

Historically, cities have also provided places for specialised business and legal transactions.[5] In *The Politics,* Aristotle proposed that a city should have both a 'free' square in which 'no mechanic or farmer or anyone else like that may be admitted unless summoned by the authorities' and a marketplace 'where buying and selling are done . . . in a separate place, conveniently situated for all goods sent up from the sea and brought in from the country'.[6] Ancient Rome had both its *fora civila* for civic assembly and its *fora venalia* for the sale of food. These Roman markets were further specialised by type of produce; the *holitorium* was for vegetables, the *boarium* for cattle, the *suarium* for pigs, and the *vinarium* for wine. Medieval marketplaces were places both for barter and exchange and for religious ritual. Modern cities have main streets, commercial districts, and shopping malls jammed with carefully differentiated retail stores in which the essential transaction takes place at the counter – the point of sale – where money and goods are physically exchanged.

But where electronic funds transfer can substitute for physical transfer of cash, and where direct delivery from the warehouse can replace carrying the goods home from the store, the counter can become a virtual one. Television home shopping networks first exploited this possibility – combining cable broadcast, tele-phone, and credit card technologies to transform the purchase of zirconium rings and exercise machines into public spectacle.[7] Electronic 'shops' and 'malls' provided on computer networks (both Internet and the commercial dial-up services) quickly took the idea a step further; here customer and store clerk do not come face-to-face at the cash register, but interact on the network via a piece of software that structures the exchange of digital tokens – a credit card number to charge, and a specification of the required goods. (The exchange might then become so simple and standardised that the clerk can be replaced completely by a software surrogate.) As I needed books for reference in preparing this text, I simply looked up their titles and ISBN numbers in an on-line Library of Congress catalogue, automatically generated and submitted electronic mail purchase orders, and received what I requested by courier – dispatched from some place that I had never visited. The charges, of course, showed up on my credit card bill.

Immaterial goods such as insurance policies and commodity futures are most easily traded electronically. And the idea is readily extended to small, easily transported, high value speciality items – books, computer equipment, jewellery, and so on – the sorts of things that have traditionally been sold by mail order. But it makes less sense for grocery retailing and other businesses characterised by mass markets, high bulk, and low margins. Cyberspace cities, like their physical counterparts, have their particular advantages and disadvantages for traders, so they are likely to grow up around particular trade specialisations. Since you cannot literally lay down your cash, sign a cheque, or produce a credit card and flash an ID in cyberspace, payment methods are being reinvented for this new kind of marketplace. The Internet and similar networks were not initially designed to support commercial transactions, and were not secure enough for this purpose. Fortunately though, data encryption techniques can be used to provide authentication of the identities of trading partners, to allow secure exchange of sensitive information such as credit card numbers and bid amounts, and to affix digital 'signatures' and time stamps to legally binding documents. By the summer of 1994, industry standards for assuring security of Internet transactions were under development, and on-line shopping services were beginning to offer encryption-protected credit card payment.[8] And the emergence of genuine digital cash – packages of encrypted data that behaved like real dollars, and could not be traced like credit card numbers – seemed increasingly likely.

In traditional cities, transaction of daily business was accomplished literally by handing things over; goods and cash crossed store counters, contracts were physically signed, and perpetrators of illegal transactions were sometimes caught in the act. But in virtual cities, transactions reduce to exchanges of bits.

Street maps/hyperplans

Ever since Ur, doorways and passageways have joined together the rooms of buildings, webs and grids of streets have connected buildings to each other, and roads have linked cities. These physical connections provided access to the places where people lived, worked, worshipped, and entertained themselves.

Since the winter of 1994, I have had a remarkable piece of software called Mosaic on the modest desktop machine that I am using to write this paragraph.[9] Mosaic, and the network of World Wide Web servers to which it provides access, work together to construct a virtual rather than physical world of places and connections; the places are called 'pages' and they appear on my screen, and the connections – called hyperlinks – allow me to jump from page to page by clicking on highlighted text or icons.

A World Wide Web 'home page' invites me to

step, like Alice through the looking glass, into the vast information flea-market of the Internet. The astonishing thing is that a WWW page displayed on my screen may originate from a server located anywhere in the Internet. In fact, as I move from page to page, I am logging into machines scattered around the world. But as I see it, I jump almost instantaneously from virtual place to virtual place by following the hyperlinks that programmers have established – much as I might trace a path from piazza to piazza in a great city along the roads and boulevards that a planner had provided. If I were to draw a diagram of these connections I would have a kind of street map of cyberspace. MUD crawling is another way to go. Software systems known as MUDs – Multi-User Dungeons – have burned up countless thousands of Internet log-in hours since the early 1980s.[10] These structure on-line, interactive, role-playing games, often attracting vast numbers of participants scattered all over the net. Their particular hook is the striking way that they foreground issues of personal identity and self-representation; as initiates learn at old MUDder's knees, the very first task is to construct an on-line persona for yourself by choosing a name and writing a description that others will see as they encounter you.[11] It's like dressing up for a masked ball, and the irresistible thing is that you can experiment freely with shifts, slippages, and reversals in social and sexual roles and even try on entirely fantastic guises. How does it really feel to be a complete unknown?

Once you have created your MUD character, you can enter a virtual place populated with other characters and objects. This place has exits – hyperlinks connecting it to other such settings, and these in turn have their own exits; some MUDs are vast, allowing you to wander among thousands of settings – all with their own special characteristics – like Baudelaire strolling through the buzzing complexity of 19th-century Paris. You can examine the settings and objects that you encounter, and you can interact with the characters that you meet.

But as you quickly discover, the most interesting and provocative thing about a MUD is its constitution – the programmed-in rules specifying the sorts of interactions that can take place and shaping the culture that evolves. Many are based on popular fantasy narratives such as *StarTrek*, Frank Herbert's *Dune*, CS Lewis's *Chronicles of Narnia*, the Japanese animated television series *Speed Racer*, and even more doubtful products of the literary imagination; these are communities held together, as in many traditional societies, by shared myths. Some are set up as hack 'n slash combat games in which bad MUDders will try to 'kill' your character; these, of course, are violent, Darwinian places in which you have to be aggressive and constantly on your guard. Others, like many of the TinyMUDs, stress ideals of constructive social interaction, egalitarianism, and nonviolence – MUDderhood and apple pie. Yet others are organised like high-minded lyceums, with places for serious discussion of different scientific and technical topics. The MIT-based Cyberion City encourages young hackers – MUDders of invention – to write MUSE code that adds new settings to the environment and creates new characters and objects. And some are populated by out-of-control, crazy MUDders who will try to engage your character in TinySex – the one-handed keyboard equivalent of phone sex.

Early MUDs – much like text-based adventure video games such as Zork – relied entirely on typed descriptions of characters, objects, scenes, and actions. (James Joyce surely would have been impressed; city as text and text as city. Every journey constructs a narrative.) But greater bandwidth, faster computers, and fancier programming can shift them into pictorial and spatial formats.[12]

Enclosure/encryption

In physically constructed cities, the enclosing surfaces of constituent spaces – walls, floors, ceilings, and roofs – provide not only shelter, but also privacy. Breaches in these surfaces – gates, doors, and windows – have mechanisms to control access and maintain privacy; you can lock your doors or leave them open, lower the window shades or raise them. Spatial divisions and access control devices are deployed to arrange spaces into hierarchies grading from completely public to utterly private. Sometimes you have to flip your ID to a bouncer, take off your shoes, pay admission, dress to a doorman's taste, slip a bribe, submit to a search, speak into a microphone and wait for the buzzer, smile at a receptionist, placate a watchdog, or act out some other ritual to cross a threshold into a more private space. Traditions and laws recognise these hierarchies, and generally take a dim view of illicit boundary crossing by trespassers, intruders, and peeping Toms.

Different societies have distinguished between public and private domains (and the activities appropriate to them) in differing ways, and cities have reflected these distinctions. According to Lewis Mumford, domestic privacy was 'a luxury of the well-to-do' up until the 17th century in the West.[13] The rich were the people who could do pretty much what they wanted, as long as they didn't do it in the street and frighten the horses. Then, as privacy rights trickled down to the less advantaged classes, the modern 'private house' emerged, acquired increasingly rigorous protections of constitutional law and public policy, and eventually

became the cellular unit of suburban tissue.[14] Within the modern Western house itself – in contrast with some of its ancient and medieval predecessors – there is a carefully organised gradation from relatively public verandahs, entry halls, living rooms and parlours to more private, enclosed bedrooms and bathrooms where you can shut and lock the doors and draw down the shades against the outside world.

It doesn't rain in cyberspace, so shelter is not an issue, but privacy certainly is. So the construction technology for virtual cities – just like that of bricks-and-mortar ones – must provide for putting up boundaries and erecting access controls, and it must allow cyberspace architects and urban designers to organise virtual places into public-to-private hierarchies.

Fortunately, some of the necessary technology does exist. Most obviously, the rough equivalent of a locked gate or door, in cyberspace construction, is an authentication system.[15] This controls access to virtual places (such as your electronic mail inbox) by asking for identification and a password from those who request entry. If you give the correct password, you're in.[16] The trouble, of course, is that passwords – like keys – can be stolen and copied. And they can sometimes be guessed, systematically enumerated till one that works is found, or somehow extorted from the system manager who knows them all. So password-protection – as with putting a lock on a door – discourages illicit entry, but does not block the most determined break-in artists.

Just as you can put the valuables that you really want to protect in a sturdy vault or crypt, though, you can build the strongest of enclosures around digital information by encrypting it – scrambling it in a complex way so that it can only be decoded by somebody with the correct secret numerical key. The trick is not only to have a code that is difficult to crack, but also to manage keys so that they do not fall into the wrong hands, and the cleverest known way to do this is to use a technique called RSA public-key encryption. In this system, which derives its power from the fundamental properties of large prime numbers, each user has both a secret 'private' key and a 'public' key that can be distributed freely. If you want to send a secure message, you first obtain the intended recipient's public key, and use that to encode the information. Then the recipient decodes it using the private key.

Under pressure from cops and cold warriors, who anticipate being thwarted by impregnable fortresses in cyberspace, the US Federal Government has doggedly tried to restrict the availability of strong encryption software. But in June 1991, hacker folk-hero Philip Zimmerman released his soon-to-be-famous, RSA-based Pretty Good Privacy (PGP) encryption program.

By May 1994, commercial versions had been licensed to over four million users, and MIT had released a free, non-commercial version that anybody could legally download from the Internet.[17] From that moment, you could securely fence off your private turf in cyberspace.

Meanwhile, the Clinton Administration pushed its plans for the Clipper Chip – a device that would accomplish much the same thing as RSA, but would provide a built-in 'trapdoor' for law-enforcement wiretapping and file decoding.[18] The effect is a lot like that of leaving a spare set of your front door keys in a safe at FBI headquarters. Opinion about this divided along predictable lines. A spokesman for the Electronic Frontier Foundation protested, 'The idea that the Government holds the keys to all our locks, before anyone has even been accused of committing a crime, doesn't parse with the public'.[19] But an FBI agent, interviewed in the *New York Times,* disagreed: 'OK, someone kidnaps one of your kids and they are holding this kid in this fortress up in the Bronx. Now, we have probable cause that your child is inside this fortress. We have a search warrant. But for some reason, we cannot get in there. They made it out of some new metal, or something, right? Nothing'll cut it, right? . . . That's what the basis of this issue really is – we've got a situation now where a technology has become so sophisticated that the whole notion of a legal process is at stake here . . . If we don't want that, then we have to look at Clipper'.[20]

So the technological means to create private places in cyberspace are available, but the right to create these places remains a fiercely contested issue. Can you always keep your bits to yourself? Is your home page your castle?[21]

Notes

1 Will Wright, 'Foreword' to Johnny L Wilson, *The SimCity Planning Commission Handbook*, Osborne McGraw-Hill, Berkeley, 1990, pxv.

2 ARPANET was funded by ARPA – the Advanced Research Projects Agency of the US Federal Government – and it was intended for use by the military and by computer science researchers. For the early history see Jeffrey A Hart, Robert R Reed, and Francois Bar, 'The Building of the Internet', *Telecommunications Policy*, Nov 1992, pp666-689.

3 For a history of the Well see Cliff Figallo, 'The Well: Small Town on the Internet Highway System', Sept 1993, available from the author at fig@well.sf.ca.us.

4 Mitchell Kapor and John Perry Barlow, 'Across the Electronic Frontier', *Electronic Frontier Foundation*, Washington DC, July 1990.

5 For historical surveys of these places see J B Jackson, 'Forum Follows Function', in N Glazer and M Lilla (eds) *The Public Face of Architecture*, Free Press, New York, 1987, and M Webb, *A Historical Evolution: The City Square*, Whitney Library of Design, New York, 1990.

6 Aristotle, *The Politics*, VII, xii.

7 Gary Gumpert and Susan J Drucker, 'From the Agora To the Electronic Shopping Mall', *Critical Studies in Mass Communication 9* (1992), pp186-200.

8 Peter H Lewis, 'Attention Shoppers: Internet Is Open', *The New York Times*, August 12, 1994, D1-D2.

9 On the development, introduction, and remarkable initial success of NCSA Mosaic see John Markoff, 'A Free and Simple Computer Link', *The New York Times*, Dec 8, 1993, D1, D5. The original work on the WWW was done by Tim Berners-Lee at CERN in Geneva in the late 80s. Mosaic was developed at the National Centre for Supercomputer Applications at the University of Illinois, Urbana-Champaign. By early 1994, more than 50,000 copies of Mosaic were being down-loaded monthly from NCSA's public server.

10 The first MUD, written by Roy Trubshaw and Richard Bartle, was based on the fantasy board game Dungeons and Dragons. There are numerous arcane variants on the generic Multi-User Something idea — TinyMUDs, MUSEs, MUSHs, MUCKs, MOOs, and so on. On the experience of MUD-crawling, see David Bennahum, 'Fly Me to the MOO', *Lingua Franca*, vol 4, no4 (May/June 1994), pp1 and 22-37.

12 This is, of course, closely related to the old literary issue of establishing a voice. 'Call me Ishmael' might be the opening ploy in a MUD interaction. So Wayne Booth's classic *The Rhetoric of Fiction* (Second edition, University of Chicago Press, Chicago, 1983) serves as a pretty good theoretical introduction to MUDding.

12 As programmers will appreciate, MUDs constitute a natural application for object-oriented programming techniques, and the developments of the MUD idea and of object-oriented programming have been intertwined.

13 Lewis Mumford, *The City in History*, Harcourt Brace and World, New York, 1961, p384.

14 One consequence is that you can get sued for invasion of privacy. Under American tort law, one who intentionally intrudes upon the seclusion of another is subject to liability if the intrusion would be highly offensive to a reasonable person. On the general idea of privacy rights, see Alan F Westin, *Privacy and Freedom*, Athenaeum, New York, 1967.

15 Authentication systems were not needed on the earliest computers, and they are not commonly used on personal computers today, since access to the machine can be controlled physically. But they are required on machines that have many potential users. Thus they first came into widespread use with the growing popularity of mainframe-based, multi-user, timesharing systems in the 1960s, and the idea carried over to computer networks in which a user logged into one machine can remotely access other machines.

16 You should not assume, though, that a password-protected place is necessarily private. In the widely reported case of Bourke versus the Nissan Motor Corporation in 1993, Nissan dismissed some employees after peeking into their password-protected electronic mail boxes. The employees sued for invasion of privacy and wrongful determination. But the California courts ruled against the employees' claim that the passwords created an expectation of privacy.

17 William M Bulkeley, 'Cypher Probe', *The Wall Street Journal*, April, 1994, ppA1, A8.

18 Peter H Lewis, 'Of Privacy and Security: The Clipper Chip Debate', *The New York Times*, April 24, 1994, pF5.

19 Jerry Berman, quoted by Steven Levy 'Battle of the Clipper Chip', *The New York Times Magazine*, June 12, 1994, pp44-51, 60, 70. In June 1994, the US Public Policy Committee of the Association for Computing Machinery (USACM) released an expert panel report entitled 'Codes, Keys and Conflict: Issues in US Crypto Policy', which took a strong stand against Clipper and urged the Clinton Administration to withdraw it.

20 Jim Kallstrom, quoted by Steven Levy, ibid.

21 For a useful summary of some of the legal issues, with particular reference to electronic mail privacy and electronic monitoring of employees, see Michael Traynor, 'Computer E-Mail Privacy Issues Unresolved', *The National Law Journal*, Jan 31, 1994.

Abridged text from William Mitchell, City of Bits, *MIT Press, Cambridge, Massachusetts, 1994, chapter 4: 'Soft Cities'. Printed with permission of MIT Press, available on the WWW: http://www-mitpress.mit.edu/ City_of_Bits/index.html.*

A.TOPOS WITH AA DIPLOMA UNIT 12
SOFT CITIES 1: FLATSCAPES
Commentary by Jane Harrison and David Turnbull

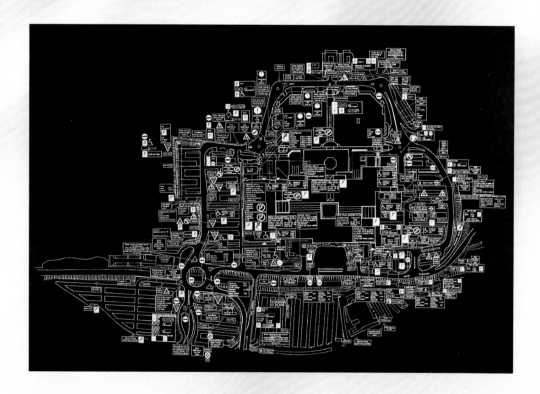

FROM L TO R: Analysis, text space of commercial field; simulation, a motile code produced through analysis of existing patterns of land use and their projected mid-term migration pattern; materialisation, variable viscosity field sample site

Flatscape

We use the term flatscape to indicate the physical condition of the *infra-urban*[1] landscape and a psychological state. This is a condition of apparently limitless horizontality, evenness and homogeneity. A flatscape is also a surface of *inclusion* which contains an overabundance of connection and a surplus of *dead ends*. Flatscapes can be found everywhere. They are non-places producing the emerging extremes of solitude and isolation identified by Marc Augé and information spaces as described by Paul Virilio.

Brent Cross

Brent Cross[2] is a paradigmatic flatscape. We have been using this environment as a test case in our work with Diploma Unit 12 at the Architectural Association. The objective of the work is twofold. One, to develop analytic methods by which such environments can be critically assimilated and two, to develop transformative techniques for projecting an optimistic future for such environments. This work explores the theory and prac-

tice of Soft Urbanism, focusing on the production and materialisation of *psyche-logical*[ß] space.

Soft Urbanism

The *infra-urban* is a global condition. It is clear that a practice of urbanism must be discovered which is based on accept-ance and transformation rather than the rejection of this condition; an urbanism which is not based on the wholesale construction or reconstruction of urban fabric but on principles of connectivity and condensation which, when material-ised as new *infrastructures,* absorb the forces of and act as catalysts for growth within developing urban contexts. We reject procedures of exclusion (that is, systems of judgement based on fantasies of order and omnipotence) in favour of models which sustain, rather than re-strain, excess to produce systems of coherent differentiation. In our research we have been developing techniques which explicitly mix, blur, distort, con-dense, and/or redistribute information found in the setting itself to produce

effects which establish continuities where none apparently exist, revealing new possibilities for social interaction, new forms and new materialisations. These techniques explore the *depthless* space of sampling, while at the same time mining the *thickness* of information as it is found in the world – demonstrating the potential of systems of inclusion rather than exclusion in the production of a complex mix, physical and social.

There are three stages to this work:

Analysis

A series of analytic techniques have been developed and expanded upon to extract and collate vast sets of data from the context of operation in the form of a series of data-fields. A data-field is understood to be always already de-territorialised. Its usefulness lies in its materiality and in the structures of combi-nation it establishes rather than in any imagined meaningful relationship to its source. Data-fields are simultaneously precise and provisional. They are the slack surfaces of information.

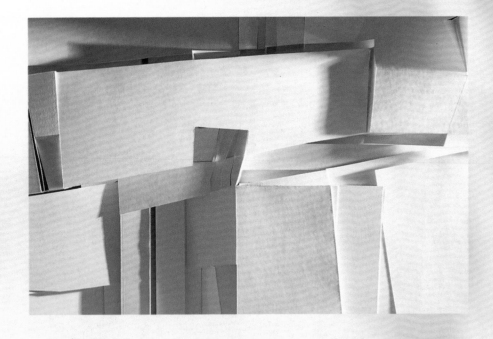

FROM ABOVE: Recreation field (sample site, Brent Reservoir) where a sports related infrastructure emerges from an analysis of the behaviour of existing patterns of mobility and materiality; maximum intensity commercial and recreational infrastructure – north circular business park

Simulation

Slack information surfaces are then manipulated systematically through procedures which simulate the probable and/or projected trajectories of development. Data is accelerated, condensed and redistributed in accordance with rules which reflect both strategic forces (political, social and economic) and errant forces (interference, accident and manoeuvre). The result of this stage of work is the production of a *motile code*, a thick construct of urban potential, simultaneously real and imaginary; excessive, complex, dense, and pointing. A code reflecting flow and movement which is capable of being interpreted spontaneously and independently.

Materialisation

The motile code carries within itself multiple possibilities and instructions for urban growth and change. To test the implications of these, sample sites are identified and performance criteria are established. Through a process of negotiation between the specific local conditions and the motile code, multiple speculative materialisations and effects – policies, infrastructures, landscapes and hybrid buildings – are produced.

Notes

1   *Infra-urban* = INFRA + URBAN: BEYOND/ BENEATH/AFTER/FURTHER THAN the URBAN.
2   Brent Cross is in North London, where the terrain has been changing continuously since the mid-19th century. The Town and Country Planning Acts of the 1940s had a profound impact on the suburban character of the area. Proximity to Heathrow airport and the M1 motorway has stimulated ribbon development at a large scale along the major roads. This is now being re-formed into cluster arrangements where shopping and entertainment zones, hotels and business parks cohabit with interwar and postwar suburban housing, the remaining 19th century infrastructure and new high speed roads: a zone of maximum potential.
3   For a discussion of the *psyche-logical* see Christine Wertheim's review of the Eidetic Images exhibition, curated by David Turnbull, in *AA Files* 30, Autumn 1995, pp74-76.

The international design and consulting practice, Wimberly
Allison Tong & Goo (WAT&G), specialising in hospitality, leisure
and entertainment, has already acknowledged the potential
market in structures for space tourism. Here the company's
Vice President and Corporate Managing Director, Howard
Wolff, introduces the exclusive resort it has conceived
for those who want to get away from it all in 20 years time.

Space Resort

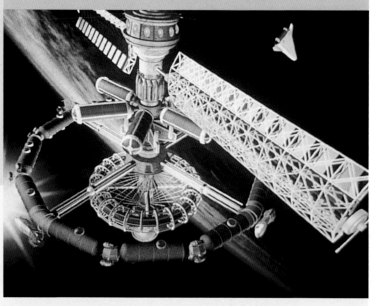

2017

Wimberly Allison Tong & Goo has designed a space resort in low earth orbit utilising recycled external fuel tanks salvaged from future space shuttle launches. This proposal faced the WAT&G design team with a set of unique architectural challenges that were completely different from those posed by their normal work designing destination resorts. The intention was to develop an orbiting hotel in this new, vast and wonderful frontier, striking a balance between creating an out-of-this-world experience and providing some of the creature comforts that travellers have come to expect in other resorts.

The privately funded project is expected to be operating in the year 2017. The hotel will accommodate 100 guests as it orbits the Earth, 200 miles above the surface of our planet. Excursions will last between three to four days and one to two weeks (like a cruise). Passengers, who will be ordinary people, not superfit astronauts, will be ferried to and from the resort by the next generation of space shuttles or reusable launch vehicles that are currently under design.

The experience to which all passengers will be looking forward will be to share the magnificent view of the Earth from space. Buzz Aldrin, one of the first men on the Moon and advocator of space tourism, describes this experience as, 'like having a globe on your desk. It's a broadening experience after looking at parts of the Earth only on maps to then see them for real'. WAT&G's designers have enabled space-resort guests to do this through viewing panels fitted with computer-aided images to help them understand what they are looking at and to show additional relevant information such as local weather conditions.

Visitors may also have a chance to dock alongside, and pay an extraordinary visit to, the international space station (ISS), which will by then be orbiting the Earth; and for those with a sense of adventure, space walks will be possible.

The designers conceive the hotel as being divided between areas of zero and artificial gravity. This will allow guests to experience floating in space, and it will also provide a refuge for those passengers who may suffer from space sickness. An area with artificial gravity will also give guests an opportunity to partake in such earthly activities as taking a shower, or sitting down for a hydroponically grown meal.

The structure's design will resemble that of a bicycle wheel, which will spin slowly to create a percentage of Earth gravity at the perimeter through centrifugal force. Guest rooms and dining areas will be located here. The hub of the structure will house spaces for zero-gravity activities including sports and recreation and will also contain honeymoon suites.

Life safety is of critical importance. In addition to the issues one would deal with in a terrestrially based hotel, in space we need to be concerned with life-support systems, emergency evacuation procedures and protection from cosmic radiation.

Architects who wish to become involved with orbital design will acknowledge that this is the chance of a lifetime to create something truly new and exciting. To many, it will sound like science fiction. To architects with imagination and vision, however, it's not a question of whether, but rather when and how. ⌀

Opposite
The basic building module for WAT&G's space resort is the space shuttle's external fuel tank. Twelve of them will be linked in a ring, end-to-end, after being released in low-earth orbit from future launches.

Above
The next generation of reusable launch vehicles will transport passengers to WAT&G's space resort, which will provide partial-earth gravity in the perimeter guestrooms and weightless recreational activities at the hub.

The Bartlett Discussion

Space Architecture

The Bartlett School of Architecture, University College London, has achieved international recognition, both for its teaching and for its research. Here, we summarise a discussion between a group of experts from the Bartlett, who speculate on the implications of space habitation.

Above and over page
Peter Cook, design for
a space resort, 2000.

At the Bartlett School of Architecture, renowned for 'thinking the unthinkable', a group of radicals including Dr Rachel Armstrong, Professor Peter Cook, Professor Colin Fournier, Stephen Gage, Neil Spiller and Charles Walker, met to address the challenges faced by our civilisation over the next 50 years. The Bartlett brainstorming reflected on all aspects of the future of the built environment, from where we will live to the incorporation of artificial intelligence and new materials. Naturally, one of the subjects addressed was the question of space habitation. For these academics and practitioners of architecture, the challenges of an extraterrestrial location were not beyond their architectural remits, since none of the technical architectural solutions that will be used to create the first public spaces in orbit will be new. 'We need not await successful revolutions in technology to solve the problems of today's high costs of access to space, nor do we need to deprive ourselves of their benefits should they occur.' [Starcraft Boosters, Inc, The StarBooster 200 System, a Cargo Aircraft for Space, prepared for AIAA/ASME/SAE Joint Propulsion Specialists' Conference, 22 June 1999, Los Angeles, CA, by Dr Buzz Aldrin and Hubert P Davis.]

Space as Utopia

Few places on Earth exist that have not been subject to the aspirations of architects, but perhaps the greatest conceptual challenge is the space beyond our own planet. Since the beginning of human civilisation, we have given the heavens structure in the form of celestial maps and astrological charts. Religious icons and the hieroglyphics of ancient Egypt have reflected the inspiration we derive from the skies. But until the 20th century, they were way beyond our reach.

214

The inaccessibility of locations has never stopped pioneers from speculating on how they may look and be reached and used by human beings. Artists and writers have often invented such speculative, entirely new worlds. Most famous, is the treatise *Utopia* by Thomas More, who coined this term, deriving from Greek and meaning 'no place', as the name of his idealised community. Utopias are imaginary places, societies or worlds that do not exist but could plausibly be created given access and unlimited resources. Those designed by architects tend to reflect the latest technological inventions and philosophies of the era.

Life in space promises a utopian ideal that weaves together many topical cultural aspirations in science, technology and human relationships. We fantasise that in the extraterrestrial environment we will be freed from the histories and legacies of the old world, and will be able to reinvent ourselves. We look to distant locations for solutions, to escape from problems such as overcrowding, pollution, war and the destruction of the Earth.

In *The High Frontier: Human Colonies in Space*, Gerard K O'Neill sought to explain how by the 1990s human colonies would be manning satellites halfway between the Earth and the Moon, pioneering the construction of solar power stations to supply inexhaustible energy to the Earth.[1] O'Neill also outlines how life styles will be shaped by these artificial environments, how climate, gravity, day-length and conditions for family life will evolve, speculating that in 200 years there could be more people living in space than on Earth.

Global Politics and Economics

The main obstacle to realising Professor O'Neill's vision has been the failure of governments to invest in space programmes that serve anything other than a military purpose. Space is a political issue before it is an economic concern. It not only reflects cultural agendas, but also unifies nations, symbolising the redemption of the human race in the event of a global catastrophe.

Since the Moon landings, the iconography of the planet Earth as seen from orbit has become a powerful symbol of international harmony and peaceful collaboration between nations. This beacon of human achievement has taken on a religious dimension and will become increasingly important as a symbol of unity as the global economy goes through its first set of major problems in the third millennium.

The principal difficulties appear to be the impending collapse of the Eastern economy and the prospect of nuclear war in Asia as Islamic countries resist the domination of the planet by a new world order orchestrated by Western superpowers.

With the end of the Cold War, the military forces of Western civilisation require a new role, and at the turn of the millennium a phenomenological milestone needs to be reached. Globalisation reflects a political shift towards international politics, by definition a shift that allows people to feel part of a larger whole, with world trade and the reversal of pollution and the depletion of the Earth's resources as the unifying goal. With the advent of technological progress and increasingly successful space missions, the public has been made aware that the planet as a whole, and not just ecology and infrastructure, is at peril.

There are two main scenarios for the future of the human race, both involving a great deal of risk. First, we can remain on this planet and eventually poison ourselves, blow ourselves to bits competing for territory or possibly experience destruction by a meteor. Second, we can leave the planet and speciate the universe. The question that our civilisation should be asking is not when space travel for civilians will happen, but why it has not happened earlier? After all, the Apollo 11 Moon landing took place a generation ago.

The first objection to space exploration is capital investment. With the advent of reusable craft, however, the cost of a space launch will decrease. The threshold for private investment will be reached when the world's multinationals, who already spend billions of dollars on advertising, consider the sponsorship of orbital craft and stations better value for money: space events currently guarantee extensive international media coverage. Advertising stunts and logos such as that commissioned for Beagle 2's launch to Mars would be likely investments. Beagle 2 is exploiting the reinvention of Britain's image under Tony Blair's New Labour as Cool Britannia by selecting the artist Damien Hirst, leader of the 'Brit pack' of talented creatives, to design a 'universally recognisable' logo, like a transmission test-card for the side of the craft. The combination of art world *enfant terrible* and the excitement that surrounds a voyage to the Red Planet has already produced many hours of high-profile media coverage.

Having a presence in orbit is the ultimate status symbol, providing a literal, metaphorical and virtual image of unlimited potential. The new millennium will increasingly reveal complex relationships between people and space, relating to a variety of physical, informational, metaphorical and virtual territories. Corporations will hope to be regarded as in some way embodying a utopian ideal, marketing not products but life styles, which will be branded and even insured, on behalf of a spectrum of investors. These may include

manufacturers, pharmaceutical companies and banks, who can agree on a united 'life style package' that will represent a particular philosophy and guarantee a certain quality of life for consumers. In the new century, we will see a proliferation of branded satellites, laser projections on to asteroids and insignia on spacecraft, brought back into our domestic worlds through the digital screen.

Communications Research

In space, the possibility of an encounter with an alien species will be ever present. Enthusiasts such as the NASA-endorsed organisation SETI (search for extraterrestrial intelligence) have been scanning the skies for contact with extraterrestrial beings for decades, pushing forward the boundaries for interplanetary communications systems and broadening our understanding of the signals coming to us from the universe.

New frequencies and means of communicating across huge distances will be established, and an interplanetary Internet system (Inter-Planet) is already under way. Information and communications in space will have their own highways, frequencies and architectures, rather like the flight pathways of aeroplanes. There will be intelligent robots and satellites to position the nodes of contact and to lay down the communications superhighways. It may be necessary to negotiate with these surveillance systems – which can be thought of as automated pilots or 'space dolphins' – if they are given artificial intelligence.

Ecology and Speciation

In the absence of natural microflora and fauna in spacecraft, the role of commensals and balanced ecosystems will be an essential design issue in space architecture since, as the human body is not a monoculture, it is not possible to create a completely sterile spacecraft. Human flesh is crawling with microbes and bacteria and in the absence of natural forces, such as abundant water for cleansing, wind for circulating fresh air, it may be possible for normally harmless organisms to produce illness and disease. It will therefore be important to ensure that natural commensal and symbiotic microorganisms are introduced into spacecraft and encouraged to thrive in orbit.

When we begin to stay for longer, it will be necessary to bring other species into orbit and establish mature ecosystems. It is likely that we will want to grow crops in orbit to reduce

the transport cost of food. These may be designer organisms that are a cross between animal, vegetable and intelligent surfaces. The intelligent surfaces could act as a source of water, minerals and artificial light. This would fuel the growth of algae and bacteria, which can be made into a variety of different products with minimum processing.

Building in Space

Space travel provides the ultimate challenge for designers and architects wishing to create an environment that is self-contained and can grow with, and is seamlessly integrated with, the human beings it protects and nurtures. One of the major challenges will be to identify substances that will be cheap and easy to assemble in space. Spacecraft and space stations will be assembled like Lego. The basic units will be manufactured from all over the world and will have standardised electrical circuitry, oxygen-carbon-dioxide-nitrogen-mixture carrying capacities, internal pressure, etc, in order to prevent negative external forces ripping environments apart.

The less human intervention and maintenance of space structures there is, the less costly habitation will be. Smart materials that are capable of self-repair will be needed, as the cost of sending up repair crews could prove prohibitive to future space stations. Not all materials will need to be artificial. Some organic materials that can grow, divide and mature in space, like bone, could be used to grow space stations from the culture of cellular 'seeds'.

To avoid disorientation, buildings able to maintain their own life cycles, mimicking the diurnal Earth patterns of sleeping and waking, and which can recycle water and organic products, will be necessary to pacify their inhabitants psychologically.

The ideal architectural material to use in a vacuum is, of course, light. Laser highways, sculptures, artworks and advertising will be part of the information and architectural structure of colonised space.

Art and Space

Artists will be sponsored and commissioned to make a new kind of public art – works geared to a leisure-seeking, extraterrestrial community on space holiday. These site-specific artworks will humanise the extraterrestrial desert and serve to test new communications, construction and image-making technologies.

The French choreographer, Kitsou Dubois, has already danced during a parabolic flight on the space shuttle, and artist Cornelia Parker has made public her desire to put a fallen meteorite back into the extraterrestrial atmosphere on one of the scheduled space flights. As televisual networks are extended into orbit, live coverage of events will guarantee exposure for commissioners of extraterrestrial artwork and remote viewers will enable terrestrial viewers to browse the antigravity gallery.

Space Fashion

The garments worn by astronauts will become an important part of their identity, not just in terms of their functional support of the body, but as a decorative covering, like a new skin. As new fabrics and intelligent materials become incorporated into spacesuits, they will not just provide a reflection of aesthetic taste and culture, but form part of the adaptive and survival mechanisms for humans themselves.

Space Sports

Survival of the fittest in the extraterrestrial environment will be more appropriately rephrased as 'survival of the most adaptable', since the first pioneers, prior to natural genetic selection, will have to resort to the use of machines and artificial devices to survive. Space sports will exploit this competition between individuals and might be enacted at the Space Olympics. These commercial events would be extensively broadcast and would offer substantial prizes to winners, generating abundant advertising revenue for sponsors. Humans and machines would compete to achieve ground-breaking feats of speed, endurance and physical adeptness. Other sports could have a more military bias, taking the form of robotic gladiatorial contests. (There are already terrestrial versions of these pirate sports in Los Angeles, conducted by Mark Pauline's Survival Research Laboratories.)

Space Entertainment

Not only will space unify humans, it will perform the additional role of consolidating the relationship between technology and people, who will be inseparable from their machines. Space travellers will be dependent on their craft and on robot surveillance to patrol inhospitable environments.

Although humans will quickly adapt to the new orbital environments and the unique demands they place on the body, our gregarious instincts will be harder to appease. The isolation and loneliness of individually manned spacecraft will have to be addressed by interaction with the environment and with communications systems. Artificial intelligences will keep people company, and holographic entertainment will stimulate

their imaginations. We will become socialised with virtual images of other humans, androids and automata. The entertainment industry will supply space travellers with regular programmes such as space-based soap operas or fantasy families with which to establish an ongoing relationship.

In order to reduce stress in the disoriented space traveller, music that samples and spontaneously composes itself could be a part of space architecture. This would disguise the perpetual hum of the power supply, which is capable of inducing psychological space sickness. Samples of the wind blowing, or the sound of the sea, may be woven into soundtrack samples to remind the space traveller or inhabitant of Earth. Remaining in touch with our human origins will be an essential part of space life.

Life and Death in Space

The mass communications networks will provide one of the first ways in which humans start to imagine what life might be like in space. With the establishment of an orbital tourist industry, people will not only begin to believe that it is possible to venture into orbit, but regard it as a right. As vacations into orbit become longer, the prospect of orbital habitation will appeal to some. This migration from the Earth will signify an important stage in human evolution as our capacity to thrive in these constructed environments will be defined by the limits of our physiology and genetics.

As orbital life is shown to have a place in human society, space will be seen as another terrain for both living and dying. Space burials will be cheaper than those on Earth and it may become popular to follow in the pathway of Star Trek visionary Gene Roddenberry with a celestial ceremony. In order to avoid the build-up of debris, there may even be designated space cemeteries for jettisoned corpses.

Pollution

Space debris is already a hazard in orbit, but as the number of visitors increases the ecology of our near orbits will need to be addressed. Space-cleansing operations should be designed to ensure that ships entering space do not collide with the rubbish that humans leave behind.

Conclusion

The concept of human habitation in space is, of course, a very old one; in some form, it can be traced back to the early days of science and even earlier, to mysticism. It has been a theme of fiction and speculation. This century has brought the first real access to extraterrestrial space and, with it, the architectural community is faced with the prospect of thinking the unthinkable about where we will live and the way in which we can best accomplish this. ◬

Notes
1 Gerard K O'Neill, The High Frontier: Human Colonies in Space, Corgi (London), 1977.

KATHARINA LEDERSTEGER-GOODFRIEND

CHALLENGING PARADIGMS

Three Variations on Housing the Homeless in Los Angeles

Homelessness is certainly not a new problem, but the 1996 Welfare Reform Bill has renewed interest in the discussion of homelessness in the United States.[1] Many fear that the urban poor could be caught in a job crisis, adding further to the numbers of homeless people that have steadily increased since the economic decline of the 1970s.

This situation poses a particular problem for Los Angeles, which became the homeless capital of the United States during the 1980s. Economic restructuring in the region exclusively increased demand for low-skilled labour. Lower wages without pension and health benefits meant that more working people were living in poverty; simultaneously, welfare programs were downsized and affordable housing units were demolished and replaced by upmarket rentals and condominiums.[2]

Even as the boom of the later 1980s spawned a renewed interest in the development and preservation of cities, it did nothing to ameliorate the situation of the urban poor. In Los Angeles, successful regeneration projects such as the Third Street Promenade and Old Town Pasadena were hailed as signs of a new sense of urbanity, but coincided with overcrowding in low-income neighbourhoods as people doubled up or moved into illegal garden and garage units. Unsurprisingly, the growing numbers of homeless people sleeping on sidewalks, beaches, and public parks did not fit the new Disneyfied image of the city. Even in more liberal areas of Los Angeles, home-owner associations worried more about keeping their neighbourhoods clean than about social responsibility.

The importance of 'home' to the housed population seems obvious: consider the current abundance of interior and gardening stores and magazines, or the popularity of books such as Witold Rybczynski's *Home*. Many cultural theorists discuss the significance of home as the most immediate environment in which the construction of personal identity through control over one's own body takes place. In this context, homelessness can be defined as 'a dramatic loss of power over the way in which one's identity is constructed, since the home no longer shields from the public gaze.'[3]

At the same time, public housing projects themselves have notably failed to shield from the public gaze. 20th-century public housing endeavours to structure occupants' private lives in their entirety. Whoever has the power to structure the space in which people's lives take place also determines the ways in which the relations of production within a particular community can, or cannot, be contested; and the belief that spacious and hygienic living conditions should function to ensure contented, productive workers and citizens remains the unacknowledged motive of many housing activists today.[4] This priority keeps those who cannot work homeless, posing a muted challenge to a paternalistic model of society. Any serious attempt to reduce the number of homeless people then requires openness to different models of social organisation demanding new types of spatial organisation.

I have selected three types of project to accompany this text in order to shed light on various ways in which architects can be involved in schemes for the homeless. Both the Simone Hotel and the Boyd Hotel by Koning Eizenberg exemplify architects' typical responses and raise doubts as to their appropriateness. Working within the constraints of their briefs, Koning Eizenberg have proved that inventive design and affordable design are not mutually exclusive. Nevertheless, the buildings could not be less welcoming: no people, no personal belongings, in fact nothing at all would indicate habitation. The buildings do not seem to foster a sense of home, pride or community for inhabitants, nor do they encourage connections with those outside.

When I asked Julie Eizenberg how they dealt with the traditionally patronising attitude towards designing for the socially underprivileged, she answered that – faced with the problem of not knowing the individual needs of future residents – their approach was to think of homeless people as equal human beings and accordingly create an environment that they themselves would feel comfortable in. With the Skid Row Housing Trust managing the project and serving as an interface between the architects and the buildings' eventual occupants, Koning Eizenberg saw as their only option a strategy of de-institutionalisation through the manipulation of formal elements. Following the criticism of post-Second World War social housing, the failure of which has largely been blamed on architects taking on the role of social engineers, Koning Eizenberg's approach is symptomatic of many contemporary architects' fear of committing their work to a strong political or social agenda. However, both the Simone and the Boyd Hotel demonstrate that an architecture of aesthetic gestures cannot provide the environment for a solution to social problems.

While it is difficult to compare projects of such contrasting scales, SAMOSHELL, the structure designed by Zeballos + Smulevich, demonstrates that architectural services can be provided in a way that is very effective. Of course, their situation was different: first, the limitations of building a temporary structure in an extremely short amount of time for very little money provoked them into abandoning architects' desire to create original pieces and instead let them realise the opportunities of prefabricated structures in this context; and second, the architects were approached by a Santa Monica agency rather than the Salvation Army with the result that they became chief co-ordinators of the project serving as the interface between all parties involved. Zeballos + Smulevich also had access to likely future residents who at the time were already using SWASHLOCK, thus enabling the architects to develop a building that would take into consideration homeless people's needs as much as the requirements of the institution that would manage the shelter.

Yet despite its success, SAMOSHELL inspires general questions about the housed population's response to homelessness. Away from any residential neighbourhoods, the shelter is located on a property directly adjacent to the freeway. Entirely enclosed by a fence and camouflaged in Santa Monica's official blue-and-white colour scheme, it exists unnoticeably amongst the surrounding public structures. While this arrangement creates privacy for the homeless who choose to use the facility, it also effectively removes the unpleasant fact of homelessness from public view.

My final example is firmly rooted in Buckminster Fuller's motto: 'to make the world work in the shortest possible time through spontaneous co-operation without ecological offence or the disadvantage of anyone.' Genesis I Transitional Village's tradition is that of the mobile home park; while it did not and will not win any architectural awards it has nonetheless received more media attention than either of the other projects. The 'dome village' really raises two questions: whether professional architects can and should be involved in projects that necessitate a new attitude towards the production of space, and whether a temporary housing solution can actually subvert architects' conventional notions of living permanently.

The project's aim was not to provide shelter that was beautiful in any conventional sense, but to create a place that a group of homeless people would be able to call their own by making it so simple that it could be built by themselves. Three years later only a fraction of the original home builders are left, but current residents continue to improve on the village. They take pride in their achievement and like to show it off. Neighbours of Genesis I have expressed their appreciation of the project, and some researchers consider it a highly successful demonstration of how vital self-determination is to the homeless with respect to creating places that allow movement back into mainstream society.[5] Others describe the project as a failure. The village apparently has a low turnover rate; also, its independence inspires fear in some that it may provide a breeding ground for criminal activities.

Where earlier sociological texts are inclined to see the homeless as voluntary drop-outs from mainstream society,[6] later texts lean towards depicting them as helpless victims of fate.[7] As Rob Rosenthal argues, 'the emphasis changed from the "agency" of homeless people themselves – that is, their individual actions and behaviours – to the "constraints" imposed on them by social processes beyond their individual control.'[8] Yet both attitudes reflect the romantic belief that all homeless persons are socially isolated vagabonds or nomads.

This belief can lead to gross generalisations about the needs of the homeless. Rosenthal describes the homeless as a heterogeneous group that does not share many characteristics besides the one of having lost a permanent residence. He identifies six subgroups that each form their own social networks and often do not interact with each other. Architects have not been sensitive to this heterogeneity. For instance, none of the projects described cater to the need of a very large group of the homeless: families and single women with children. Few places target these groups

because they tend to lead a less visible, peripatetic existence, relying on the generosity of relatives and friends to share their homes.

Moreover, while many homeless people share mainstream aspirations, their requirements and expectations on the way to fulfilling those aspirations will differ significantly from those of the housed population. Architects' difficulty in accepting this difference is evident in the criticism of Genesis I. Despite the fact that mobile homes are the predominant form of unsubsidised affordable housing, they are still not widely appreciated because they do not fulfil the mainstream American demand for conventionally constructed dwellings.[9] Such standards of acceptability are preserved by private and public institutions such as mortgage bankers, zoning and building authorities, state and federal housing agencies and, of course, professional organisations of architects. These institutions are less interested in finding new models for living than in ensuring the predictability of the market through the protection of market values.[10] Housing reformers may create public support for responsible capitalism but, as I suggested earlier, they are simultaneously complicit with a system that has historically given housing not to the poorest but to workers. As a result they ensure that housing is produced by institutions that completely control the planning process in an attempt to create rationalised environments necessary for the preservation of the existing social order.

The difficulties to be overcome for architects in trying to find successful solutions for housing the homeless generate more general questions concerning the significance of architecture for housing. Rybczynski claims that the impact of architects is negligible in relation to the way most people live. By turning away from an involvement in mass production in the 1930s and concentrating on the image of the architect as artist, the architectural profession has deprived itself of the knowledge needed to produce good housing. The majority of people in the United States and Canada see no connection between architects and their private living environment. This should come as no surprise: 20th-century avant-garde architectural theory, which continues to dominate contemporary architectural teaching and discourse, is inherently anti-domestic. The ultimate validation for being modern is to despise the function of the home as a refuge and to deny its occupants' needs for privacy in which to develop and define individual and family identity.[11]

Significantly, none of the articles I found on either the Simone or the Boyd projects discuss the social connotations of Koning Eizenberg's designs. Instead, they assure us that our compassionate liberal souls may rest in peace now that the homeless can relax in surroundings straight out of a tasteful architectural or interior design magazine. SAMOSHELL and Genesis I, on the other hand, are projects that challenge accepted architectural paradigms. They are both projects that would not usually find their way onto the pages of a design-oriented architecture magazine because their original design is not what makes them interesting. In contrast to the interior of the Boyd Hotel – which still looks untouched a full year after opening – SAMOSHELL and Genesis I constitute an architecture of the everyday in which the process of appropriation by inhabitants and their daily needs overwhelms any concern with aesthetics. They provide shelter that allows identity to be established as a result of inhabitation rather than design. The difference between the Simone and Boyd Hotels and projects such as SAMOSHELL and Genesis I is perhaps best expressed by saying that one approach exemplifies the desire of modern architects to stage the life of their clients, whereas the other approach is characterised by the flexibility necessary to enable inhabitants to define and live their particular differences.

Notes

1 It requires each state to have 30 per cent of welfare recipients either engaged in work or enrolled in work training by the end of 1998. While this goal may be reached in rural and suburban areas it appears elusive in cities where the welfare population is concentrated.

2 Jennifer Wolch, 'From Global to Local: The Rise of Homelessness in Los Angeles during the 1980s', Allen J Scott and Edward W Soja (eds), *The City: Los Angeles and Urban Theory at the End of the Twentieth Century*, University of California Press (Berkeley, Los Angeles and London), 1996, pp390-425.

3 Neil Smith, 'Homeless/Global: Scaling places', Jon Bird et al (eds), *Mapping the Futures: Local Cultures, Global Change*, Routledge (London and New York), 1993, pp87-119.

4 Don Mitchell, 'Public Housing in Single-Industry Towns: Changing Landscapes of Paternalism', in James Duncan and David Ley, *Place/Culture/Representation*, Routledge (London and New York), 1994, pp110-27.

5 See, for instance, Michael Dear and Jurgen von Mahs, 'Housing for the Homeless, by the Homeless, and of the Homeless', in Nan Ellin (ed), *Architecture of Fear*, Princeton Architectural Press (New York), 1997, pp187-200.

6 See, for example, Jacob A Riis, *How the Other Half Lives*, Hill and Wang (New York), 1957, orig pub 1890, p148: 'It is a mistake to think that they are helpless little creatures, to be pitied and cried over because they are alone in the world. [. . .] The *Street Arab* has all the faults and all the virtues of the lawless life he leads. *Vagabond* that he is, acknowledging no authority and owning no allegiance to anybody or anything, with his grimy fist raised against society whenever it tries to coerce him, he is as bright and sharp as a weasel, which among all the predatory beasts, he most resembles' (my emphasis).

7 See, for example, Alexander Cockburn, 'On the Rim of the Pacific Century', in David Reid (ed), *Sex, Death and God in L.A.*, University of California Press (Berkeley and Los Angeles), 1992, p10: 'In the interval of a couple of blocks we could see the class war fought out at the level of the built environment. Amid the corporate towers of the prime redevelopment zones there were pleasant little spaces, gardens, bowers amid the reflecting glass, along with avant-garde street furniture inviting you to linger and repose. Move toward skid row, and the destitute *urban nomad* pushing his purloined shopping cart finds himself the object of low-intensity civic warfare: rounded bus seats he can't lie down on, sprinkler system drenching areas where he might sleep, spikes and bars guarding trash he might try to sort through' (my emphasis).

8 Rob Rosenthal, *Homeless in Paradise: A Map of the Terrain*, Temple University Press (Philadelphia), 1994, p3.

9 Allan D Wallis, *Wheel Estate: The Rise and Decline of Mobile Homes*, The Johns Hopkins University Press (Baltimore & London), 1991, pp12-29.

10 To give just two examples of many I mention the following:
In a recent exhibition about new models of housing in Los Angeles, Re: American Dream, architects demonstrate how to maximise the use of downsized city lots while the underlying ideology of ownership, privacy and individuality remains untouched;
The Department of Housing and Urban Development's new policy is not to built emergency shelters nor to improve existing bad housing but to reconstruct entire neighbourhoods based on New Urbanist principles that consist of rules such as: mixed-use developments, access to public transport, pedestrian friendly streets and last but not least the construction of traditional brick town houses with columns, gabled roofs, etc.

11 Christopher Reed, 'Introduction', in Christopher Reed (ed), *Not at Home: The Suppression of Domesticity in Modern Art and Architecture*, Thames and Hudson (London), 1996, pp7-17.

Zeballos + Smulevich, SAMOSHELL, Santa Monica Homeless Shelter, Los Angeles, 1994

SAMOSHELL

In 1994 a law was passed that prohibited sleeping in public spaces; an emergency shelter to house those affected by the new law was needed urgently. Santa Monica's Human Affairs Division contacted architects Zeballos + Smulevich who in 1993 had re-designed a group of existing buildings to serve as a shower/laundry/locker-storage facility, SWASHLOCK, for the City of Santa Monica SAMOSHELL, the Santa Monica Homeless Shelter, would be built on the same property – leased for a temporary period from the Santa Monica Department of Transportation. Several Santa Monica agencies participated in the design and construction, collaborating with Sprung Instant Structures Inc. of Calgary, Canada, the architects, and the Salvation Army, who would ultimately manage the shelter.

The project had to be completed within a four-month period, so a pre-engineered structure seemed the only feasible solution. Sprung Instant Structures' system consists of aluminium wide flange members spaced ten-feet apart and bolted on to a concrete slab. Once the vinyl stressed skin membrane is stretched over this skeleton, it forms a 37x18 metre lightweight shell. Attempting to domesticise the scale of the building, the architects modified the manufacturer's standard CAD shop drawings to include translucent panels at window height as well as a series of 'dormer windows' at a higher level. Inside the vaulted structure, human scale is achieved through the height of partitions, suspended ventilation and fluorescent lighting.

Space for communal activities is located between the building's entrance and an office area in the back. Altogether the structure provides shelter for 100 people of both sexes. The intention was to separate women's and men's sleeping quarters by a box-shaped volume containing restroom and washing facilities. Yet due to an increase in the number of homeless women seeking shelter, the general sleeping area has now been partitioned into two spaces. Besides designing the shelter and managing its construction, Zeballos + Smulevich obtained used commercial kitchen equipment, second-hand storage lockers, and beds from military surplus.

Genesis I Transitional Village

This is located a few blocks west of Los Angeles' downtown financial district. A corporate grant, the help of downtown property developer David Adams and the approval of both mayor's office and city council enabled homeless activist Ted Hayes, founder of Justiceville/Homeless USA, to begin constructing 18 domes that would house the experimental community he had envisaged. The structures are engineer Craig Chamberlain's variation on Buckminster Fuller's geodesic dome. They are bolted together from curved non-toxic polyester fibreglass panels that sit on a concrete footing. They take about two hours to built, are earthquake and water proof and, at the time, cost approximately $6,500 each.

Twelve domes house two residents each. The other domes accommodate communal kitchen, office, storage and meeting space. Governed by the conviction that the 'best form of government is self government', residents must show both willingness to stabilise their lives and commitment to supporting the village. Responsibility for management, maintenance of personal and property appearance and village security are supposed to improve organisational abilities and imbue homeless people with a sense of self-esteem and self-reliance. The village is also linked with social agencies that provide counselling and work-related services.

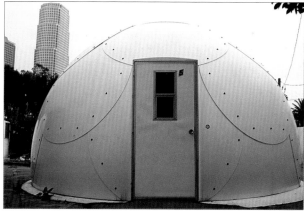

Genesis I Transitional Village, Los Angeles, 1993